DAYMOND R. DUCK

ON THE BRINK

D0368148

DAYMOND R. DUCK

ON THE BRINK

STARBURST PUBLISHERS

P.O. Box 4123, Lancaster, Pennsylvania 17604

To schedule Author appearances write:
Author Appearances, Starburst Promotions, P.O. Box 4123
Lancaster, Pennsylvania 17604 or call (717) 293-0939

Credits:
Cover design by Bob Fuller Creative

Unless otherwise stated all Scripture references are from the King
James Version of the Bible. All Jerusalem Post quotations are from
the International Edition of the Bible.

ON THE BRINK

Copyright ©1995 by Starburst, Inc.
All rights reserved.

This book may not be used or reproduced in any manner, in whole
or in part, stored in a retrieval system or transmitted in any form by
any means, electronic, mechanical, photocopy, recording, or otherwise,
without written permission of the publisher, except as provided by
USA copyright law.

First Printing, October 1994

ISBN: 0-914984-58-6
Library of Congress Catalog Number 94-85140
Printed in the United States of America

This book is dedicated to my loving wife,

Rachel.

I prayed that God would let me know if
He wanted me to write this book.
My prayer was answered a few days later
when Rachel presented me with a
word processor for my birthday.

Contents

Introduction

As a student of prophecy, Sunday School teacher and lay pastor, I have studied, taught and preached on prophecy for more than twenty years. Three comments keep popping up.

First, there are those who say, "I did not realize prophecy makes so much sense." People seem to think all prophecy is a mystery. They speculate on whether God ever intended them to understand it.

Second, there are those who say, "I have been wondering what 'they' (Hal Lindsey, Dave Breese, Marlin Maddoux, Noah Hutchings, Pat Robertson and others) are talking about." These people have heard the great men of God preach and teach, but they know so little prophecy they do not understand what is being said.

Third, there are those who say, "I know what 'they' are talking about, but where is it in the Bible?" These people do not want to be told what the Bible says. They want to read the prophecies with their own eyes.

This book is an effort to present an in-depth prophetic study in language which is easily understood; to help the reader learn what pastors and the "heavyweights" of Christian prophecy are talking about and to show where these prophecies and their interpretations can be found in the Bible.

Some of the more important points in this book are marked with a (✦) sign. They are prophetic points of light. Psalm 119:105 reads, *Thy word is a lamp unto my feet, and a light unto my path.* II Peter 1:19 says, *We have a more sure word of prophecy whereunto ye do well that ye take heed, as unto a light that shineth in a dark place, until the day dawn, and the day star arise in your hearts.* These points of light from the Word of God are singled out to assist the reader in finding the main ideas.

I thank God for the opportunity to write **On The Brink** and pray His wisdom will rest upon you as you study these *300 Points of Light On The Soon Return of Jesus.*

Chapter **1**

The Tribulation Period

The Lord of all still loves this old earth, and an essential part of His love is to change those things which are ripping it apart. While He does plan to bring destruction upon those who are polluting His name and destroying His creation, His main purpose is to heal and remake what He started. This may give us a sense of foreboding at first, but when we look beyond the calamity, we picture a better world where the kingdom, the power, and the glory are His. We see a mended and improved society; a kingdom of peace, righteousness, justice and love; hearts lifted with joy, happiness and praise; an earth full of His grace and glory. We visualize a world filled with beautiful people doing everything possible to make this marvelous planet a wonderful place to live.

Jesus was prophesying about the end of the age when He said, *Then shall be great tribulation, such as was not since the beginning of the world to this time, no, nor ever shall be* (Matthew. 24:21). "Great tribulation" speaks of our planet's darkest hour. The entire world is On The Brink of a catastrophe for which it is totally unprepared. We are not moving toward a new era of peace and cooperation. We are plunging toward distress of nations, world-wide conflict, famine, pestilence and death. These will ravage and lay waste the earth.

The pale horse has been bridled. He is saddled and ready. Death has his foot in the stirrup. He awaits only the authority to mount and ride forth to kill and destroy one-fourth of earth's population. Hell will follow to gather the souls of the dead (Revelation 6:8). The four Satanic angels have been prepared. They are eager to be loosed to slay one-third of the remaining inhabitants with fire, smoke and brimstone (Revelation 9:14–18).

The human race has never experienced anything like the tragic scenario predicted in the Bible. People will be confused; unable to cope. Disaster will pile upon disaster with widespread devastation and destruction. Only a small percentage of mankind will survive the seven long rigorous years of a world turned upside-down; bathed in blood and torment.

Has anyone told you about this? Should these judgments occur in your lifetime, are you ready? Do you know what it takes to be ready?

The Names of the Tribulation Period

The names of the tribulation period reveal much about the terrible events to come. Some are as follows:

Jeremiah 30:7	The time of Jacob's trouble.
Zephaniah 1:14–16	The great day of the Lord.
	A day of wrath.
	A day of trouble and distress.
	A day of wasteness and desolation.
	A day of darkness and gloominess.
	A day of clouds and thick darkness.
	A day of trumpet and alarm.
Isaiah 26:20	The indignation.
Isaiah 34:8	The day of the Lord's vengeance.
Daniel 9:24–27	The seventieth week.

The Purpose

The Holy Bible gives many reasons for the great Day of the Lord. Some manifest God's infinite love, but others demonstrate His fierce anger and purging fury. Both natures exist. And His overwhelming goodness and overpowering severity are found in all the end-time events. If this sounds strange to you, just remember He did create the rose, but He also brought forth the rattlesnake. He did ordain the joy of marriage, but He also allows the sorrow of death to break it up. God did send His own Son, but He allowed Him to be despised, rejected, bruised and smitten. His love is greater than we can imagine, but we would be foolish to believe it is impossible to ignite His burning wrath when His real goal is to bring an end to evil.

The Love of God

The awe-inspiring love of God is the nature often overlooked by those who study the indignation. Our great and gracious God will use the unparalleled sufferings of that dreadful time to usher in special blessings the world has not known since the days of Adam. The ever escalating disasters will bring people to God and make things right on earth. The tribulation period will cause people to be less proud (Isaiah 13:11). One-third of Israel will call upon God (Zechariah 13:9). A great revival will be unleashed among all the nations of the earth (Revelation 7:9-17). It will be a revival greater than the one Jonah preached in Assyria; a revival that will move an uncountable number to Christ. Praise and exultation will break forth in heaven with people shouting, *Salvation to our God which sitteth upon the throne, and unto the Lamb* (Revelation 7:10). Angels will sing, *Blessing, and glory, and wisdom, and thanksgiving, and honour, and power, and might, be unto our God for ever and ever. Amen* (Revelation 7:12). The immense distress of nations will bring in reconciliation, righteousness, the fulfillment of prophecy and the return of Jesus Christ (Daniel 9:24). And the people *shall beat their swords into plowshares, and their spears into pruninghooks: nation shall not lift up sword against nation, neither shall they learn war any more* (Isaiah 2:4).

A good example of what hard times will do occurred in Russia when Dr. Billy Graham preached there in the fall of '92. Attendance records were broken every night. Thousands were turned away. Multitudes, including several top leaders and many military personnel, made commitments to Christ. And on the last day of services, the doors had to be locked 90 minutes early. But people hungry for the Word of God broke them down and entered.

God's judgment comes from God's love. He uses it to make things better. He is not a tyrant. He is a loving Father who does not refuse to use a "paddle" when it will correct a bad situation. The Apostle Paul said, *My son, despise not thou the chastening of the Lord, nor faint when thou art rebuked of him: For whom the Lord loveth he chasteneth, and scourgeth every son whom he receiveth. . . . Now no chastening for the present seemeth to be joyous, but grievous: nevertheless, afterward it yieldeth the peaceable fruit of righteousness unto them which are exercised thereby* (Hebrews 12:5-6, 11).

The Wrath of God

We do not hear much about the wrath of God because the thought is almost repugnant to us. All good preachers want to stress the love of God. God is love, but He can be very harsh too. Please listen to what Dr. Billy Graham has to say in his book *Storm Warning,* "When we tell only the stories of victory, we tell only a part of the truth. When we recount only the answered prayers, we oversimplify. When we imply that the Christian faith involves no yoke and no burden, we tell less than the whole truth. And half-truths, easy answers, and convenient lies are the weapons of deceit."[1]

Yes, God is good, long-suffering and merciful, but He is also *a consuming fire* (Hebrews 12:29). Yes, He prefers to guide the world with a hand of love, but unrepentant men will resist His guidance and refuse to respond to anything but chastisement. Evil men will create this head-on collision forcing a swat from that mighty loving hand whose purpose is to change, refine and improve the situation.

The divine judgments will come upon a world that does not know the true God or His precious Son Jesus. It will be a generation of people who misinterpret His character and personality. Mankind will neither heed nor love Him. Idolaters will rule. Blatant iniquity will abound. Sinners will persecute the righteous. Wicked people will tear the best fabrics of society apart. The organized Church will be lukewarm. Blasphemers will trample upon the pure blood of Jesus Christ. False doctrines will create confusion. Multitudes will be in danger of hell. Family relationships will fracture. Human spirits will be confused and broken. Nations will be in an uproar. Weapons of mass destruction will proliferate. Tempers will be short and times will be frightful and perilous.

The Lord of Hosts is very patient, but He *can* be provoked. He is kind, but the rest of the story is: He *hates* sin. He will bear some persecution of His people, but should He sit still forever while the fierce and violent wage all-out war on the righteous? He will tolerate some idolatry, some irreverence and some blaspheming of Jesus, but should He allow the toothless roaring lion to lure the whole world into hell? Should He ignore the fervent prayers of the righteous man and permit the disintegration, deterioration and degradation of His creation? The Almighty will not punish without cause. But when the folly of this God-rejecting world goes too far, and men will no longer repent, the severity of His wrath will bring forth the appalling and unequaled tribulation period.

The Judge of the living and dead will use the day of trouble and distress to punish the world for sin (Isaiah 13:11). He will doom those on earth who ignore the truth and take pleasure in unrighteousness (II Thessalonians 2:8–12). It will be a time of severe testing for every individual alive; a reminder to the world the living God expects more out of mankind than He is receiving (Revelation 3:10).

Setting the Stage

There are three indicators which unlock the mystery of the tribulation period:

1. The appearance of Jesus;
2. The land of Israel;
3. The circumstances for remaining on the land.

In studying the appearance of Jesus, we see He was required to come out of the nation of Israel. We also discover He must appear twice. These two appearances are called His first and second comings or His first and second advents.

Concerning the land, Jehovah God gave it to Abraham and his descendants. When Abraham died, the glorious land was given to Isaac and his descendants. After Isaac, the eagerly desired territory went to Jacob and his descendants.

Regarding the circumstances for remaining on the promised land, occupation was always conditional. If the descendants of Abraham, Isaac and Jacob ever ceased to follow God, a curse would come upon them and they would be temporarily removed from that special place. The land would become desolate and remain so until they were allowed to return.

The Beginning

It all started in the Garden of Eden when Satan tempted Adam and Eve to eat the fruit of the tree of the knowledge of good and evil placed there by the Creator. The Old Serpent should not have tempted them, but he did. God responded by placing a curse on him. He told the Wicked One the seed of woman would bruise his head (Genesis. 3:1-15).

This is an unusual thing God said because physically speaking, there is no such thing as the seed of woman. It would make more sense, if He said the seed of man would bruise Satan's head. The only way to have a seed of woman bruise his head was to have a miracle birth.

Such a miracle is exactly what God had in mind. The curse He placed upon Satan is really a prophecy about the virgin birth of Jesus and His two appearances. The seed of woman is the Christ. He came the first time to die for the sins of the world and to buy back this majestic creation Adam and Eve lost. The gentle Jesus came to bruise Satan's head and He did.

But there is more. The Son of God defeated Satan at the cross, but He did not bind and chain the Evil One at that time. He will do that when He returns at the end of the tribulation period to stop the Tempter's work and to establish His own kingdom here on earth.

✦ *It (Jesus) shall bruise thy (Satan's) head.*
(Genesis 3:15)

The Spread of Sin

When Satan's temptation of Adam and Eve consummated in the corruption of the entire world, God decided to destroy everyone except one preacher of righteousness and his family. This religious man was Noah.

Noah had an active faith in God. He believed the Lord when He revealed His plan to destroy the world with a flood. Noah built the giant ark as God instructed him, gathered his family and rode out the flood. With his life spared, Noah became God's channel for the first coming of Jesus (Genesis. 6: 8).

Only three generations passed before Noah's descendants became corrupted. Noah's great-grandson Nimrod led the rebellious group who tried to build the Tower of Babel. God confused their tongues and scattered them around the world. Then He chose another man and again started a new nation (Genesis 11).

God's Promise to Abraham

Immediately after the incident at the Tower of Babel, God called Abraham and asked him to move to the land of Canaan. The Lord told Abraham He would make a great nation out of him, bless him, make him a blessing to others and bless all the families of the earth through him.

These are exciting promises. God was saying, "I will give you descendants, they will become a nation, and one of your descendants will be a blessing to every family on earth." Other Scriptures bear out the fact that He was referring to the nation of Israel and His only begotten son Jesus.

Abraham accepted this fantastic offer. He went forth into the land of Canaan and came to Shechem. There God appeared to him again to say He would give the country to his descendants (Genesis 11:31–12:7).

✦ *I will make of thee a great nation.*
(Genesis 12:2)

✦ *In thee shall all families of the earth be blessed.*
(Genesis 12:3)

✦ *Unto thy seed will I give this land.*
(Genesis 12:7)

God's Promise to Isaac

Abraham fathered several children by his concubines and wives. The Lord blessed all of them, but the special promises made to Abraham were passed on to Isaac. Isaac's descendants would become the nation to receive the land and bring forth Jesus (Genesis 26:1–5).

✦ *Unto thee (Isaac), and unto thy seed, I will give all these countries.*
(Genesis 26:3)

✦ *In thy (Isaac's) seed shall all the nations of the earth be blessed.*
(Genesis 26:4)

God's Promise to Jacob

Isaac had twin sons named Jacob and Esau. Both prospered, but Jacob and his descendants became the beneficiaries of the splendid promises made to Abraham and Isaac (Genesis. 28:1-22).

✦ *The land whereon thou liest, to thee (Jacob) will I give it.*
(Genesis 28:13)

✦ *In thee (Jacob) and in thy seed shall all the families of the earth be blessed.*
(Genesis 28:14)

Jacob is Israel

The tribulation period earns its name "time of Jacob's trouble" from Jacob. The "time of Jacob's trouble" refers to Jacob's early life when he did not trust God to lead him. He was an unbeliever with many problems. The name indicates Jacob's descendants will have trouble trusting God for guidance during the tribulation period. As unbelievers, they will have many problems they will not know how to solve.

Jacob did not remain an unbeliever. The time came in his life when he began to trust God. Then his name was changed to Israel

and His descendants became known as the children of Israel and
the nation of Israel (Genesis 32:24-32).

God's Promise to Israel

Israel and his children wound up in Egypt. They were there for
430 years and their numbers multiplied to several hundred thousand. Moses led them out and forged them into a nation.

They went to Mount Sinai where God announced He had chosen them to be a special people. He gave them two reasons: (1) He
loved them; (2) He wanted to keep the promises He made to their
fathers (Deuteronomy 7:6-8).

✦ *The Lord thy God hath chosen thee to be a special people.*
(Deuteronomy 7:6)

✦ *Because the Lord loved you.*
(Deuteronomy 7:8)

✦ *And because he would keep the oath which he had sworn
unto your fathers.*
(Deuteronomy 7:8)

God's Covenant with Israel

God made a special covenant with the children of Israel at
Mount Sinai. He would be their God if they would follow Him. They
listened to instructions pertaining to offerings, sacrifices, cleans-
ings, holiness, the land and so forth. Those instructions are included
in the Law of Moses. Many of them can be found in the book of
Leviticus and the 25th and 26th chapters are of particular interest.

The Land's Sabbath of Rest

God's instructions for the land are found in Chapter 25. The
people were to keep a sabbath. That is, the soil was to *rest every
seventh year.* This is a major key which unlocks much of the mystery surrounding the length of Israel's captivity in Babylon and the
length of the tribulation period.

Concerning the land and crops, God wanted Israel to follow a
week of years. The Jews could plant crops for six consecutive years,
but the land was to be allowed to rest the seventh year. The seventh
year was called *a sabbath of rest unto the land* (Leviticus 25:1-4).

It is helpful to understand that the Hebrew word translated "week" means seven. One week of days equals seven days and one week of years equals seven years. It is possible to have a week of minutes, a week of hours, a week of days, a week of weeks, a week of months, a week of years and so on. We will soon see that the Bible even speaks of a week of weeks (seven weeks) and a week of years (seven years).

+ Seven years equals one week of years.
+ The seventh year shall be a sabbath of rest.
  (Leviticus 25:4)
+ *Thou shalt neither sow thy field, nor prune thy vineyard.*
  (Leviticus 25:4)

What Would Happen
If Israel Broke the Covenant (The Curse)?

Chapter 26 of Leviticus suddenly turns prophetic. After giving a series of specific instructions for rituals, morality and soil use, God abruptly placed several choices before the new nation. These choices would drastically affect the Jewish future by giving the people a chance to choose their history in advance. The Jews could choose the narrow road of obedience to God and their history would become a history of blessings or they could choose the broad road of rebellion and make their history a record of chastisement and judgment.

Those who study the chapter quickly notice the word "if." *If* occurs nine times in this one chapter. It means God would respond to the peoples behavior. He would bless their loyalty and punish their disobedience. He is a God who reacts to personal conduct. *If* Israel was obedient, they would be blessed.

If Israel obeyed God, the people would receive rain, have good crops, dwell safely in the land, live peacefully, triumph over their enemies, have many children and experience God's presence. They would greatly prosper and be permanently secure.

On the other hand, *if* the people rebelled against God, their initial judgments would include fear, disease, sorrow, crop failure and death at the hands of their enemies. *If* they continued to rebel,

God would punish them seven times more. He would humble them by stopping the rain, hardening the soil and causing even more severe crop failure. *If* Israel still rebelled, God would punish the people seven times more for their sins. He would send plagues and wild animals and their cattle and children would die. *If* the Jews still would not reform, God would punish them seven times. He would cause their enemies to attack them and send diseases and famine upon them. Finally, *if* the people still refused to repent, God would chastise them seven times. The Jews would cannibalize their children, God would destroy their cities and sanctuaries and He would make the country desolate. He would scatter the people among the heathen and *cause the land to rest and be desolate for as long as it had not enjoyed her sabbaths* (Leviticus 26: 27-35).

These harsh words are found in Deuteronomy 28:15-20. *But it shall come to pass, if thou wilt not hearken unto the voice of the Lord thy God, to observe to do all his commandments and his statutes which I command thee this day; that all these curses shall come upon thee, and overtake thee: Cursed shalt thou be in the city, and cursed shalt thou be in the field. Cursed shall be thy basket and thy store. Cursed shall be the fruit of thy body, and the fruit of thy land, the increase of thy kine, and the flocks of thy sheep. Cursed shalt thou be when thou comest in, and cursed shalt thou be when thou goest out. The Lord shall send upon thee cursing, vexation and rebuke, in all that thou settest thine hand unto for to do, until thou be destroyed, and until thou perish quickly; because of the wickedness of thy doings, whereby thou hast forsaken me.*

✦ *I will chastise you seven times for your sins.*
(Leviticus 26:28)

✦ *I will scatter you among the heathen.*
(Leviticus 26:33).

✦ *Then shall the land enjoy her sabbaths.*
(Leviticus 26:34)

✦ *As long as it (the land) lieth desolate it shall rest; because it did not rest in your sabbaths, when ye dwelt upon it.*
(Leviticus 26:35)

✦ *All these curses shall come upon thee.*
(Deuteronomy 28:15)

Jeremiah's Warning

From the days of Moses unto the days of Jeremiah, Israel went through many cycles. Beginning with Moses, Israel served God for several years and enjoyed the blessings He promised. But in spite of His goodness, a new generation arose who began to rebel. When God called for repentance, the people did not respond. So He withdrew His help, the blessings evaporated and times were hard. Then the reeling nation sought out God. He restored her and the blessings returned.

Israel repeated this cycle over and over again. God always took the Jews back and blessed them. He never wanted to apply the curse. He loved the children of Israel; wanted to be their God.

By the time Jeremiah came along, Israel was divided. The Northern Kingdom of Israel had been destroyed and the Southern Kingdom of Judah was in dire circumstances. The chosen people were unwilling to obey God and stopped their ears to what true prophets were saying. They worshiped false gods and did not let the soil rest as God instructed them. Their sins provoked His wrath.

God moved on Jeremiah to deliver a warning. He told Judah to repent immediately from their sins and dwell in the land or He would bring Nebuchadnezzar, the king of Babylon, against the nation and make the whole land a desolation. He would make the people serve the king of Babylon for seventy years. Jeremiah wrote these things in Jeremiah 25 verses 1–13.

✦ *The whole land shall be a desolation, and an astonishment; and these nations shall serve the king of Babylon seventy years.*
(Jeremiah 25:11)

✦ Jeremiah's prophecy was written in a book.
(Jeremiah 25:13, Author's translation)

What God Did

Judah did not heed the warning God told Jeremiah to deliver. The people continued in their sin, mocking the messengers of God and despising His words. They pushed their jealous God too far and finally triggered the curse.

II Chron. 36:11-21 records that God brought the king of the Chaldees (Nebuchadnezzar the king of Babylon) against Judah. Many people were killed; the country looted and burned. Captives were taken to Babylon to be servants to the king and his sons. The loot was also taken to Babylon.

Why did God do this? He did it, *To fulfil the word of the Lord by the mouth of Jeremiah, until the land had enjoyed her sabbaths; for as long as she lay desolate she kept sabbath, to fulfil threescore and ten years* (II Chronicles 36:21).

Some people do not understand how long 70 sabbaths are. Since it would take 7 years to steal one sabbath, 14 years to steal two sabbaths, 21 years to steal three sabbaths and so on, it can be determined that it took 490 years to steal 70 sabbaths. Both of these numbers (490 and 70) are important and we will see them again.

 ✦ *Them that had escaped from sword carried he away to Babylon.* (II Chronicles 36:20)

 ✦ *To fulfil the word of the Lord by the mouth of Jeremiah, until the land had enjoyed her sabbaths to fulfil threescore and ten years.* (II Chronicles 36:21)

God's Promise

Judah made a serious mistake by ignoring the warning of Jeremiah. He was truly speaking the Word of the Lord. The fact God fulfilled his prophecy demonstrates that.

After Judah was taken captive to Babylon, God told Jeremiah to send a letter to the elders, priests, prophets and people. The letter is found in Chapter 29. God told the people to build houses, plant gardens, get married, have children and pray for peace. The Lord said He would cause them to return to the land after 70 years (Jeremiah 29:1-29; Leviticus. 26:44, 45).

✦ *After seventy years be accomplished at Babylon I will visit you,*
and perform my good word toward you, in causing you to
return to this place.
(Jeremiah 29:10)

Daniel's Discovery

Daniel was among the group of captives taken to Babylon. While
reading some books in Babylon he made an interesting discovery:
The Word of the Lord had come to Jeremiah the prophet and Jerusalem was to be desolate for 70 years. It is most likely Daniel was
reading the Book or scrolls Jeremiah wrote and he read the 25th and
29th chapters of the Prophet's Book.

✦ *I understood by books the number of the years.*
(Daniel 9:2)

Daniel's Prayer

Daniel understood the situation and began to fast and pray. His
prayer supports the conclusions already set forth. The people
sinned by departing from God's precepts and judgments. They refused to heed God's prophets. They failed to walk in the law. Their
sin and rebellion was against God Himself. God drove them out of
the country because of their sin. They were under a curse. God's
oath written in the law of Moses, was against them and even though
the people suffered, they had not prayed for repentance or understanding (Also see Deuteronomy 30:1-3; Joshua 8:34).

Daniel continued the prayer. He confessed the people had
sinned. He asked God to turn away His anger and fury; to take note
of the desolate sanctuary and to hear and observe the people's problems. He prayed, not because the people were righteous, but because God is merciful. He asked the loving Father to hear and forgive.
He also asked Him to not delay for His sake because Jerusalem and
the people were called by His name (Daniel 9:3-19; Leviticus 26:40-46).

✦ *The (God's) curse is poured upon us.*
(Daniel 9:11)

✦ *And the (God's) oath that is written in the law of Moses.*
(Daniel 9:11)

Daniel's Visitor

While Daniel was praying, a remarkable thing happened. The angel Gabriel appeared. He came to give Daniel skill, understanding and a message. It is one of the most incredible communications the world has ever heard. It contains information about when Israel would be forgiven, when Israel would return to the land and when Jesus would come (Daniel 9:20-23).

+ *Gabriel touched me.*
    (Daniel 9:21)

+ *I (Gabriel) am now come forth to give thee skill and understanding.*
    (Daniel 9:22)

+ *Understand the matter, and consider the vision.*
    (Daniel 9:23)

+ *I am come to shew thee.*
    (Daniel 9:23)

Gabriel's Message

Gabriel's message is found in Daniel 9:24-27. It is one of the most important passages in the entire Bible and very complicated. It requires a great deal of study to really understand it.

Gabriel said, *Seventy weeks are determined upon thy people and upon thy holy city, to finish the transgression.* He was saying, *Reconciliation for Israel will come, but not until after seventy weeks of additional judgment has occurred. Then God will bring an end to Israel's judgment.*

"Seventy weeks" does not mean weeks of days. It has already been noted the Bible speaks of a week of days (seven days), a week of weeks (seven weeks) and a week of years (seven years). When viewed in the light of history, it is apparent Gabriel was speaking of 70 weeks of years, or 490 years.

There are at least three references in the Bible verifying one week can mean seven years. The first reference tells us seven sabbaths of years equals 49 years (Leviticus 25:8). That translates into one sabbath every seven years. The second reference tells Ezekiel to lay on his side for the iniquity of Israel. It states each day has been appointed for a year. If one day is a year, then one week is seven years (Ezekiel 4:4-6). The third reference states Laban told Jacob to fulfill a week for Rachel's hand in marriage. Jacob did so by working seven years (Genesis 29:21-30).

Therefore, one week in the Bible often signifies one week of years (seven years) and history verifies Gabriel was speaking of weeks of years. So how long is 70 weeks or how long is 70 weeks of years? The answer is 70 weeks equals 490 years (70 weeks x seven years/week = 490 years).

Why did Gabriel say 490 years? Where did this number come from? It is how long it took Israel to steal 70 sabbaths (seven years/sabbath x 70 sabbaths = 490 years) and seven times more punishment for Israel's sins over-and-above their 70 years of captivity (Leviticus 26:18,21,24,28).

When Would the Additional 490 Years Begin?

The 70 weeks (490 years) would begin when the commandment was given to restore and rebuild Jerusalem. That commandment is found in Nehemiah 2:1-8. Other commandments can be found that refer to rebuilding the temple, but they do not apply because they make no mention of rebuilding Jerusalem. Thus, the commencement date of the 70 weeks (490 years) *is the month of Nisan, in the twentieth year of Artaxerxes the king.*

> ✦ *From the going forth of the commandment to restore and to build Jerusalem.*
> (Daniel 9:25)

How Would the Additional 490 Years be Broken Up?

Gabriel did not say the 70 weeks (490 years) would be broken up into three time periods, but he divided them that way in his message. In the first place, he mentioned a time period of seven weeks (49 years). In the second place, he mentioned a time period of 62 weeks (434 years). Finally, he talked about the concluding one week (7 years).

> ✦ *Seven weeks.*
> (Daniel 9:25)

✦ *And threescore and two weeks.*
(Daniel 9:25)

✦ *And he shall confirm the covenant with many for one week.*
(Daniel 9:27)

What Would Happen During the First 483 Years?

Gabriel had a wonderful message for the Jewish captive. For one thing, when the people returned, they would rebuild the main street of Jerusalem and the wall around the city. The brush and weeds would be cut, the heaps of rubbish would be removed and the beautiful city would be laid out again.

We read about this in the Book of Nehemiah. The commandment was given in the 20th year of Artaxerxes the king (445 B.C.). Nehemiah secured assistance and protection from the king. He gathered supplies and returned to the land and the former city. When he reached his destination, the opposition was there and the "troublous times" began, but Nehemiah and his hard-working people persevered. After seven weeks (49 years), the street and wall were there. This concluded the first time period in Gabriel's message.

✦ *The street shall be built again, and the wall, even in*
troublous times.
(Daniel 9:25)

When Would Messiah the Prince Come?

Not only was the beginning of the 490 years identified, but we are given an incredible prophecy about the appearance of Messiah. The first seven weeks (49 years) would pass and then 62 more weeks (434 years) would bring us to the arrival of Messiah the Prince. This totals 69 weeks (7 weeks + 62 weeks = 69 weeks) or 483 years (49 years + 434 years = 483 years) between the commandment and the arrival of Messiah. (See chart on next page).

This is exactly what happened. Sir Robert Anderson, a highly respected English lawyer and former head of Scotland Yard, determined 483 years-to the exact day-elapsed between the commandment and the triumphal entry of Jesus. He took leap year into consideration and used the Jewish prophetic year of 360 days per

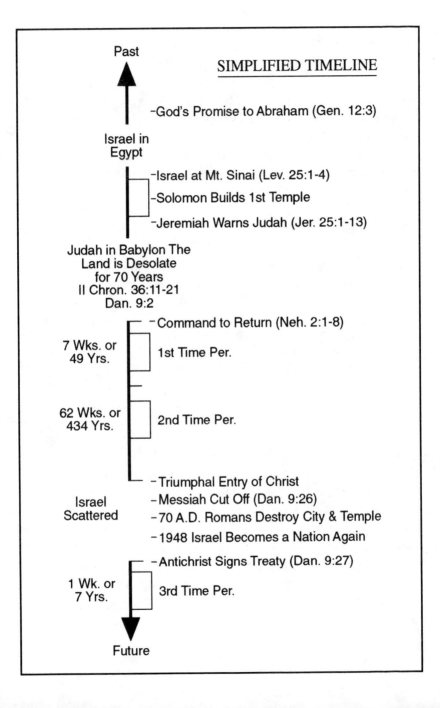

year to show 483 years equals 173,880 days and he calculated exactly this number of days elapsed between the two events. The following information is taken from his book:[2]

The 1st Nisan in the twentieth year of Artaxerxes (the edict to rebuild Jerusalem) was 14th March, B.C. 445.

The 10th Nisan in Passion Week (Christ's entry into Jerusalem) was 6th April, A.D. 32.

The intervening period was 476 years and 24 days (the days being reckoned inclusively, as required by the language of prophecy, and in accordance with the Jewish practice).

But 476 x 365 equals	173,740 days
Add (14 March to 6th April, both inclusive)	24 days
Add for leap years	116 days
	173,880 days

69 weeks of prophetic years of 360 days (or 69 x 7 x 360) equals 173,880 days.

It may be well to offer here two explanatory remarks. First: in reckoning years from B. C. to A. D., one year must always be omitted; for it is obvious, ex. gr., that from B. C. 1 to A. D. 1 was not Two years, but one year. B. C. 1 ought to be described by B. C. 0, and it is so reckoned by astronomers.

✦ *From the going forth of the commandment . . . unto the Messiah the Prince shall be seven weeks, and threescore and two weeks.*
(Daniel 9:25)

What Would Happen to Messiah the Prince After the 62 Week Period?

He would appear and then be killed. And we know shortly after the Lamb of God made His triumphal entry into Jerusalem, He was literally tortured and killed. But it was not for Himself. The Messiah died for the sins of all who will believe in Him.

✦ *After threescore and two weeks shall Messiah be cut off, but not for himself.*
(Daniel 9:26)

What Would Happen to the City and Temple After the 62 Week Period ?

Gabriel made another astounding and shocking prediction that was bound to bring consternation to the righteous Daniel. He told Daniel his dearly loved Jerusalem would be rebuilt and then he said it would be destroyed again and the house of the Lord too.

This was carried out in 70 A.D. by a Roman General named Titus. He overran the city, slaughtered 5 million Jews and tore the temple apart stone by stone.

✦ *The people of the prince that shall come shall destroy the city*
   and the sanctuary.
   (Daniel 9:26)

Another Prince

Jerusalem and the temple would be destroyed by *the people of the prince that shall come.* Notice, it is the people of the prince (not the prince himself) who would do this. Also, this is a different prince from Messiah the Prince. Gabriel spoke of Messiah the Prince (capital P) and the prince (small p) that shall come.

We are told a prince would appear sometime after the destruction of Jerusalem and the temple. This prince will come from the same group of people who destroyed the city and the sanctuary. Since it is known that the Roman army did this, it is concluded a prince is coming who will be from a group of nations who will arise out of the old Roman Empire.

✦ *The people of the prince that shall come shall destroy the city*
   and the sanctuary.
   (Daniel 9:26)

The End of the Seventy Weeks

How will it end? The 70 weeks will wind up with a flood of destruction and desolation. Israel and Jerusalem will experience terrible disasters and some—but not all—of that area will be made desolate. This will complete the 490 years of additional judgment upon Israel.

✦ *The end thereof shall be with a flood.*
   (Daniel 9:26)

✦ *Unto the end of the war desolations are determined.*
(Daniel 9:26)

The Final 7 Years

The final week is often called the 70th week, the tribulation period, etc. and the events herein described are all future. Notice they occur after the death of Jesus and after the destruction of Jerusalem and the temple. Most Bible scholars place the triumphal entry and the death of Jesus around 32 A.D. And there is great consensus that Jerusalem and the temple were destroyed in 70 A.D.

This 70th week did not occur before the triumphal entry of Jesus because that ended the first 69 weeks. This 70th week did not occur between 32 A.D. and 70 A.D., because Jerusalem and the temple had to be destroyed before it could begin. This means there is a gap in time between the end of the 69th week and beginning of the 70th week.

This gap in time is the Church Age. The Church was brought into existence after the first 69 weeks of Israel's judgment, and at some point in the future, the Church will be removed (the rapture). Then, when all things are ready, God will restart His time clock for the final week (seven years) of Israel's judgment.

Notice the entire 70 weeks (490 years) of judgment is separate from the 70 years of Babylonian captivity and all of it requires Israel to be in the land. In other words, God did not start counting on the 490 years until the commandment was given to restore and rebuild Jerusalem. He waited until some of the Jews returned and the commandment was issued. He stopped counting at the triumphal entry; but before He started counting again, the Jews were put off the land a second time. It will be necessary for them to return again before He starts the final countdown.

✦ *He shall confirm the covenant with many for one week.*
(Daniel 9:27)

The Covenant

The 70th week begins when someone signs a seven year covenant with many (many nations, the U.N., Israel, etc.). Some wrongly believe the tribulation period begins with the rapture of the

Church. It does not. It begins with the signing of a well publicized seven year covenant that pertains to Israel. This covenant is usually called a peace treaty.

✦ *He shall confirm the covenant with many for one week.*
(Daniel 9:27)

The Covenant Maker

It is generally agreed by conservative scholars the person who brokers the covenant is the one referred to *as the prince that shall come* in verse 26. We usually call this bloody and deceitful man the Antichrist.

People want to know, "What nation or group of nations does the Antichrist come from? This has already been answered. The Antichrist comes from the same group of nations that destroyed Jerusalem and the temple in 70 A.D. He comes from the revived Roman Empire.

Do not miss this point. Since the Antichrist will sign a seven year covenant pertaining to Israel, it stands to reason the nation of Israel would have to come back into existence again. It ceased to exist as a nation in 70 A.D., so in order for this prophecy to be fulfilled, Israel would have to become a nation again. This is one reason why the nation of Israel exists today. It exists so prophecies can be fulfilled.

✦ *He shall confirm the covenant.*
(Daniel 9:27)

The Tribulation Mid-point

In the middle of the 70th week, the prince that shall come will *cause the sacrifice and the oblation to cease.* This implies the re-building of the temple in the last days because the sacrifice and oblation (animal sacrifice, gifts, offerings, worship, etc.) were always done at that place. It also implies a system of priests for the services; equipment for the sacrifices; furniture for the temple; clothing for the priests and such. All of this is being done this very day. There have been two unsuccessful attempts to lay the temple cornerstone; one in 1989 and another in 1990. Talmudic schools have been established and priests are now in training. For the last six years, weavers have been working on garments for the high priest and his attendants; most of their clothes are ready for use. The high priest's solid gold crown has been made; his breastplate is almost complete. Most of the temple furniture and hundreds of musical instruments have been manufactured. The pans for the incense and the forks for the sacrifices are ready. And a six-foot tall $10 million gold menorah is ready to set in the new building.

This is all being done, but the Antichrist will put a stop to the services in the middle of the tribulation period. He will cause them to cease three and one-half years from the signing of the covenant.

✦ *In the midst of the week he shall cause the sacrifice and the oblation to cease.*
(Daniel 9:27)

The Desolation

The Antichrist will defile the new temple at the middle of the tribulation period and a reign of bloody terror will begin. Many of the Jewish people will flee into the wilderness and the temple will remain desolate until the end of the tribulation period.

✦ *He shall make it desolate.*
(Daniel 9:27)

Everlasting Righteousness (The Millennium)

We need to recognize one more very important point before we move on. There are some who believe the Church will succeed in bringing everlasting righteousness to this earth without the world going through the tribulation period. But that is not what the prophet Daniel said. He wrote that the angel Gabriel told him, *Seventy weeks are determined upon thy people . . . to bring in everlasting righteousness* (Daniel 9:24). The Living Bible says it this way, *The Lord has commanded 490 years of further punishment upon Jerusalem and your people. Then at last they will learn to stay away from sin, and their guilt will be cleansed; then the kingdom of everlasting righteousness will begin, and the Most Holy Place (in the temple) will be rededicated, as the prophets have declared.* The kingdom of everlasting righteousness (the Millennium) will not begin until Israel completes all 490 years of punishment God decreed.

The nation only completed 483 years of its punishment when they killed Jesus. God stopped counting and the nation was destroyed. He has called the Jews back so they can complete the last seven years. *Then* the time of everlasting righteousness will begin.

✦ *Seventy weeks are determined upon thy people . . . to bring in*
   everlasting righteousness.
   (Daniel 9:24)

The Proof is in the Pudding

The test of a true prophet is the accuracy of his message. If God inspired the message, it will come true. If Gabriel was a false prophet, people need not concern themselves with the tribulation period, but if he was a true prophet, people should be greatly concerned.

Listed below are some of the things that were required to happen *if* Gabriel's message came from God :

✦ There had to be a commandment to rebuild Jerusalem.
   (Daniel 9:25)

✦ Israel had to be released from Babylon.

✦ Israel had to return.

✦ Jerusalem had to be rebuilt.
   (Daniel 9:26)

✦ The temple had to be rebuilt.
   (Daniel 9:26)

✦ Jesus had to come the first time.
   (Daniel 9:26)

✦ 483 years had to pass before Jesus came.
   (Daniel 9:25)

✦ Jesus had to be killed.
   (Daniel 9:26)

✦ Jerusalem had to be destroyed.
   (Daniel 9:26)

✦ The temple had to be destroyed.
   (Daniel 9:26)

There is none like God and the reason is He can declare the end from the beginning and foretell things that are not yet done (Isaiah

46:9, 10). He demonstrated that. The above list of events is incredible, and yet, all of these events actually happened. It is enough to cause many to believe the remainder of the prophecy will be fulfilled.

Gabriel's Unfulfilled Prophecies

The remaining events Gabriel foretold for the future are as follows:

✦ The Antichrist must come.
   (Daniel 9:27)

✦ The Antichrist must sign a seven year covenant to protect Israel.
   (Daniel 9:27)

✦ The Temple must be rebuilt.
   (Daniel 9:26)

✦ The animal sacrifices must begin.
   (Daniel 9:27)

A Personal Message

God makes the same offer He made to Israel to every individual today. Obey Him and He will bless you. Base your life on His Word and He will care for you. He will keep you and receive you into heaven. Repudiate His offers of mercy through Jesus and keep ignoring His standards and values and He will bring you before His throne of judgment. Everyone has a choice, but the choice each one makes will affect his history in advance.

Chapter 2

Israel

Gabriel's message to the prophet Daniel reveals, God has a definite plan for Israel. The world is now living out the fulfillment of that plan. If you need any proof there is a God, this is it. The Everlasting Father is not dead or in vacation mode. He is alive and well; and working out His plan.

The Holy Spirit inspired the prophets of old to write it down and He miraculously preserved it. We can read what Moses had to say and what Isaiah wrote. We can find part of the plan in Jeremiah's Book and another part in Ezekiel's Book. It's all there and nothing else is needed to understand what is going on in the world today.

Moses

The intriguing things Moses wrote in the first five books of the Holy Bible will continue in effect until every detail is fulfilled. Everything he said is important and nothing can be overlooked. Jesus said, *Think not that I am come to destroy the law, or the prophets: I am not come to destroy, but to fulfil. For verily I say unto you, Till heaven and earth pass, one jot or one tittle shall in no wise pass from the law, till all be fulfilled* (Matthew 5:17,18).

Religion and the Land

Religion and ownership of the land are at the heart of the never- ending Arab-Israeli conflict. The two groups are diametrically opposed to each other because each group thinks it worships the only real God and each group thinks He gave the promised land to it. The conflict over this blessed place is theological and directly linked to the question, "Whose god is God and who worships the true God?" The land issue can never be settled until the theological conflict over God's identity is settled. The religion of the loser is dead.

An article by Joel Greenberg in The Jerusalem Post entitled *Peace as a Betrayal of God*, dated December 14, 1991, reveals the view of a group of Moslem clerics, called The Palestine Council of Ulema (religious scholars) who gathered in Jerusalem to condemn peace negotiations with Israel. Mr. Greenberg writes:

"Religious law forbids participation in the Madrid Conference because it is aimed at achieving peace with Israel, subsequently legitimizing its existence on the blessed land of Palestine, confirming its aggression and theft of the Moslems' land, homes, holy places and property, and ultimately assisting it in achieving its aggressive objectives.

"The fatwa goes on to cite a series of arguments based on Koranic verses, against making peace with Israel, and including the following assertions:

'If the Moslems circumstances require a cessation of fighting, a truce is permitted, not peace or reconciliation. A temporary truce is permitted by religious law. . . but permanent peace is sanctioned by no one, especially when it entails abandoning the lands of the Moslems . . . .'

'Salah ed-Din made peace at Ramle with the Crusaders, but this was not really peace, but a truce, limited to three years and three months . . . .'

'The Moslem ruler chosen by the nation can conclude a truce for the benefit of the nation; he is not authorized to make a permanent peace, and any such pact is forbidden, null and void . . . . Such a peace is a grave sin and a betrayal of God and his messenger to the believers (Mohammed).' "

✦ *And the Lord appeared unto Abraham, and said, Unto thy seed will I give this land.*
(Genesis 12:7)

Ownership of the Land is Permanent

It is useless to discuss territorial compromise or the so-called swapping of "land for peace." Abraham's seed has a God-given right to the land and the decision is eternal. The immutable God will never give the beautiful land of Canaan to another nation and never take it back. He has chosen one group of descendants to receive it forever.

✦ *For all the land which thou seest, to thee will I give it, and to thy seed forever.*
(Genesis 13:15)

God's Name is at Stake

God made a covenant to give a tract of land between the Nile and the Euphrates rivers to the seed of Abraham. The covenant is His solemn and binding pledge that Abraham's offspring will receive the land. It is very important to see this, because a holy God cannot allow His name to be tarnished. The true God committed Himself to give that much desired territory to Abraham's descendants and He must do it or His name will be blasphemed.

Everything is bound up in this. God's honor is at stake. His renown and glory are on the line. His Word, character, authority and reputation are all wrapped up in this covenant. He obligated Himself to give the land to Abraham's descendants. And if He does not do it, mockers will bring the name of God and the entire Bible into question.

✦ *The Lord made a covenant with Abram, saying, Unto thy seed have I given this land, from the river of Egypt unto the great river, the river Euphrates.*
(Genesis 15:18)

The Land Cannot be Divided

The blessed land will not be partitioned. Wicked world leaders want to carve on Jerusalem and Israel like they would slice on a slab of untrimmed meat. But they will fail because the East Bank and the West Bank will become the property of the same group of Abrahamic offspring.

✦ The covenant includes all the land of Canaan.
   (Genesis 17:1-8)

The Arabs are Descendants of Abraham

The Arabs proudly trace their ancestry to Abraham. He bore one son, Ishmael, by his wife's maid, Hagar, and six sons by his second wife (or concubine) Keturah. (Genesis 16:1-16; 25:1-6; I Chronicles 1:32)

The Arabs will not get the Land

God promised to bless Ishmael and to make him a great nation. But He did not make a covenant to give him or any of his descendants the land. The fact is, He sent Ishmael out of the country. *And Ishmael married an Egyptian and dwelt in the wilderness of Paran* (Genesis 17:18-21; 21:9-21).

The offspring of Keturah did not receive the land either. They moved eastward when Abraham sent them away and gave all he possessed to Isaac (Genesis 25:1-6).

The Jews are Descendants of Abraham

The Jews proudly trace their ancestry to Abraham too. He bore Isaac through his first wife Sarah. Then Isaac bore Jacob and Esau. And Jacob's name was changed to Israel (Genesis 21:1-8; 25:20-26; 32:24-32).

The Jews will get the Land

The all-important covenant with the land went to the descendants of Isaac. Esau was the first-born, but he sold his birthright to Jacob. His descendants will serve the offspring of Jacob (Genesis 17:21; 25:23-34; 26:1-5; 28:10-15).

We have seen this taking shape in recent years. In 1917, a Jewish Professor named Dr. Chaim Weizmann was teaching Chemistry at Manchester University in England. He also served as president of a Jewish movement called Zionism. This movement was working to establish a national homeland in Palestine for the Jews.

World War I was in progress and England was fighting to win control of the very area the Jewish people wanted. At that critical time, Dr. Weizmann discovered a new process for producing two components used in the manufacture of high explosives, acetone and butyl alcohol. With World War I going on, this was a very valuable finding. High explosives were needed to sustain the war effort.

Dr. Weizmann knew the value of his discovery. So he offered his new process to England in exchange for British help in obtaining the land of Palestine for the Jews. England accepted his offer and signed an agreement known as the Balfour Declaration.

When the war was over, England was on the winning side. The British even had control of the land the Jews wanted. They went to the League of Nations requesting a mandate to rule over the area and got it. The mandate expired in 1947, but England pursued the issue of a Jewish homeland with the United Nations. And on November 29, 1947, the United Nations agreed to a British plan to divide Palestine into an Arab state and a Jewish state. The Jews accepted this plan, and the nation of Israel came into being the following year. The Arabs rejected it, but could not do anything about it.

It is quite interesting that God gave a Jewish Chemistry Professor a new way to produce materials for high explosives at the same time World War I was going on. The discovery was so valuable, England was willing to secure a homeland for the Jews in order to get it. Also it was so important it helped win World War I.

The Tribulation Period

Today's Middle East situation bears out the pure concentrated truth of the Old Testament. Long ago, Moses predicted the scattering of the Jews and a later return before the tribulation period of the latter days. It is plain in the Scriptures that God gave all of Canaan to the Jews, but an unbelieving world has made itself blind and numb to this (Deuteronomy 4:24-31).

The children of Israel were scattered, but they have returned and possess part of the glorious land today. However, it is only a fraction of what Moses said they will receive. And although it is just a portion of their inheritance, there is a tremendous effort by the United Nations, the United States, the European Community, the Arabs and a whole host of other nations to get Israel to give back some of the small part they have. These groups are stepping into an issue Israel's God seems to have already decided. It is a dangerous thing to challenge the great and terrible God.

Israel is the rod of God's inheritance, the battle ax and weapon of war He plans to use to "break in pieces the nations" and to "destroy kingdoms." He will use this ticking time bomb to show the world He is the only God. The movers and shakers of this world will learn the hard way that men cannot give away land the omnipotent God has given to Israel (Jeremiah 51:19-23).

> ✦ *I call heaven and earth to witness against you this day, that ye shall soon utterly perish from off the land where- unto ye go over Jordan to possess it.*
> (Deuteronomy 4:26)

> ✦ *When thou art in tribulation, and all these things are come upon thee, even in the latter days.*
> (Deuteronomy 4:30)

Isaiah

The Book of Isaiah is the beginning of the prophetic books in the Holy Bible. A copy was delivered unto Jesus in the synagogue in Nazareth when He began His ministry. Our Lord took the Book and read from it. The Scripture He read was fulfilled on that day (Luke 4:16-21).

Isaiah foretold the lineage of Jesus, the coming of John the Baptist, the virgin birth of Jesus, the death of Jesus, the fall of Babylon and the rebuilding of Babylon. He foretold some amazing and unusual things that have come to pass. This is what makes his prophecies about Israel's future so important. His record demonstrates he was speaking for God.

The Tribulation Period

Isaiah looked into the future and he saw a day when the nation of Israel will be restored. It will be a time of boundless joy; a time when multitudes will praise God for their deliverance. But the great joy will not last. An indignation will come and the Jews will need to hide. Indignation is one of the names of the tribulation period and many of the Jews will flee into the wilderness where they will be safe (Isaiah 26:1-21; 34:1-8; Jeremiah 10:10; Habakkuk. 3:12; Zephaniah 3:8).

✦ *Hide thyself as it were for a little moment, until the indignation be overpast.*
(Isaiah 26:20)

Blossoms in the Desert

When the great prophet looked beyond the indignation, he focused his attention on the Israeli desert. Most people would see boulders, rocks, outcroppings, dry plants, hot sand and a blazing sun, but Isaiah saw blossoms. He saw a desert adorned with beautiful blossoms.

The fragrance of flowers fills the air over the Negev Desert today. And the sweet smell of profits is everywhere because flowers are Israel's leading agricultural export. The Jews have built an extensive system of canals, pipelines and tunnels to move badly needed water there. They have been so successful in pushing back the desert and bringing large sections under cultivation, that several nations, including the United States, are studying their methods. These nations intend to apply Israeli techniques to deserts in other countries with the hope of helping underdeveloped nations all over the world.

✦ *And the desert shall rejoice, and blossom as the rose.*
(Isaiah 35:1)

Springs of Water

As his eyes walked across the future desert laden with flowers in full bloom, Isaiah looked down at the soil. But he did not see cracks in a parched land. He did not see dust blowing here and there. No, he saw marshes, springs and puddles of water.

Today, blankets of snow and sheets of rain are covering the land of Israel. But think about it. Only God can do this. He is the only One who can provide the abundant amounts of water Israel is receiving on a regular basis.

In 1992, Jerusalem experienced record-breaking rain and snow on three different occasions. The Negev Desert received snow for the first time ever. And when the snow reached 68 feet deep on

Mount Hermon, it didn't stop snowing, but the officials had to stop measuring. Torrential rains and melting snow turned fields into lakes; creeks became raging rivers. And several people died when flash floods swept them away in swollen streams.

✦ *And the parched ground shall become a pool, and the thirsty land springs of water.*
(Isaiah 35:7)

Bring My People Home

The regathering of Israel is causing the population to grow "by leaps and bounds." The population, which stood at approximately 800,000 in 1948, reached 5,192,000 by the beginning of 1993. Jews have arrived from 120 nations, they speak 83 different languages and demographers are now predicting the majority of the world's Jews will live in Israel within 10 years (Isaiah 43:1-13).

✦ Bring my sons from far, and my daughters from the ends of the earth.
(Isaiah 43:6).

The Narrow Land

Isaiah predicted the Jews would return to a land too narrow for all its inhabitants. Israel is a long narrow country today with a land area about one-fifth the size of the state of Tennessee. It is not more than ten to twelve miles wide at its narrowest point, only seventy miles wide at its greatest point and about two-hundred and sixty miles long (Isaiah 49:8-26).

✦ *And the land of thy destruction, shall even now be too narrow by reason of the inhabitants.*
(Isaiah 49:19)

Gentiles Will Carry Israel Home

It is a sure truth that Isaiah believed Gentiles would help Israel return to the land. He said, *For the Lord will have mercy on Jacob, and will yet choose Israel, and set them in their own land: and the strangers shall be joined with them, and they shall cleave to the house of Jacob. And the people shall take them, and bring them to their place* . . . . (Isaiah 14:1,2).

Concerned Gentile Christians from all over the world are doing exactly what Isaiah said they would do. In the fall of 1990, Christians from 65 nations raised close to $1 million to fly twelve plane loads of Soviet Jews to Israel. Representatives from twelve nations working with the International Christian Embassy presented checks to Prime Minister Shamir.

In July of 1991, a group called the Religious Roundtable hosted a rally in Memphis, Tennessee to kick off a $1 million drive to fund "freedom flights" for Soviet Jews. UnitedStates Housing Secretary Jack Kemp was present.

Also in 1991, Christians in England, who call themselves the Ebenezer Emergency Fund, sponsored three flights of immigrants from the Commonwealth of Independent States to Israel. And they raised $500,000 to hire ships for three voyages.

> ✦ *I will lift up mine hand to the Gentiles, and set up my standard to the people: and they shall bring thy sons in their arms, and thy daughters shall be carried upon their shoulders.*
> (Isaiah 49:22)

Flying as a Cloud

Some scholars do not believe *fly as a cloud* implies on an airplane, but many Jews interpreted it that way when they returned in 1948. They saw their flights on American planes as a fulfillment of Isaiah's prophecy.

In 1984, George Bush, Vice-President of the United States, made a personal appeal to the government of Ethiopia to release its Jewish population. His efforts on behalf of Operation Moses helped obtain the release of 8,500 Jews who were airlifted to Israel.

In May of 1991, George Bush was President of the United States and the Ethiopian government was on the brink of collapse. President Bush interceded again by asking for the release of the Jewish population. His request was granted and planes were sent in to get the people.

The Jews in Ethiopia are descendants of King Solomon and the Queen of Sheba. This airlift, called Operation Solomon, involved at least forty flights by IAF and El Al planes. As many as twenty-one planes were in the air at the same time. Some 14,400 Jews were taken home in about thirty-six hours.

The Deliverer worked in a mighty way again. Instead of parting the waters of the Red Sea for the Jews to walk through, He provided airplanes and they flew over it.

✦ *Who are these that fly as a cloud?*
(Isaiah 60:8)

The Sons of Strangers

Isaiah predicted the sons of strangers will help rebuild Israel. And Gentiles are causing the hammers to bang and the saws to buzz there. The United States alone contributes $3 billion a year to the new nation. The National Association of Home Builders in Washington, D.C. predicts United States companies will build 30,000 houses there each year over the next five years.

In June of 1991, there was a move in the U.S. House of Representatives to cut $82.5 million from Israel's aid package to punish her for establishing settlements in the occupied territories. This was the amount the U.S. State Department estimated Israel spent on settlements in 1990. Several other countries are also contributing to the rebuilding of Israel.

✦ *And the sons of strangers shall build up thy walls, and their kings shall minister unto thee: for in my wrath I smote thee, but in my favour have I had mercy on thee.*
(Isaiah 60:10)

The Glory of Lebanon

Isaiah also foresaw the reforestation of Israel. And the modern fulfillment is well underway. From the beginning of the nation, emigrants have been pouring into Israel without jobs or sufficient income. Many have been given the task of setting out seedling trees. Now lofty trees line most inter-city roads and many of the major highways.

A group called the Jewish Nation Fund (JNF) has been working with organizations from all over the world in a reforestation program for several years and they are achieving fantastic results. They have planted more than 185 million trees on 200,000 acres of flourishing land. They manage another 100,000 acres of thriving natural woodlands and plan to increase that to 250,000 acres by the turn of the century. Bridges for Peace and Southwest Radio Church are two other organizations helping to raise money to plant a wide variety of new trees.

> ✦ *The glory of Lebanon shall come unto thee, the fir tree, the pine tree, and the box together, to beautify the place of my sanctuary; and I will make the place of my feet glorious.*
> (Isaiah 60:13)

Jeremiah

Jeremiah is the prophet who warned Israel of the destruction of Jerusalem and the impending captivity in Babylon. His message was true, but very unpopular. Delivering so much bad news broke his heart; caused him pain and anguish; got him beaten, branded a traitor and cast into prison. He only did it because God told him to. But we cannot leave it there because his prophecies were not all bad. He saw many good things. Its just that they would not come to pass for awhile. They were in Israel's distant future and it would be the latter days before they occurred.

Operation Exodus

One good thing Jeremiah saw was a future deliverance of Jews from a land lying north of Israel. It will be a deliverance greater than the estimated 2 million Jews who changed countries when Moses led the children of Israel out of Egypt. It will even cause them to stop talking about the one Moses led. And they celebrate that one as the single greatest event in their entire history.

There are only four countries directly north of Israel. The largest and farthest north is Russia. From 1971 to 1979, 250,000 Jews left Russia. Slightly more than half went to Israel and most of the remainderst moved to the United States. In the early '80s, the Russian goverment almost stopped the flow. The total for seven years dipped to approximately 7200 people. In 1987, approximately 8500 moved; in 1988, 18,000; in 1989, more than 71,000; in 1990, almost 185,000; in 1991, more than 170,500; in 1992, it dropped to

64,000; and in 1993 it hovered between 8,000–10,000 per month. But the number is expected to rise sharply as Russia continues to slide into the sinkhole of misery and despair.

Leaving the country was difficult at first because the Soviets would not allow direct flights to Israel. Most of the Jews had to travel to foreign countries before they could head on to Israel. Most took only one piece of luggage. And many of them have never heard of Moses. Religious persecution has prevented most from owning, or even being taught, the Scriptures. It is easy to see why they would recall their own exodus instead of the one in Moses day.

> ✦ *Therefore, behold, the days come, saith the Lord, that it shall no more be said, The Lord liveth, that brought up the children of Israel out of the land of Egypt; But, The Lord liveth, that brought up the children of Israel from the land of the north.*
> (Jeremiah 16:14,15)

The Time of Jacob's Trouble

One bad thing Jeremiah saw in Israel's distant future is called "the time of Jacob's trouble." He said Israel will return and possess the land given to Abraham, Isaac and Jacob. But they will not have peace. They will experience the worst time in their entire history. They will go through great destruction, but they will survive as a nation. This "time of Jacob's trouble" is also called the tribulation period (Jeremiah 30:1–7).

> ✦ *Alas! for that day is great, so that none is like it: it is even the time of Jacob's trouble; but he shall be saved out of it.*
> (Jeremiah 30:7)

The Lord's Message for The Latter Days

The 30th chapter of Jeremiah is filled with God's promises to the children of Israel. It was meant to console and inspire the people by offering hope to the nation. It certainly did; and still does.

One promise tells us Jerusalem would be rebuilt in the same place. After saying it would be destroyed, the Lord said it would be rebuilt on top of the old ruins. That is why Jerusalem stands where it does today. God decreed it would be rebuilt there.

Another promise tells us Jerusalem would have a population increase. The number of Jews in Jerusalem was 40,000 in 1905; 99,500 in 1946; and 353,900 in 1990. Another 200,00 are expected to move there by the year 1995 and Israeli Housing Minister, Ariel Sharon predicts there will be 1 million Jews in the greater Jerusalem area "during our days."

God also promised to punish anyone who hurts Israel in the latter days. In 1948, exactly one day after Israel became a nation, the Jews were attacked by Arab armies from Egypt, Syria, Lebanon, Iraq and Transjordan. With God's help, a very unusual Israeli army defeated all of them.

On July 26, 1956, Egypt seized the Suez Canal from Britain and France; refused Israel use of the canal; blocked all ships going there; and initiated several border clashes. On October 9, 1956, Israel responded with a counterattack. Britain and France helped out. The Jews were winning big when the United Nations, backed by the United States and Russia, pulled them off. A United Nations Emergency Force was sent in to police the border.

In 1966, Egypt resumed the border clashes and the following year asked the United Nations to withdraw the peace keeping force. The United Nations complied and Egypt moved her army toward the border. Israel feared an eminent attack and struck first. The Israeli military attacked Egypt, Jordan and Syria at the same time. God gave the Jews a victory over all three nations in just six days.

On October 6, 1973, Egypt and Syria attacked Israel again. They were assisted by troops from Iraq, Jordan, Algeria, Morocco, Kuwait and Saudi Arabia. God graced Israel with a victory over Syria, Egypt was almost defeated and the remainder of the forces were pushed way back. The conflict lasted only seventeen days.

In 1990, Iraq invaded Kuwait and became entangled in the Persian Gulf War. The Iraqis launched thirty-nine Scud Missiles toward Israel in an effort to involve the Jews with the idea of turning this war into another Arab-Israeli conflict. The thirty-nine missiles resulted in the direct death of one Israeli and the indirect death of a dozen more. Combined forces defeated Iraq in one hundred hours.

The Israelis were also promised that their leaders would come from their own people. It would not be like it was during the earthly days of Jesus when leaders of another nation ruled over them. That is why they are ruled by their own people today.

Finally, when these things come to pass, the Lord said *consider it the latter days.* Make no mistake about it . . . God is setting the stage for the tribulation period and the second coming of Messiah. He is not only rebuilding and regathering the nation; He is preparing to judge the world.

+ *Thus saith the Lord.*
  (Jeremiah 30:18)
+ *The city shall be builded upon her own heap.*
  (Jeremiah 30:18)
+ *I will multiply them.*
  (Jeremiah 30:19)
+ *I shall punish all that oppress them.*
  (Jeremiah 30:20)
+ *Their nobles shall be of themselves.*
  (Jeremiah 30:21)
+ *In the latter days ye shall consider it.*
  (Jeremiah 30:24)

An Example of God's Love and The Work of The Holy Spirit

The Lord said He loves the Jews with an everlasting love. And He also said He would pull them into the land in the latter days. Multiplied thousands are pouring out of the land of their birth; giving up almost all their earthly possessions; enduring incredible persecution and hardship; moving to a land they have never seen. The sick and afflicted; mothers and expectant mothers are returning by plane, by boat, and by any way they can possibly make it. Why? Because God loves them and the Holy Spirit is drawing them.

Between 1985 and 1990, Ethiopian Jews were released in groups of 200 to 500. They left two to four times per year. Each group contained 50 to 70 refugees who required immediate hospitalization. Many of them were children suffering from the likes of malnutrition, malaria and tuberculosis. Ambulances met them when they arrived in Israel and transported them to the hospital.

During Operation Solomon, 81 of the 14,400 Jews who relocated needed hospitalization. Eleven babies were born within a period of thirty-seven hours twenty-three minutes. At least two babies were born aboard flights. When the people landed at the airport, their only possessions were the clothes they had on. Many were not even wearing shoes. The Spokesman for the Israeli Defense Forces commented, "It's like watching a scene from the Bible."

✦ *At the same time, saith the Lord.*
(Jeremiah 31:1)

✦ *With lovingkindness have I drawn thee.*
(Jeremiah 31:3)

✦ *I will gather the blind and the lame, the woman with child and her that travaileth with child.*
(Jeremiah 31:4)

Ezekiel

Ezekiel began prophesying before the fall of Israel. His early messages were filled with warnings of the nation's impending defeat and Jerusalem's destruction. After those things happened, his messages changed to words of hope and restoration.

The Brag

Ezekiel prophesied the enemies of Israel would brag, "Aha, even the ancient high places are ours in possession." Arabs have bragged they possessed the land and the holy places. They even built the Dome of the Rock on the temple mount. They still say, "The temple mount is ours and the holy city is ours."

When the face-to-face Arab-Israeli peace conference convened at the Royal Palace in Madrid in the fall of 1991, Syria immediately staked out a hard-line position. Farouk al-Sharaa, Syrian foreign minister, told the conference Israel must give up "every inch" of the land it conquered in 1967. This includes East Jerusalem, Bethlehem, Shiloh, Bethel and the temple mount.

Think about this. There are twenty-two Arab countries and one Jewish nation. The Arabs occupy almost 5,000,000 square miles of land and the Jews have about 8,000 square miles. The Arabs possess more than 600 acres for each Jewish acre. Arab land area is almost twice the size of the United States and the land of Israel is smaller than the state of New Jersey. But the Arabs want Israel to give up land.

✦ *The enemy hath said against you, Aha, even the ancient high*
  places are ours in possession.
  (Ezekiel 36:2)

The Real Landlord

When Esau left the land of Canaan, he settled in Idumea (or Edom). He overcame the former residents who lived there. Later, his descendants took over the land and they are numbered among the Arabs today. Ezekiel said, "the residue of the heathen" and the descendants of Esau will anger God by appointing the land of Israel into their possession.

The omnipotent God is the real Landlord in the land of Israel and the right to decide who lives there belongs to Him. He said the land will be Israel's inheritance. Those who say otherwise question the Lord's name, authority, power and the Bible.

✦ *Surely in the fire of my Jealousy have I spoken against the resi-*
  due of the heathen and all Idumea, which have appointed my
  land into their possession.
  (Ezekiel 36:5)

Fruit Trees on the Mountains

Not only will God decide who gets the land, but He will also determine who gets the fruit. And some, who once called Israel the land of milk and honey, are beginning to call it "the land of citrus." The once bleak hills are alive today with healthy, vigorous fruit trees. God is blessing them with ever-increasing yields. And Israeli farmers are selling millions of tons of high-quality citrus products; earning millions of dollars by exporting lemons, limes, oranges, grapefruit, tangerines, mandarin and other fruits.

> ✦ *But ye, O mountains of Israel, ye shall shoot forth your branches, and yield your fruit to my people of Israel; for they are at hand to come.*
> (Ezekiel 36:8)

The Cities of Israel

The ancient cities of Israel are another one of those great modern fulfillments of Bible prophecy. The fact that Ezekiel and others said they would be rebuilt has offered comfort and hope to the Jews for centuries. They longed for the day when God would allow construction to begin.

The southwestern section of Tel Aviv was formerly an ancient port city called Jaffa. It dates back to Bible times and has many historic sites. In 1909, it was re-established as an all-Jewish city. By 1918, it had grown to a population of 2,000. In 1935, 125,000. In 1937, 150,000. In 1990, it exceeded 325,000. Today, the metropolitan area is home to approximately 1,350,000 Jews.

Beersheba is the place where Abraham settled. It was a small town when Israel was first established. Today, it is a bustling city with more than 112,000 residents. Sing praises to the Lord, O heavens, and exult, O earth; for the Lord is comforting His people with the rebuilding of Israel.

> ✦ *And I will multiply men upon you, all the house of Israel, even all of it: and the cities shall be inhabited, and the wastes shall be builded.*
> (Ezekiel 36:10)

The Mountaintops

People say Israel and Judea belong to the Arabs; and to the Moslems; and to the Palestinians. And people say the Golan Heights belong to Syria. But the Word of God says the children of Israel will walk upon the mountains; and possess them. Different people say different things, but the last word belongs to the Lord.

Mount Carmel is where Elijah faced the doomed prophets of Baal during the days of Ahab and Jezebel. The city of Haifa stands there today and is home to almost 270,000 Israelis. The Jews also walk on, and possess, Mount Moriah, Mount Olivet, Mount Zion and more. Some have even requested permission to establish settlements on the Golan Heights.

> ✦ *Yea, I will cause men to walk upon you, even my people Israel; and they shall possess thee.*
> (Ezekiel 36:12)

The Great Name of God

God's name is very important. The world cannot know whose religion is right; whose teachings to follow; or who to worship, unless it knows who to call on. Is God's name Jehovah, Allah, Ishtar, Mother Earth, Gaia, Diana or what? Whose name do we declare among the nations?

Ezekiel knew many would not understand what was happening when God drove Israel out of the land; skeptics would doubt the holy character of Israel's God; unbelievers would associate the Jewish Deity with weakness and indifference; pagans would refuse to give Him the glory He deserves; some would ridicule His name; and some would turn to other gods. He knew people would misinterpret Israel's calamity and believe the Jewish God no longer reigns. He sits upon a throne, high and lifted up, but people do not understand. So they worship a variety of false gods.

The great prophet said that is why the Lord God would regather Israel. He would call His people home to set apart His hallowed name. He would work through Israel again to show the world who He is and to re-establish His reputation. When He gets through, there won't be any doubts about who is God (Ezekiel 36:16–23).

> ✦ *And I will sanctify my great name, which was profaned among the heathen.*
> (Ezekiel 36:23)

Heart Surgery

Did Ezekiel think the Jews would worship the true God when they return? No. But he believed they would come to the light because God will change their hearts and give them a new spirit. They will return in unbelief, but it won't last. God will bring them to the truth; give them wisdom and understanding.

Very few of the returning Jews are devout. Some say they have never heard of God. One poll of Soviet refugees revealed seventy-two percent considered themselves secular. Many were born and raised in communities void of synagogues and rabbis, exposed to other religions, married to a spouse of another nationality, and so forth. They do not really know the God who is calling them home. Even the devout Jews are misguided. They have not accepted Jesus. But that is only temporary.

> ✦ *A new heart also will I give you, and a new spirit will I put within you.*
> (Ezekiel 36:26)

Prosperity

A coalition of nations will attack Israel in the latter years to capture a great spoil. They will seek money, cattle and goods. Israel is not without hardship, but the land is more productive and prosperous than ever before. Israeli fields are alive with loaded fruit trees, great-looking crops, cattle, sheep and the like. The fact is, this young nation led the industrialized world in economic growth three years in a row; 1990, 1991 and 1992. And its growth rate was still increasing at the beginning of 1993. This prosperity serves as a magnet to Jews all over the world.

The Tel Aviv Stock Exchange had to halt trading in July 1991 when Naphtha Israel Petroleum Corp. struck oil near Gaza. Mud and oil gushed forth uncontrollably. Geological surveys indicate there is an abundance of "black gold" there.

Israel's cattle industry is flourishing. One large dairy recently celebrated its 30th birthday. It is just one of many dairies, but its sales are topping $20 million dollars a year. It keeps expanding and is even thinking about exporting many of its products.

Israel sits at the south end of the Dead Sea which is loaded with large quantities of valuable minerals. Some have said they are worth more than all the minerals in the rest of the world combined. Every element known to man is there, including silver and gold. And Israeli companies are extracting many of them.

> ✦ *Art thou come to take a spoil? hast thou gathered thy company to take a prey? to carry away silver and gold, to take away cattle and goods, to take a great spoil?*
> (Ezekiel 38:13)

Ravenous Birds

Ezekiel had a sure word of prophecy about birds too. When that great northern army comes against Israel in the last days, it will suffer a terrible defeat. And the Lord God will heap additional shame and dishonor upon it by sending birds of prey to feast on the "flesh of kings, and the flesh of captains, and the flesh of mighty men, and the flesh of horses, and of them that sit on them."

Some say there are birds of prey in Israel today. Others say there aren't any. We can only tell you what David Rudge wrote in the Jerusalem Post on September 14, 1991. His article entitled, *Birds of Prey Start Migration*, says,

> "The annual migration of birds of prey has started with a flock of over 55,000 honey buzzards, tracked by radar from Ben-Gurion Airport, flying over Israel "en route" from Eastern Europe and Asia to their winter watering grounds in Africa. The migration period usually lasts until the end of October, during which time 450,000 storks, 70,000 pelicans and 140,000 other birds of prey are expected to fly over the country."

> ✦ *I will give thee unto the ravenous birds of every sort.*
> (Ezekiel 39:4)

Amos

Amos was a "herdman" and a "gatherer of sycamore fruit" when God called him to be a prophet. He is noted for saying, *Prepare to meet thy God* (Amos 4:12). He had some good news too.

Crops

Amos probably made more than a few people squirm when he predicted God would send fire upon Judah to devour the palaces of Jerusalem. And it was no light thing when he predicted the slaying of thousands in Israel. But it was a wonderful thing when he said

God would restore the nation and cause the land to produce bountifully in the last days.

Today, Israel is using some of the most modern Agricultural techniques in the world and reaping remarkable results. Jewish farmers are irrigating, rotating crops, double-cropping and more. Their unique skills are paying off with a rich bounty of fruits, nuts, grain, cotton, poultry, herbs and vegetables. They meet their own needs and then export thousands of tons of avocados, tomatoes, persimmons, strawberries, red peppers, peanuts, almonds, pecans and Gali melons.

Every year, students from more than 100 nations travel to Israel to study the Jewish methods. Many of them are from countries having no diplomatic ties with the Jewish nation. They go because they want to learn how Israel is becoming the breadbasket of the Middle East.

✦ *The plowman shall overtake the reaper.*
   (Amos 9:13)

Waste Cities

At the beginning of his ministry, Amos prophesied the Philistine cities of Ashdod and Ashkelon would be cut off and the remnant of the people would perish (Amos 1:8). Zephaniah agreed when he said Ashkelon would become a desolation and the people of Ashdod would be driven out (Zephaniah 2:4).

Did it happen? The Bible says that the good King Hezekiah smote the Philistines in all that region (II Kings 18:8). He destroyed all that area and literally fulfilled the prophecies of Amos.

But Amos didn't stop with the bad news. He said the people would return and rebuild the waste cities. And today, 68,000 people live in Ashdod. And more than 54,000 have made Ashkelon (Ashqelon) their home. How do you explain the great harbor in Ashdod? What do you say about that large refinery there? Why have all those houses and apartments been built in Ashqelon? When the Word of God says something will happen, you better believe it.

✦ *And I will bring again the captivity of my people Israel, and they
shall build the waste cities, and inhabit them.*
(Amos 9:14)

Zechariah

Zechariah is known for predicting the triumphal entry of Jesus.
He said our Lord would be betrayed for thirty pieces of silver and
announced what would happen to the money. He prophesied the
disciples would be scattered and Jesus would be pierced in the side.
Since he was so accurate, what should we think about his visions of
Israel and Jerusalem in the last days?

God's Plan for Confronting the World

Zechariah believed God would use Israel in the last days to con-
front the world. He said God would make Jerusalem and Israel a
problem for the whole world. And every nation that harmed Israel
would be harmed in return.

Arab forces and Arab proxy powers have attacked Israel, waged
an economic boycott against the nation, published anti-Semitic lit-
erature against the people, boycotted companies doing business
with the Jews, terrorized the populace, desecrated the cemeteries,
stoned the police, killed the citizens and stolen their property. They
have mistreated the Jews and harmed them all over the world in
every way they could. They have taken extreme measures to embar-
rass, weaken and destroy the young nation.

While they were doing all of that, those same Arabs fought "like
cats and dogs" with each other. Some had civil wars, massacred
their own citizens, created famines, terrorized other nations and
used poison gas in violation of the Geneva Convention. Up until
Iraq's invasion of Kuwait, the United Nations overlooked all of that.
It was willingly ignorant and self-blinded to any and all Arab atrocities. The United Nations never condemned, warned or censured an
Arab state for anything.

Over the same period, the United Nations placed Israel under a
microscope and turned the new nation into its own personal
punching bag. According to the Jerusalem Post for the week ending

June 22, 1991, Israel was "condemned" 49 times, "warned" 7 times and issued 31 "expressions of concern." The situation would have been even worse except for United States and European vetoes. Now even that is changing. An article in Newsweek magazine entitled, *A Marriage on the Rocks,* dated September 30, 1992 says,

> Washington no longer sees Israel as its key strategic ally. There was always an inherent tension between U.S. support for the Jewish state and its ties with conservative Arab states such as Saudi Arabia. But in an unstable region where Moscow was arming radical regimes from Baghdad to Tripoli, democratic Israel was considered Washington's most reliable "strategic partner." Now the collapse of the Soviet Union and the gulf war have paved the way for a stronger U.S. tilt in the direction of the oil sheiks. Arab states expected a more sympathetic hearing from Washington after co-operating in the war on Saddam. Now they are getting it, along with access to the latest American military hardware.

God is preparing the world for a confrontation over Israel and Jerusalem. We call it the tribulation period and it will determine who has the clout on this globe. If world leaders would study the Scriptures on this matter, and seek to do God's will, they could avoid "the faithful lightening of His terrible swift sword." Since they will not, this onslaught is inevitable.

The nations of the world will gather against tiny Israel. Two-thirds of the Jews will be killed and Jerusalem will be captured. The remaining one-third will escape. These Jews will accept Jesus and He will personally intervene on their behalf (Zechariah 13:8-9; 14:1-3).

✦ *And in that day will I make Jerusalem a burdensome stone for all people.*
(Zechariah 12:3)

✦ *All that burden themselves with it shall be cut in pieces.*
(Zechariah 12:3)

✦ *And it shall come to pass in that day, that I will seek to destroy all the nations that come against Jerusalem.*
(Zechariah 12:9)

Food for Thought

When we pray The Lord's Prayer, we pray, *Our Father which art in heaven, Hallowed be thy name. Thy kingdom come. Thy will be done in earth as it is in heaven.* When we conclude, we pray, *For thine is the kingdom, and the power, and the glory, for ever. Amen.* We pray for God to have a kingdom on earth and for His will to be carried out here just like it is in heaven.

Devout Jews have expected their King to come and rule from the throne of David for ages. Some even thought Jesus might be that King. To Christians, He is that King.

If Jesus is that King and He is planning to rule over this earth from Israel to make things better, do you think our global leaders will accept Him? Do you think our blind misguided leaders are ready to cede their sovereignty to an Israeli King? Do you think the Russians, Iranians, Libyans, or Communists will obey the King of Israel? The answer is, "No." They will not willingly grant their authority to Him and they will not willingly obey Him.

If God's will is to be done on earth, leaders and nations must know who God is. The world's wickedness and the rise of Israel means we are **On The Brink** of finding out. Our steadfast and loving God has not cast Israel aside and He is not about to allow the world to be buried in the pit of sin. The Jews are His means of protecting His name so the planet can be healed. The Church should rally behind them (Romans 11:13–27).

Chapter 3

Russia

Ezekiel was called to be a watchman unto the house of Israel (Ezekiel 3:17; 33:7). His task was comparable to the man who stood on the city wall at night looking and listening for signs of approaching danger. If he saw an enemy or heard a suspicious noise, he was required to sound an alarm and awaken the people.

Ezekiel stood on the wall of time, looking far off into the future, when he spotted Israel's return to the magnificent land. He saw the chosen people going home full of hope and joy, the holy people singing praises to our faithful and loving God, the dearly beloved nation being restored, the famous ancient cities being rebuilt, mountains covered with trees, brooks of water, bountiful crops, lush green gardens, lovely meadows, flowering fields; a land of wheat, and barley, and vines, and fig trees, and pomegranates; a land of olive oil and honey; a good land with many marvelous things. But when he looked a little further into the future, he saw frightening signs of impending danger. Some of the old enemies would still be there. They would team up with new adversaries and all of them would seek to invade the holy land together.

The Word of the Lord

Keep in mind, this is not a message from Ezekiel, but one that was given to Ezekiel. The Spirit of God called him to receive it and

equipped him to deliver it. That is the only way he could possibly
know these spine-tingling things. The information was given too
long ago and is far too incredible for the human mind to conceive.
Think about it. Ezekiel lived during the hard times of the Babylonian
captivity. He was a contemporary of Jeremiah and Daniel. He was
born about 625 B.C., in the eighteenth year of the good King Josiah.
That was more than 600 years before the birth of Christ and nearly
2100 years before Columbus discovered America. Ezekiel could not
know these mind-boggling events on his own. Without a doubt, this
is a message from our omniscient God.

+ *And the word of the Lord came unto me.*
  (Ezekiel 38:1)

Prophesy Against Russia's Leader

There are four things that cause students of prophecy to believe
Ezekiel was told to prophesy against Russia's wicked leader. They
are his title, his territory, the cities under his control and the location
of his country in relation to Israel.

(1) His Title

The word of the Lord came to Ezekiel telling him to prophesy
against Gog. So the problem at this point is to identify Gog. Dr. J.
Vernon McGee says:

> "Gog is a word for ruler, meaning roof, which actually means 'the
> man on top.' I can't think of a better name for a dictator than Gog.
> If he is not on top, he is not a dictator, and if he is on top, he is a
> dictator."[1]

Gog is a title describing the leader of a territory. He is its dictator.

+ *Set thy face against Gog . . . and prophesy against him.*
  (Ezekiel 38:2)

(2) His Territory

When we try to identify Gog's territory, we find ourselves tan-
gled in the brier patch of Bible translations. It gets thorny because
the King James Version calls Gog *the chief prince of Meshech and
Tubal,* and the New King James Version calls him *the prince of
Rosh, Meshech and Tubal.* The old translation calls this leader *the*

chief prince, but the corrected version calls him *the prince of Rosh.* "Chief" is the Hebrew word "Rosh."

Is Gog "the chief (Rosh) prince" or is he "the prince of Rosh?" Is "Rosh" a descriptive name or is "Rosh" a proper name? One needs to decide between the two versions.

William Kelly, who has written several commentaries and is often quoted says:

> "It is true that . . . (Rosh), when the context requires it to be a common appellative, means 'head' or 'chief'; but it is this sense which in the present instance brings confusion. There can be no doubt therefore that it must be taken as a proper name."[2]

The hard-working translators of the New King James Version Bible understood this and corrected the wording. "Rosh" is a proper name and Gog is "the prince of Rosh." He is the evil dictator who rules the Bible region called Rosh.

✦ Gog is the "chief" prince.
(Ezekiel 38:2)

The Identity of Rosh

The list of scholars who teach Rosh in Russia is very impressive. After reviewing the works of William Kelly, Arno C. Gaebelein and Louis Bauman, Dr. J. Dwight Pentecost says:

> "Thus the identification of Rosh as modern Russia would seem to be well authenticated and generally accepted."[3]

Dr. J. Vernon McGee writes:

> "Bishop Lowther made the statement that Rosh taken as a proper name in Ezekiel signified the inhabitants of Scythia from whom the modern Russians derive their name."[4]

Dr. Robert Lindsted supplies the following information:

> "If you buy a Jerusalem Post newspaper which is written in Hebrew, any article concerning Russia has the word Rosh in it. It has not changed in twenty-eight hundred years, being exactly the same word that is used here in Ezekiel."[5]

The esteemed Dr. C. I. Schofield concluded:

> "The reference is to the powers in the north of Europe, headed by Russia."[6]

In summary, Rosh is Russia and "the prince of Rosh" is the prince of Russia. He is the hard-line authoritarian ruler of the land of Russia.

Since the word "Russia" is analogous to the republic of Russia and to the former Soviet Union, it must be understood Russia is here taken to mean the republic of Russia. "The prince of Rosh" is the dictator of the republic of Russia. But this does not preclude the fact that he may also rule other republics, states or nations at the same time he rules his own territory.

(3) The Cities Under His Control

Dr. J. Dwight Pentecost was quoting from *Russian Events in the Light of Bible Prophecy* by Louis Bauman when he said:

> ". . . Gesenius, whose Hebrew Lexicon has never been superseded . . . identified 'Meshech' as Moscow, the capital of modern Russia in Europe. 'Tubal' he identified as Tobolsk, the earliest province of Asiatic Russia to be colonized . . . Moscow bespeaks Russia in Europe, and Tobolsk bespeaks Russia in Asia."[7]

Moscow and Tobolsk are two cities ruled by the republic of Russia. And the "prince" of those cities is the dictator of that republic.

> ✦ *Set thy face against Gog, the land of Magog, the chief prince of Meshech and Tubal.*
> (Ezekiel 38:2)

(4) The Location of His Country in Relation to Israel

The King James Version places Gog in the "north parts" and the New King James Version puts him in the "far north." There are only four countries north of Israel. They are Lebanon, Syria, Turkey and Russia. The nation in the "far north" is the republic of Russia. All other nations are ruled out.

Those who are trying to buy democracy in Russia with the hard-earned wages of their citizens should take a good look at this. God knows the future before it happens and He has told us this powerful nation will end up with a dictator. Democracy will not succeed in Russia.

> ✦ *Thou shalt come from thy place out of the north parts.*
> (Ezekiel 38:15)

Do not be Fooled

Since the failed military coup in the former Soviet Union, in August 1991, many ill-advised people want to cast aside this important prophecy. They want us to believe Russia is no longer dangerous. But one failed coup does not justify downplaying any message from God. And it is a poor reason to assume the Bible is incorrect. There is no evidence Boris Yeltsin is not Gog, or another dictator will not arise in his place. There is no reason to assume the current hard times, or some other crisis, will not cause an unstoppable demand for the restoration of the Communist Party. "It isn't wise for the United States to say, 'We fully support Yeltsin,'" says Mikhail Afstaviev, a Yeltsin critic in the Russian parliament. "I suppose that very quickly, even by June, he'll be out of power."

The fact is, there has already been an attempt to assassinate Yeltsin, an attempt to impeach him, and an attempt to restore the Communist regime of the former Soviets. Keep in mind that Samson was weakened when Delilah helped shave his head. But his hair began to grow back. And he regained his strength. It is true that the bear's claws have been clipped, but claws grow back too.

When Soviet Vice-President Gennady Yanayev announced he was taking over during the failed coup, he said a "committee of eight" would be running the government for the foreseeable future. After that failed, Boris Yeltsin said there were "controlling factors behind the scenes." The "committee of eight" was not alone. A mysterious figure, or figures, was standing in the wings. Can we be sure they are not still there? Do we know they are not behind the ongoing challenge to Yeltsin's leadership?

Mr. Yeltsin also said, "Russia must have help from the West or the possibility of a great civil war and global conflict may be upon us. And now deceased former United States President Richard Nixon wrote in The Wall Street Journal, "If Mr. Yeltsin fails, the prospects for the next 50 years will turn grim." And German Chancellor Helmut Kohl warned, "Failure of democratic reforms could threaten global stability and unleash a refugee exodus not seen since World

War II." Are we sure Mr. Yeltsin won't fail? Are we sure his reforms won't be scuttled? Are we sure his health won't fail? He has led a charmed life so far. But how long can it last? He is a mortal human being too.

It is good to want to think and hope for the best. But it is better to remember every word of God is sure and certain. The heads of nations will come and go, but the identification of Meshech, Tubal and the country to the far north of Israel will not change.

Instead of downplaying true prophecy, we should examine how the failed coup affects it. It was God's instrument for tearing down the Iron Curtain. At least, for the time being, Russia has been opened up for the gospel. God has sent in missionaries and preachers with the Bible. We should not wish problems on any people. But we can rejoice over this. It gave the Church an amazing opportunity to give the Word of God to millions of people. We can praise God because many soldiers will receive grace and salvation before this great battle rages.

The Message

One can only speculate as to why the all-knowing God gave this message. But there is no need to speculate about the truth of it. Almost every newscast reveals it is precisely correct.

God's Attitude Toward Russia

Newspapers and magazines are filled with alarming articles about the ever-worsening conditions in the former Soviet Union. Some reports even say they are now more severe than in the Great Depression. Earthquakes have left thousands homeless. Coal, oil and gas production have constantly declined. Crop failures and food shortages are common. Rationing has started. Store shelves are empty. Essential medicines are scarce. Basic necessities are hard to find. Unemployment is rampant. Markets have collapsed. Factories have closed. Hyperinflation has arrived. Prices have soared. Alcoholism is widespread. Trade Unions have struck. Poverty has spread. Troops have defected. Ethnic groups have clashed. Tempers have flared. Economic reforms have failed. Government deficits have soared. Gross national product has gone into a free fall. Debt has multiplied. Credit sources have dried up. Art treasures have been sold. Weapons have been sold. Politicians have resigned. Communists have been jailed. The military is demoralized. Corruption is unchecked. Fears of disintegration and chaos abound. Dire warnings are commonplace. The hammer and sickle have been pulled down. The new fragile democratic movement is in danger. And many of the reforms have gone haywire.

Several nations have tried to help, but they have been unsuccessful. Russia's vexing problems boil down to something beyond human control. Our Everlasting Father knew ages ago He would have to bring "the evil empire" down. So He ordained it's judgment. Conventional wisdom may say otherwise, but the issue is settled. Russia is hanging by a thread and squirming in her death throes. It is the judgment of the Lord God upon a nation that went too far in opposing Him and His kingdom in Israel.

✦ *Behold, I am against thee, O Gog.*
(Ezekiel 38:3)

Russia's Turnaround

In 1922, the Union of Soviet Socialist Republics (U.S.S.R.) consisted of Russia, Byelorussia, Transcaucasia and the Ukraine. During the '20s, Russia added Tajikistan, Turkmenistan and Uzbekistan. In 1936, Transcaucasia was divided into Azerbaijan, Armenia and Georgia and the union added Kazakhstan and Kirghiz. In 1939, it seized Poland and part of Finland. In 1940, it grabbed Estonia, Latvia, Lithuania, Moldavia and part of Romania. East Germany was taken in 1945. By 1948, it controlled the East European governments of Albania, Bulgaria, Czechoslovakia, Hungary, Poland, Romania and Yugoslavia. Russia was ever-expanding and constantly gobbling up more of the world's land and population. It seemed like the power-hungry nation took whatever it wanted and got away with it. Where was the moral outrage?

The situation began to turn around in 1989 and 1990. The Berlin Wall was breached and Germany was reunified. Poland elected a non-Communist prime minister and a non-Communist president.

The "velvet revolution" toppled hard-line Communists in Czecho-slovakia. The Communist Party resigned in Hungary. The government of Romania was toppled and a new cabinet was elected. Estonia, Latvia and Lithuania all elected parliaments with non-Communist majorities and all of them began seeking independence. Next came "the shock of a lifetime." On August 18, 1991, Soviet hard-liners, under Vice-President Gennady Yanayev, attempted a coup. World leaders were stunned when the KGB, the Communist Party and the General Staff of the Armed Forces seized control of the government. Seventy-two hours later, it was all over, but the Soviet Union was forced to restructure itself and it will never again be the same.

At first, Soviet President Mikhail Gorbachev tried to hold onto power and the former Soviet Union central authorities tried to resist the fast-paced changes that were taking place. They quickly tried to compromise with Boris Yeltsin on a new "Union of Sovereign States." A new State Council was elected to replace the Congress of People's Deputies. Both sides agreed to several radical changes as the former authorities tried to preserve what power they had left. But it was too late. A dramatic "turnaround" was taking place.

The Baltic States were granted independence, shrinking the Soviet Union for the first time since the Communist Party took over. Communism was declared a failure and the Communist Party was suspended. Hundreds of thousands of KGB troops were transferred to the Defense Ministry. The KGB lost control of government communication systems. Reformers were put in charge of the military. The leaders of the newly independent states began to exert themselves and the new Union of Sovereign States fell apart.

Next, the leaders of the three Slavic states—Russia, Byelorussia and Ukraine—announced they were forming a new "Commonwealth of Independent States." Mikhail Gorbachev called this unconstitutional. But most of the other republics soon joined. President Gorbachev's power was gone. His position was meaningless. The remnants of the former Soviet ministries were out of power. And they could no longer stop the rapid changes taking place.

✦ *I will turn thee back.*
(Ezekiel 38:4)

A Hook in the Jaw

If a person has a hook in his jaw, he loses control to whoever or whatever controls the hook. He will go wherever the hook goes. God is using a hook to take control of the Russian stronghold. His hook is Russia's need for food, goods, money, medicine and such. With many of the problems unresolved and strategic mistakes still being made, fear and anxiety are mounting. Hunger and deprivation are real and people worry about starvation and famine. It has caused former Soviet President Gorbachev to say the situation has reached an "explosive critical mass." His country is on-the-ropes and nothing short of dramatic action can prevent total disaster.

✦ *I will put hooks into thy jaws.*
(Ezekiel 38:4)

Pulling on a Bear

In June 1991, Mikhail Gorbachev traveled to Oslo, Norway to receive the Nobel Peace Prize for 1990. He used the occasion to announce a peaceful "new world order" depends upon massive aid from the West to finance Soviet reforms. He also said, "If perestroika fails, the prospect of entering a new peaceful period in history will vanish, at least for the foreseeable future." The former Soviet leader may not have realized it, but he was being prophetic.

God will pull the weakened bear into Israel. This will be the Lord's doing. Taking control of Russia will be His decision. Some people do not think like this, but they fail to understand everything the uncorruptible God does is good. He can even bring good out of war and turn war into good.

✦ *I will bring thee forth.*
(Ezekiel 38:4)

The Russian Coalition

Five of the republics in the new Commonwealth of Independent States—Kazakhstan, Uzbekistan, Kyrgyzstan, Turkmenistan and Tajikistan—are predominantly Moslem. It has long been rumored by supposedly reliable intelligence sources that the former Soviet leaders promised Islamic countries they would help do something about Israel in exchange for their not interfering in the religious affairs of the Soviet republics. It was a mutual agreement. The former Soviets would help liberate Palestine. The Islamic countries would not stir up religious hatred in Moslem republics of the Soviet Union. Those leaders are no longer in power. And those agreements no longer exist. But the time will come when a Russian dictator will think an evil thought; dream the impossible dream; and decide to plunder Israel. He will gather a coalition of nations to help him. And they will head south toward Israel.

+ *Persia, Ethiopia, and Libya with them.*
  (Ezekiel 38:5)

+ *Gomer, and all his bands; the house of Togarmah of the north quarters, and all his bands.*
  (Ezekiel 38:6)

+ *Thou shalt think an evil thought.*
  (Ezekiel 38:10)

Iran

Most dictionaries and encyclopedias will tell you Persia is Iran. The nation is bitterly opposed to Israel. It claimed neutrality during the Persian Gulf War. But it admitted sending milk and medicine to Iraq. It's leaders opened a bank account for contributions to Iraq. And they permitted supplies to be smuggled across their borders into Iraq. They denounced the United States for bombing civilian targets there. And threatened to enter the war against Israel, if Israel got involved.

An article by Moshe Zak in the Jerusalem Post entitled *The Price of Not Helping Gorbachev,* dated December 21, 1991, says,

"If Gorbachev is deposed and the Soviet Union, recently a stabilizing factor, falls apart and gives rise to a bloc of Moslem states siding with fundamentalist Iran, hater of Israel and hater of peace, the damage to the world and the region could be great."

It happened. President Gorbachev was toppled. The Soviet Union crumbled like a cookie. And Iran immediately embarked on a program to influence the religious attitudes of the former Soviet Moslem republics. This got the attention of Newsweek magazine on February 3, 1992. Under the heading *A Scramble for Influence,* the writers say,

"The breakup of the Soviet Union has spurred a regional contest to shape the political, economic and religious fate of the five resource-rich Central Asian republics. Rivals include: Iran.

"Eager to secure allies to the north, Teheran has been courting the Muslim republics with diplomatic and trade overtures. It has also been accused of exporting Islamic fundamentalism to Tajikistan, with which Iran shares a comon language."

The magazine quotes a Suadi official as saying, "Iran would like nothing better than to have five mini-Irans, completely under their sway." The fear that these five Moslem republics will influence the Russian republic to form a coalition of armies to attack Israel and liberate Palestine is real and Scriptural.

A story by Douglas Waller in Newsweek magazine entitled *Sneaking in the Scuds,* on June 22, 1992 says,

" 'The diplomats may be talking peace,' a Western ambassador in the region says, 'but the generals are preparing for war.' "

An article by Louise Lief in U.S. News & World Report under the title, *Iran's Familiar Face,* includes the following:

"While Rafsanjani's technocrats are wooing foreign investors and implementing free-market reforms, Iran also has launched what United States government analysts estimate is a five-year, $10 billion military buildup. At the same time, the Islamic Republic is making new threats against its neighbors and Rafsanjani's opponents have begun an anti-Western social counterrevolution . . . .

"Iran is now the chief opponent of Israel and of the United States-sponsored Mideast peace talks. Days after the United States elections, President Rafsanjani told worshipers at Friday prayers at Tehran University that if the Clinton administration is preoccupied with reviving the United States economy, 'the people here will settle accounts with (Israel).' Iran supports radical Palestinian groups that oppose the peace talks, and also the Lebanese Hezbollah that is firing rockets into northern Israel in an apparent effort to derail the negotiations."

Among the nations of the world, Iran is the most adamant in its opposition to Israel. It has vowed to destroy Israel; vowed to destroy anyone friendly to Israel; vowed to wreck the Israeli-Palestine Liberation Organization (PLO) peace agreement; and vowed to acquire the weapons to do it. Despite all its internal problems, the nation is squandering its badly needed resources on such things as missiles, planes, tanks, bombs and poisoned gas. It is reported to be manufacturing nerve gases, including mustard gas, and is suspected of acquiring at least three nuclear warheads from one of the former Soviet republics. And the equipment is not cheap. It is the best money can buy. It includes computer systems, communication systems, MiG-29 fighter planes, T-72 battle tanks, surface-to-air missiles and surface-to-surface missiles. Some of it is defensive. But most of it is offensive.

All of this combines to make the nation one of the single greatest threats to peace and stability in the entire world. It has targets. And is preparing to strike.

✦ Persia (Iran) will join the coalition.
    (Ezekiel 38:5)

Ethiopia and/or Iraq and/or Sudan.
Some versions of the Bible say Ethiopia and some say Cush. The word rendered Ethiopia in some translations is Cush in the original Hebrew.

This causes a problem. Some interpreters say this is a reference to the modern nation of Ethiopia. Others say it is a reference to the Old Testament nation of Cush. And to make matters worse, two different areas were known as Cush during Old Testament times.

The modern nation of Ethiopia is not very strong, but it could join the Russian coalition. This is especially true because Iran is trying hard to destabilize the nation so it can be turned into an

Islamic state. Such a state would take its cues from Iran and be ready and willing to attack Israel.

The Old Testament locates the earliest area called Cush. Moses wrote, *And a river went out of Eden to water the garden; and from thence it was parted, and became into four heads. The name of the first is Pison: that is it which compasseth the whole land of Havilah . . . And the name of the second river is Gihon: the same is it that compasseth the whole land of Ethiopia (Cush). And the name of the third river is Hiddekel (the Tigris): that is it which goeth toward the east of Assyria. And the fourth river is Euphrates* (Genesis 2:10-14). The Garden of Eden was in modern Iraq. And the Pison, Tigris and Euphrates rivers are in the general area of Iraq and Iran. They are on the continent of Asia, not Africa.

Soviet Foreign Minister Eduard Shevardnadze shocked the world by resigning his post in December of 1990. He said he resigned partly because of severe criticism at home over his stance against Iraq during the Persian Gulf crisis. His country had strong ties with Iraq and many of its citizens expected Russia to support Iraq in the conflict.

On February 11, 1991, U.S. News & World Report wrote United States intelligence sources were saying Washington had evidence the Soviet Union was supplying Iraq with information it could use to target and conceal Scud missiles. A spokesman for the Bush administration denied it.

One week later, the same magazine wrote intelligence sources were implicating the Soviet Union in shipments of "cargoes of military significance" across Jordan to Iraq. The Bush administration was reluctant to verify the report.

Other reports indicated the Soviet Union established routes across Afghanistan and Iran into Iraq. The routes were supposedly used to supply Iraq with arms, chemical weapons, food and other essential supplies.

And the flurry of raids during the closing days of the Bush administration shed more light on the subject when the Russian government admonished the United States for acting without the explicit approval of the United Nations. Russia even announced, one week later, that it was prepared to use its veto power in the United Nations Security Council to stop the American-led attacks. And Russian President Boris Yeltsin criticized the United States tendency to dictate its terms to Iraq.

Some Old Testament scholars think the area just south of Egypt was also known as Cush. They teach this because Cush and Egypt are frequently mentioned together in the Old Testament and it looks like they shared a common border. This area is occupied by the modern nation of Sudan (Isaiah 11:11; 18:1; 20:3; Ezekiel 29:10; 30:4,5,9; Daniel 11:43; Amos 9:7).

Sudan is a militant Islamic state today. Its army, navy and air force are being equipped and trained by Iran. It maintains training camps for the PLO. It helped broker an alliance between the PLO and the Hamas movement. And it has vowed to spread Islam throughout the Middle East.

✦ Ethiopia (Cush) will join the coalition.
  (Ezekiel 38:5)

Libya

Some versions of the Bible say Libya and some say Put. The word translated Libya is Put in the original Hebrew.

It is difficult to positively identify Put. Some writers locate it in the area of Iraq and Iran. Others place it in North Africa with modern day Libya. Both places have Arabs who would join Russia in an all-out attack on Israel.

✦ Libya will join the coalition.
  (Ezekiel 38:5)

Germany

Virtually all Bible scholars agree Gomer is Germany. But it is hard for people to believe Germany would do this. Nevertheless, the Bible says, "Gomer (Germany), and all his bands" will join Russia in this invasion.

Germany was a divided nation prior to October 3, 1990. Up until that time, prophecy buffs were willing to overlook "all his bands" and apply this prophecy to East Germany. That all changed when the division ended. "Gomer, and all his bands" have been reunited.

Germany and Russia have signed a "friendship treaty" and Germany's first important foreign visitor was no less than Mikhail Gorbachev. In exchange for Russian approval of German reunification, Germany gave Russia about $9.5 billion and agreed to allow Russian troops to stay in East Germany until the end of 1994.

Germany is Russia's largest trading partner. The two countries have strong ties and they will become even stronger. They hope to strengthen each other so both can have more influence over the affairs of Europe.

In the fall of 1990, Germany was put in the position of deciding between the United States and Russia. The United States did not want to give Russia the food supplies Moscow requested. Germany rejected the United States position, sided with the Russians, and sent the food anyway.

Germany gave President Bush problems during the Persian Gulf Crisis. He was organizing the coalition against Iraq, but Germany resisted. Chancellor Kohl's government wanted to negotiate with Saddam Hussein.

In February of 1992, Germany stopped all weapons shipments to its North Atlantic Treaty Organization (NATO) partner Turkey. The angry Turkish President Turgut Ozal ominously warned "Germany changed a lot after unification. It is as if it is trying to intervene in everything, interfere with everyone, trying to prove it is a great power. In the past, Hitler's Germany did the same thing."

In August of 1991, Mikhail Gorbachev asked the Group of Seven leading industrial powers, the G-7, for massive aid to shore up Russia's ailing economy. The United States took the position throwing money at the problem would not cure it and called for major reforms first. Germany had made $35 billion in commitments to Russia and accused the G-7 of being "stingy." By May of 1992, Germany's commitments to the former Soviets had increased to $47 billion.

And another $19 billion had been designated for other Eastern European countries.

Polls conducted in Germany show strong opposition to Israel. Antisemitism and neo-Nazism are growing and many Germans blame Israel for exploiting the Holocaust. German companies helped Iraq with its efforts to acquire chemical weapons and offensive nuclear weapons. And there have been reports Germany is selling nuclear weapons technology to Iran even though there is general agreement Iran wants to use those weapons against Israel.

It all boils down to a lot of cooperation between Russia, Germany, Iraq and Iran and a lot of animosity between the Germans and Israelis. The unthinkable will happen.

✦ Gomer (Germany) will join the coalition.
   (Ezekiel 38:6)

Armenia and/or Turkey and/or the Baltic States

Togarmah of the north quarters and all his bands will join the alliance, but they are hard to identify. According to Dr. Charles R. Taylor, Togarmah had two divisions. It is his opinion the southern division settled in Turkey and the northern division settled in the Baltic States region of Latvia, Estonia and Lithuania.[8] Hal Lindsey concludes Togarmah is part of modern southern Russia.[9] Harry Rimmer says, "Togarmah has always been the land which we now call Armenia."[10] Louis Bauman says it is "probably the Turkoman tribes of central Asia, together with Siberia, the Turks and the Armenians."[11] Dr. J. Dwight Pentecost adds, "how far this people extends beyond Turkey or Armenia cannot be positively determined, but it could include Asiatic peoples federated with Russia."[12]

Armenia is in a difficult position. The nation wants its independence from Russia, but is bordered by old enemies and hostile neighbors—Turkey, Iran and Azerbaijan. Consequently, many Armenian citizens believe they need Russia for protection.

Turkey may not have a choice either. It is becoming expedient for the country to cooperate with the Russians. Turkey has been a pro-Western nation and member of NATO for many years, but the West is placing less importance on this ally because it now assumes the Russian threat is diminishing. This is making the nation more vulnerable to Russian intimidation and pressure.

President Turgut Ozal, who often opposed his own large Moslem population to side with the West, is now dead. And Turkey is moving closer to Iran. High-level meetings, designed to improve relations between the two, are succeeding. Both are Islaamic republics. They share many things in common.

The three Baltic States have declared, and been granted, independence. But Communists occupy many of the seats in Parliament, Lithuania has elected a Communist to be its first president, Russian troops are still on Baltic States soil and many former Soviet officials are still calling for a restoration of the former Soviet empire. That empire may be gone forever, but it is probably too early to place your bets.

✦ Togarmah will join the coalition.
(Ezekiel 38:6)

God's Advice to Russia's Leader

The Russians have now completed two arms reduction treaties with the West, but they are still allowed to have 3500 nuclear warheads. So even if these treaties are signed, they will remain a very powerful and dangerous force for many years. An article in Newsweek magazine entitled, *Nukes on the Loose,* dated December 16, 1991 asks, "As the Soviet Union breaks up, who will get control of the 27,000 warheads in its far-flung arsenal?" The article reads,

> "Under the new Strategic Arms Reduction Treaty (START), Washington and Moscow are supposed to destroy some of their long-range weapons. And Presidents Bush and Gorbachev have promised to withdraw and dismantle many tactical nukes. But a weakened Soviet government cannot carry out such tasks promptly. Sergei Rogov, a Soviet arms-control expert, estimates it would take at least 25 to 30 years to dismantle all of the weaponry."

George J. Church wrote an article with an amazingly similar title for Time magazine with the same date, December 16, 1991. His article was entitled, *Soviet Nukes On the Loose,* and he says,

"Western experts do not doubt the sincerity of Ukraine and the other republics in wanting to carry out massive nuclear disarmament—for the moment. Their fear is that minds might change in six months or so if no satisfactory arrangements for control can be worked out and if republic leaders become enamored of the diplomatic and political clout that possession of nukes confers. Ukraine and some other republics fear they will be unable to resist Russian domination if they turn over responsibility for any of their nuclear arsenal to Yeltsin's government. The danger would become greater still if military or right-wing coups overthrew the present Kremlin and republic leaders, as could happen if winter food and fuel shortages touch off street riots. Talk of just such a coup is rampant these days in Moscow."

The former Soviet Union spent all its years preparing for war and many years will pass before it is unprepared, if ever. Much of that power has passed on to the republic of Russia. Most of the time, the Soviets spent 20–25% of their Gross National Product (GNP) on the military. They continue to maintain 3 to 4 million troops. They continue to build naval bases, nuclear submarines, aircraft carriers, fighter planes, bombers, super-bombers and tanks. And they still have 11,000 nuclear warheads aimed at the United States. We must never forget the Russians were preparing for war and they will remain prepared until they assail Israel.

✦ *Be thou prepared.*
(Ezekiel 38:7)

The Time of the Coalition Attack

The coalition will attack in the latter years and the latter days after the long expected regathering of the Jews.

✦ *In the latter years thou shalt come into the land.*
(Ezekiel 38:8)

✦ *It shall be in the latter days.*
(Ezekiel 38:16)

✦ *Thou shalt come into the land that is brought back from the sword, and is gathered out of many people.*
(Ezekiel 38:8)

Security Agreement and/or Peace Treaty

Ezekiel prophesied Israel will be "dwelling safely." And virtually all Bible scholars interpret this to mean "under a peace treaty." A majority of them even believe the peace treaty being referred to is the covenant the Antichrist makes pertaining to Israel. If that assumption is correct, the Russian onslaught will occur during the tribulation period (Daniel 9:27).

Dr. Emil Gaverluk does not agree with that. He points out the Hebrew word for peace is "shalom," but the word in Ezekiel 38:8,11,14 is "betakh" and the word for confirm in Daniel 9:27 is "gabar."[13] His point is the three different Hebrew words indicate three different situations.

"Shalom"would indicate peace, but there is no "shalom" in the Ezekiel or Daniel passages. The Jews will not obtain "shalom" until they accept Jesus.

"Betakh" in the Ezekiel passages means Israel will have the false impression the nation is dwelling securely. It indicates the Jews will be duped into signing a worthless security agreement.

"Gabar" in the Daniel passage is more than the impression of a security agreement. "Gabar" is a confirmed agreement. It is a strong covenant the Antichrist pushes on Israel.

If Dr. Gaverluk is right, the Russian coalition of nations could beset the Jews before the tribulation period. It remains to be seen, but the ongoing Middle East peace talks may have already resulted in Israel being duped into thinking it has a security agreement. We should keep in mind these talks, which began in October, 1991, have now produced an agreement to give the Palestinians limited self-rule over the Gaza Strip and the West Bank city of Jerico. They call for a more definitive recognition of Israel. And a permanent settlement within two years. This bears very close scrutiny.

✦ *They shall dwell safely all of them.*
   (Ezekiel 38:8, 11, 14)

Another Desert Storm

Many prophecy buffs have been watching for the nations to slowly and steadily align into the predicted coalition. But Ezekiel said they will arise and come like a storm which suggests the idea this alliance will come up fast. It will be Russia's last-ditch effort to save the union and it will be quickly-but poorly-organized.

The Persian Gulf crisis is an example. Iraq invaded Kuwait on August 2, 1990. The UN Security Council condemned Iraq just one day later. It imposed sanctions just four days later. The United States deployed troops to Saudi Arabia just five days later and on November 29, 1990, the United Nations authorized the use of force if Iraq failed to cease its occupation of Kuwait by January 15, 1991. It took less than five months to assemble twenty nations into a coalition.

"Like a storm" is a suggestion of turbulence and violence. Storms roar, blow, damage and destroy. They often come up in a hurry and pass by just as fast.

After a time of "softening-up," Desert Storm broke forth immediately with incredible violence and destruction. The storm lasted about 100 hours and then it suddenly stopped before total victory was achieved. That is a good example of how the Russian alliance will act. It will organize very fast; attack quickly and violently; and suddenly stop short.

For whatever it's worth, President Bush was criticized for stopping short. Many believe Iraq could have been "taken over" or obliterated with just a few more hours of Desert Storm. Bear in mind if Iraq had been "taken over" or obliterated, it might not have been available for Russia's ill-conceived desert storm.

✦ *Thou shalt ascend and come like a storm.*
(Ezekiel 38:9)

Airplanes

The Russian-led forces will fill the skies with airplanes. They will opt for an all-out air strike against the tiny nation. For many years, the Russian air force grew at a terrific pace. Up until the failed coup, they were adding 45 more super-bombers and 700 more fighter planes each year. They currently possess more than 5000 fighter/bombers, a multitude of helicopters, and at the time of the coup, they had three aircraft carriers under construction. And lest we forget, they increased their 1993 military procurement by 10 percent. Upgrading is also a key word in Iran. Western intelligence sources are reporting that Iran is trying to buy more than 100 military planes from Russia. They want to spend $2.2 billion to enlarge their air force by a whopping 40 percent.

A majority of Iraq's planes survived the Persian Gulf War. It was strange, but most of them were not even used. Iraq flew 132 of them to Iran for safekeeping. Others were stored near religious sites, museums, archaeological sites, and so forth. Those planes are still available for a future storm provided Iran and Iraq both agree to use them.

Germany's planes made the headlines during the Persian Gulf War too. Some were flown to Turkey. It was the first deployment of German planes on foreign soil since World War II. They will do it again.

Airplanes received a lot of attention during the Persian Gulf War. Military spokesmen kept reporting how many sorties their planes flew. Lt. Gen. Thomas Kelly reported United States planes flew approximately 10,000 sorties the first week. The figure reached 72,000 sorties in just five weeks. The total sorties for all coalition forces was approximately 100,000. A cloud of fighters and bombers covered the land of Iraq.

✦ *Thou shalt be like a cloud to cover the land.*
(Ezekiel 38:9)

An Evil Thought

Russia's leader will develop a fatal attraction. His nation will need food, but he will not have the money to buy it. He will see the Jews possess what he needs and wants and believe he can get away with rapidly plundering Israel. He will think the Moslems will be supportive and grateful so he will gather his coalition of nations and make a desperate move.

+ *Thou shalt think an evil thought.*
  (Ezekiel 38:10)
+ *And thou shalt say, I will go up to the land of unwalled villages.*
  (Ezekiel 38:11)
+ *To take a spoil, and to take a prey.*
  (Ezekiel 38:12)

Others Will Question His Intentions

Sheba, Dedan and the merchants of Tarshish, with all the young lions, will ask questions about this attack. Sheba and Dedan are cities in Saudi Arabia. The merchants of Tarshish refers to Great Britain. The young lions are those nations that grew out of Great Britain. The United States and Canada are included.

Observe these four nations were all on the same side during the Persian Gulf War in opposition to Iraq. They will still be allies when the Russian leader decides to assail Israel. Isn't it interesting they are properly aligned today.

+ *Sheba, Dedan, the merchants of Tarshish, and all the young lions thereof, shall say unto thee, Art thou come to take a spoil?*
  (Ezekiel 38:13)

God's Response to the Evil Thought

Russia could not attack Israel if the invincible God did not permit it, but He will allow it when the plans are formulated. He will even bring the Russian alliance into Israel and turn their evil thought into good by using the assault to sanctify His name. He will use this battle to rewrite the book of defeats and to let the world know Israel's covenant-making God is the Omnipotent One.

+ *I will bring thee against my land, that the heathen may know me, when I shall be sanctified in thee, O Gog, before their eyes.*
  (Ezekiel 38:16)

The Great Battle

The new union of nations will make a fatal mistake. This is the land Almighty God gave to Israel. He gave it to the Jews "forever" and these people will have the gall to think they can march right in and take it.

The God of Heaven will be angry when the coalition attacks. His presence will cause the land to shake violently. Every creature on earth will feel the furious vibrations and thunderous quakes, including the fish, fowls, animals and all human beings. While that is going on, the Lord Jehovah will bombard the invaders with pestilence, blood, rain, hail, fire and brimstone. The Russian alliance will be terrorized and the invasion will quickly turn sour. Many of the coalition troops will begin to fight amongst themselves.

We can easily see how this alliance would do that. The Iranians and Iraqis have been bitter enemies and did not set aside their differences until the Persian Gulf Crisis. Also, since the attempted coup, we have seen many rifts between the former Soviet republics and have witnessed a great amount of animosity and infighting.

In an Associated Press article in The Jackson Sun newspaper entitled, *Soviet Union flag, Morale Lie in Tatters,* dated December 26, 1991, we read,

"Rifts between republics of the new commonwealth were also coming into sharper focus.

"Ukraine on Wednesday accused Russia of refusing to distribute new rubles to other republics and renewed its complaint about the dominant former Soviet republic's unilateral decision to free prices, Radio Russia reported."

Another Associated Press article in The Jackson Sun newspaper entitled, *Ukraine Warned on Army,* dated January 5, 1992, says,

"The commonwealth military chief on Saturday warned Ukraine not to violate defense pacts and accused all member states of 'hastiness' in forming separate armies.

"The statement could worsen divisions over military issues in the four-week-old post-Soviet alliance. It came as Ukraine's military chief reiterated the republic's claims to the fleet in the Black Sea, where many of the former Soviet Union's western warm-water ships were based. Some of the ships are nuclear powered or carry nuclear weapons."

An article in U.S. News & World Report entitled, *New Year, Old Fears*, dated January 13, 1992, says,

> "Last week this fault line rumbled ominously. Ukrainian officials bitterly attacked the Russian-ordered price hikes and in retaliation decided to introduce a coupon system that spells the end of a workable ruble currency zone. Belarus and Uzbekistan say they will follow suit. Ukraine and Russia fell out over ownership of the Soviet Black Sea fleet. Tajikistan announced that it may seize a secret plant on its territory and try to set up a uranium-development consortium with Arab countries."

The eleven republics in the new Commonwealth of Independent States fear they will be dominated by the republic of Russia because it has long ridden roughshod over them. When Russia forms the coalition to attack Israel, her chickens will come home to roost.

✦ *My fury shall come up in my face.*
(Ezekiel 38:18)

✦ *There shall be a great shaking in the land of Israel.*
(Ezekiel 38:19)

✦ *Every man's sword shall be against his brother.*
(Ezekiel 38:21)

✦ *I will plead against him with pestilence and blood.*
(Ezekiel 38:22)

The Great Feast/Bonfire/Burial

The outcome of this great battle is going to be the exact opposite of the much celebrated Persian Gulf victory. That war cost the lives of about 200 coalition troops and up to 100,000 Iraqis. This suicidal mission will cost the lives of very few Israelis (if any) and multitudes (perhaps millions) of coalition troops. Five out of every six coalition troops will die. The death toll will be so great the birds and animals will devour many of the dead before they can be buried. Some will not be buried for seven months. The Jews will collect so many weapons of destruction it will take seven years to dispose of them.

> ✦ *I will give thee unto the ravenous birds of every sort, and to the beasts of the field to be devoured.*
> (Ezekiel 39:4)

> ✦ *They shall burn them with fire seven years.*
> (Ezekiel 39:9)

> ✦ *And seven months shall the house of Israel be burying of them.*
> (Ezekiel 39:12)

The Great Revival

People have forgotten the Deliverer of Israel is God. They do not appreciate the Lord of Hosts anymore. They do not know Him, respect Him or believe His Word. They do not believe the land still belongs to Israel. They do not seem to understand a faithful God will arise and lead His people Israel again.

He will change much of this by bringing a suicidal onslaught upon the land. The coalition defeat will be so great it will cause defiant and unbelieving men to change their minds about the mighty God. The Church rolls will grow again when He stands up to make His name known in many nations.

> ✦ *I will be known in the eyes of many nations, and they shall know that I am the Lord.*
> (Ezekiel 38:23)

An Incredible List

Look at the list of prophecies in Ezekiel 38. It is incredible how they fit current events.

> ✦ A country north of Israel (Russia) will be Israel's enemy.
> (vs. 15)

> ✦ Moscow will be ruled by that country.
> (vs. 2)

> ✦ Tobolsk will be ruled by that country.
> (vs. 2)

> ✦ Russia will lose control of her destiny.
> (vs. 4)

> ✦ Iran will be Israel's enemy.
> (vs. 5)

- ✦ Iran will align with Russia.
  (vs. 5)
- ✦ Iraq will be Israel's enemy.
  (vs. 5)
- ✦ Iraq will align with Russia.
  (vs. 5)
- ✦ Iran and Iraq will align with each other.
  (vs. 5)
- ✦ Libya will be Israel's enemy.
  (vs. 5)
- ✦ Libya will align with Russia, etc.
  (vs. 5)
- ✦ Germany will reunite.
  (vs. 6)
- ✦ Germany will be Israel's enemy.
  (vs. 6)
- ✦ Germany will align with Russia, etc.
  (vs. 6)
- ✦ Russia will prepare for war.
  (vs. 7)
- ✦ Israel will go back to the land.
  (vs. 6)
- ✦ Israel will sign a security agreement.
  (vs. 8)
- ✦ Israel will have cattle and goods.
  (vs. 12)
- ✦ Russia will need cattle and goods.
  (vs. 13)
- ✦ There will be a split in Arab unity.
  (vs. 13)
- ✦ Saudi Arabia will align with England, United States, etc.
  (vs. 13)
- ✦ Saudi Arabia will oppose Iraq, Iran, etc.
  (vs. 13)

Some people have difficulty believing Ezekiel could foretell a Russian invasion of Israel. It is just too incredible for them to accept. But predicting a Russian assault is no more difficult or unusual than predicting a virgin birth or the resurrection of the dead.

Some think the Soviet collapse means Russia is no longer a dangerous threat to anyone. Russia is in a "state of flux," but it is not yet on the ash-heap of history. There is still a very powerful military and women and children to feed.

Something to Think About

Shortly after the crucifixion of Jesus, the Apostles were gathered with Mary, the brothers of Jesus and others to discuss a replacement for Judas Iscariot. Peter stood up and said, *Men and brethren, this Scripture must needs have been fulfilled, which the Holy Ghost by the mouth of David spake before concerning Judas* . . . . (Acts 1:16). He was saying the Spirit of God spoke by David and because it was the Holy Spirit speaking, the prophecy had to be fulfilled.

That is the way the early Church viewed the Scriptures. The living and true God was speaking through the prophets. He can not lie and the Scriptures can not be broken. A wise person would rest upon that and permit the Scriptures to affect his/her life. A wise nation would pray, trust the Lord of Hosts and prepare. It is a loving God who tells you how to avoid disaster.

Chapter 4

Europe

Daniel should be recognized for many reasons, but one of the most important is he introduced us to the concept of a false Messiah. We call this deceptive man the Antichrist. Daniel called him the little horn, a king of fierce countenance, the prince that shall come, a vile person and the king who does according to his will (Daniel 7:8, 8:23, 9:26, 11:21,36).

But Daniel didn't leave it there. He connected this pseudo-Christ to the revived Roman Empire. The angel Gabriel told him, *the people of the prince that shall come shall destroy the city and the sanctuary* (Daniel 9:26). The Roman army did that in 70 A.D. They are the "people" who destroyed Jerusalem and the temple. The Romans are the "people of *the prince that shall come.*"

This presents a problem. *The prince that shall come* is to be a Roman, but he has not arrived and the Roman Empire no longer exists. This causes liberal scholars, who have eaten the wrong spiritual food, to suggest the prophecy and the Bible are wrong. But the bottom line is the prophecy and the Bible can still be right, provided the Roman Empire is revived. If that were to happen, the terrible desolator could rise over a Revived Roman Empire.

That is what we see developing in Europe today. The steady emergence of the European Community (EC), the shake-up in Eastern Europe and the collapse of the former Soviet Union are nothing more than the fulfillment of Bible prophecy. They are the birth-pangs of the Revived Roman Empire. The dramatic events of recent months are setting the stage for the last Gentile kingdom and the appearance of the wicked prince called Antichrist.

The Place

Daniel was in Babylon when Gabriel revealed the Antichrist and the Revived Roman Empire. Babylon was the seat of power. It was the first global empire and its king was the first world ruler. Nebuchadnezzar was his name.

He was mighty; extremely rich; a haughty arrogant man with the "I disease"—I did this, I did that, I have this and I have that. And it is quite likely he gave a lot of thought to what the future held for him and "his" vast domain. He was definitely concerned about the future and troubled to the very point of sleeplessness.

The Forgotten Dream

It was the second year of Nebuchadnezzar's glorious reign. He dreamed a dream that deeply disturbed him. He was awe-struck; overwhelmed; and terribly upset. Sleep abandoned him. And he woke up worrying about what he had envisioned.

He called in the magicians, astrologers, sorcerers and Chaldeans. The magicians understood mysteries; the astrologers read horoscopes; the sorcerers talked to dead spirits; and the Chaldeans supposedly understood philosophy and science. They were purported to be men of learning and Nebuchadnezzar counted on them to tell him the meaning of his disquieting dream.

Nebuchadnezzar explained he had a dream and was troubled to know what it was. He sensed it was something very important, but could not lay his hand on it. He was tormented by it and wanted to know the significance of it.

The Chaldeans said, "tell thy servants the dream, and we will shew the interpretation." Nebuchadnezzar answered, "the thing is gone from me." Even though he sensed the dream was literally filled with meaning, he could not remember what it was (Daniel 2:1-5).

It Turned Ugly

Nebuchadnezzar was a violent man with a quick temper. He excelled in mass murder. So he told his counselors to reveal the dream and its meaning or they would be cut in pieces and their houses destroyed. He was serious.

He followed the threat with bribery; offering the wise men gifts, rewards and great honor to do as he asked. He was the leader of the world and could be very generous, if he wanted to be. He could make it well worth their time to tell him what he wanted to know.

The Chaldeans asked him a second time to disclose the dream; even promised the greatly desired interpretation if he would. They were in a tough spot with this hothead. They carefully suggested the interpretation would be possible, if he could come up with the worrisome dream.

Nebuchadnezzar accused his advisers of trying to buy time. He charged them with stalling in hopes he would give up on the whole matter. He reasoned they had been lying to him if they could not reveal the thing that made him so anxious and restless.

His wise men countered by saying he was asking the impossible. They replied no man can do what you ask and no king has ever asked his advisers to do anything like this before. They added no one can do this, but the gods.

Nebuchadnezzar flew into a rage and ordered the death of all the wise men in Babylon. The order not only included these men; it also took in Daniel and some of his friends.

Daniel's Request

Troops were dispatched to locate Daniel and his associates so they could be killed. When the soldiers arrived, Daniel wondered why Nebuchadnezzar had acted so hastily. He was puzzled as to what could be so urgent. He inquired about it and the captain of the guard explained what happened.

Daniel received permission to visit the angry king. He did not go to ask what the dream was; that would be a waste of breath. He went to request time to come up with it. He believed God would supply both the dream and the interpretation.

Daniel's request was granted and he returned home. He gathered his most loyal friends and quickly explained the situation. They joined him in urgent prayer for God's mercy concerning the dream. This was truly a matter of life and death (Daniel 2:13–18).

An Answer to Prayer

Daniel and his friends prayed and then retired for the night. During the night, Daniel had a vision. It is impossible to say exactly what happened, but Daniel most likely dreamed the same dream as Nebuchadnezzar. We only know God revealed the mysterious dream and its far-reaching meaning.

✦ *Then was the secret revealed unto Daniel in a night vision.*
(Daniel 2:19)

The Kingmaker

God is the ultimate authority. He overthrows kings and He establishes kings. He removes governments and nations to accomplish His will; sets them up to fulfill His promises. He is always in control. And all nations, governments and rulers exist only because He permits them to exist.

✦ *He removeth kings, and setteth up kings.*
(Daniel 2:21)

Who Knows What the Future Holds?

Who can reveal the future? The answer is all-important because Daniel is going to reveal the dream and its interpretation. He wants everyone to know human beings do not have the ability to do this. He could do it because there is a great God in heaven who knows history before it is written. The Lord knows the future and often outlines it before it happens.

✦ *The secret which the king hath demanded cannot the wise men, the astrologers, the magicians, the soothsayers, shew unto the king.*
(Daniel 2:27)

✦ *But there is a God in heaven that revealeth secrets.*
(Daniel 2:28)

The Latter Days

We immediately learn from Daniel that God was providing Nebuchadnezzar with details of the latter days. His dream was a portrait of things to come; things that people can watch for so they can see the day approaching.

✦ *God hath made known what shall be in the latter days.*
(Daniel 2:28)

The Dream

Daniel told Nebuchadnezzar he dreamed about an enormous dazzling statue. It frightened him because its form was so terrible. Its head was gold; its chest and arms were silver; its belly and thighs were brass; its legs were iron; and its feet were part iron and part clay. A stone struck this grisly image on its feet and they broke into pieces. Then the whole thing crumbled into dust and the wind blew it away. The stone became a great mountain and filled the earth (Daniel 2:31–35).

The Interpretation

Daniel began by reminding Nebuchadnezzar where he got his kingdom and who made him a monarch. He said, *The God of heaven hath given thee a kingdom, power, and strength, and glory.* There are no kings or kingdoms on earth except those God permits. There is no power, or strength, or glory except that which He allows. They all exist by His permission or they do not exist at all.

Daniel also told Nebuchadnezzar God gave all men into his hand and made him ruler over every one of them. There are no other gods who can set up kings or kingdoms. It cannot be done without approval from above.

NEBUCHADNEZZAR'S IMAGE (Daniel 2)

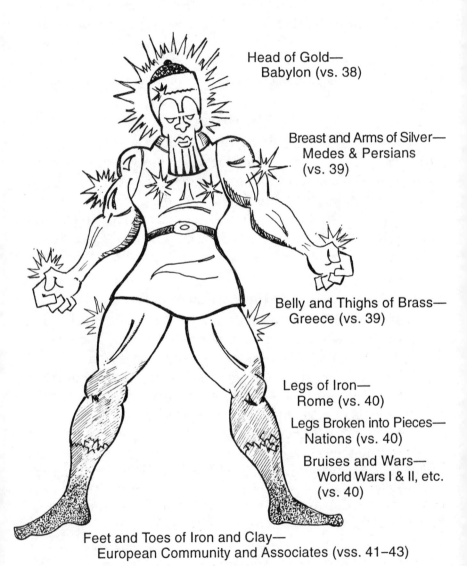

Head of Gold—
Babylon (vs. 38)

Breast and Arms of Silver—
Medes & Persians
(vs. 39)

Belly and Thighs of Brass—
Greece (vs. 39)

Legs of Iron—
Rome (vs. 40)

Legs Broken into Pieces—
Nations (vs. 40)

Bruises and Wars—
World Wars I & II, etc.
(vs. 40)

Feet and Toes of Iron and Clay—
European Community and Associates (vss. 41–43)

The Head of Gold

Daniel quickly began to interpret the stunned king's dream. He used the words "king" and "kingdom" interchangeably. He presented the great statue as a broad outline of the Gentile age. The age came into existence when Babylon destroyed Israel. Gentiles will move through four world kingdoms and see the beginning of a fifth. While the fifth is still in its infancy, God will suddenly bring their rule to an end. Daniel told Nebuchadnezzar that he was the head of gleaming gold.

✦ *Thou art this head of gold.*
(Daniel 2:38)

The Breast and Arms of Silver

The Bible tells us who the next Gentile world kingdom was. The second world kingdom came into being the very night the defiant king Belshazzar made a great feast and foolishly drank wine out of the sacred temple vessels. The ghostly fingers of a great hand suddenly appeared and wrote a message on the wall. Beautiful Babylon was numbered and finished. God had checked the glorious empire out and it came up short. The shiny gold kingdom was divided and given to the silver empire led by the Medes and Persians (Daniel 5:1-28).

✦ *After thee shall arise another kingdom.*
(Daniel 2:39)

The Belly and Thighs of Brass

Daniel prophesied the Medes and Persians would be replaced by a third world empire of brass. This was accomplished by the nation of Greece under Alexander the Great (Daniel 8:1-21).

✦ *A third kingdom shall rule over all the earth.*
(Daniel 2:39)

The Legs of Iron

Daniel did not identify the fourth world kingdom, but there is general agreement iron represents the Roman Empire and history bears it out. The Romans were the major power on earth when Jesus came the first time.

✦ *The fourth kingdom shall be strong as iron.*
(Daniel 2:40)

The Broken Legs

Daniel predicted the Roman Empire, represented by the legs of iron, would crack and break into pieces (nations). The pieces would bruise (fight wars and oppress people).

That is exactly what happened. The Roman Empire fractured into the nations of France, Germany, England and so forth. They fought many wars. England and France warred, Spain fought England, Germany fought England, France, Russia, and other nations, ulitmately culminating in World Wars I and II. *Wars and rumors of wars* continue to this very day.

✦ *It shall break in pieces and bruise.*
   (Daniel 2:40)

The Feet and Toes of Iron and Clay

What about the fifth Gentile world kingdom? Daniel said the last kingdom will be divided. It is difficult to say exactly what he meant, but it seems likely he was saying it would organize into two divisions at first. And later on, it would have ten sub-divisions. It is probable that the two feet implies two primary divisions at the outset. And the ten toes most likely represent ten secondary divisions that would come afterwards.

This is not far-fetched. Notice, the statue had two arms of silver which represented two groups of people–the Medes and the Persians. The statue had two legs of iron which represented the Roman Empire that split into two divisions–Eastern and Western. This historical pattern suggests the Revived Roman Empire will come on the scene with two main divisions. Then, when it reaches its final form, it will have ten sub-divisions.

But it will not come strictly out of the old Roman Empire. It will be an odd mixture of iron and clay; an incohesive alliance of old Roman Empire nations and non-Roman Empire nations.

And most of its power will come from the iron nations that were in the old Roman Empire. They will give the kingdom its power by transferring their weapons, resources and military to it.

The kingdom will lack uniformity. It will be "partly strong and partly broken" signifying a mixture of strong nations and weak nations; strong established democracies from Western Europe and weaker ex-Communist countries from Central Europe.

What kind of allies will the last Gentile world kingdom have? It will "mingle with the seed of men" by forging covenants with corrupt rulers in the world. And for lack of cohesion, it will come under the control of the profane wicked prince called Antichrist.

And the last Gentile world power will lack unity because member nations will not merge, or cleave, their cultures, nationalities and customs. Individual leaders may try to combine these things, but their people will not fully co-operate.

✦ *The kingdom shall be divided.*
(Daniel 2:41)

✦ *Thou sawest the feet and toes, part of potters' clay, and part of iron.*
(Daniel 2:41)

✦ *There shall be in it the strength of the iron.*
(Daniel 2:41)

✦ *The kingdom shall be partly strong, and partly broken.*
(Daniel 2:42)

✦ *Thou sawest iron mixed with miry clay, they shall mingle themselves with the seed of men.*
(Daniel 2:43)

✦ *But they shall not cleave one to another, even as iron is not mixed with clay.*
(Daniel 2:43)

The Kingdom of Stone

The fifth Gentile world kingdom of iron and clay will abruptly end when a great stone smashes it. This mighty rock represents Jesus who will appear in the twinkling of an eye to totally crush the wicked empire, capture its charismatic leader and bring in the final restoration of Israel.

✦ *God will replace the ten kings with his own kingdom.*
(Daniel 2:44,45)

A Sure Thing

The scary dream that so greatly disturbed Nebuchadnezzar, was a prophetic vision given by God to reveal future world empires. It began with Nebuchadnezzar and ended with the second coming of Jesus. It is an ironclad dream that cannot be changed and the Biblical interpretation is absolutely correct.

✦ *God has revealed what shall come to pass.*
(Daniel 2:45)

✦ *The dream is certain.*
(Daniel 2:45)

✦ *The interpretation is sure.*
(Daniel 2:45)

The Revived Roman Empire

This intriguing vision means the Gentile governments of the world are living on borrowed time. When the bottom of the statue is reached, Jesus will return. The head of gold lasted about 66 years and was overthrown. The breast and arms of silver continued for 207 years. The belly and thighs of brass ended after about 269 years and the legs of iron lasted approximately 539 years. The pieces of iron have been around for more than one thousand years, but we do not know how much longer they will last. The feet of iron and clay are now forming, but the rapture of the Church will occur before they are fully organized. The feet will last just seven years from the time the Antichrist signs his highly publicized covenant with Israel. This final seven years is the seventieth week described in chapter one.

The Iron

For several years, conservative writers have been saying the Revived Roman Empire is coming on the scene in the form of the Common Market. Some call it the European Community (EC) and others call it the European Economic Community (EEC). Hal Lindsey says:

"One of the reasons I'm convinced we're living in the closing days of the world's history is because of the emergence of the

European Common Market, also known as the European Economic Community. There is no doubt in my mind that it's the forerunner of the Revived Roman Empire which the prophet Daniel spoke about with such certainty. He predicted that the number of nations in it would be limited to ten. This is the very number which the Common Market has set as its goal for inner membership!"[1]

David Wilkerson has written:

"I believe that the European Common Market is the foundation for the revival of Rome and the ten-nation confederacy."[2]

And this is the view of Dr. Tim F. LaHaye:

"It is inconceivable that a one world controlled government be established without an interrelated one world economy. Such an economy has been suggested in the European common market. Although it is still in its infancy, because of economic necessity it could spread throughout the entire world and eventually become the type of instrument used to control the monetary and financial affairs of the world by the anti-Christ."[3]

It is very important to observe these men are not saying the EC, as it now stands, is the Revived Roman Empire. Hal Lindsey called the EC the "forerunner" of the Revived Roman Empire. David Wilkerson suggested the EC is the "foundation" for the Revived Roman Empire. And Dr. LaHaye suggested the EC "could spread" and "eventually become" the Revived Roman Empire. These men realize the EC must undergo major changes before it satisfies the known prophetic requirements.

This is what is happening. Keep in mind that the Revived Roman Empire will begin with two primary divisions as you read this excerpt from an article by Russell Watson, Ruth Marshall, Karen Breslau and Daniel Pedersen entitled, *In Europe, Three's a Crowd*. It appeared in Newsweek magazine on October 5, 1992:

"Prime Minister John Major wants to make Britain one of the three pillars of the European Community. But last week, during an acute crisis of confidence in the future of European unification, it became clear that three's a crowd. Kohl and Mitterrand pressed ahead with unification on their own terms, which could lead to the creation of not one new Europe but two—with Britain the most conspicuous occupant of the second-class carriage.

"The only nations really prepared for 'more Europe' were Germany, France and the three small but economically sturdy countries located between them: Belgium, the Netherlands and Luxembourg. As long as they stand up to speculative pressure in the foreign-exchange markets, they can participate fully in the European monetary system, which requires their currencies to stay closely in line with each other. They may even be able to move on to a single currency and other forms of cooperation. Economically weaker members of the EC—Britain, Italy, Spain, Portugal, Denmark, Ireland and Greece—may not qualify for full membership in the rich men's club. 'The most probable outcome is a two-speed Europe,' says Ireland's Peter Sutherland, a former member of the European Commission, the Community's executive body."

The Clay

The EC is just half the picture. It contains the iron in the feet of iron and clay. Its central government, economic power, resources and militaries will combine to make it the seat of power in the last generation of Gentiles. It will be the heavyweight in the economic and military colossus that vainly tries to rule the world in the last days.

The other half of the picture is the group of weaker nations trying to affiliate with the EC. They will become the clay in the feet of iron and clay. It will be an unusual union to say the least, but both groups are making steady progress toward consolidation.

An article by James Walsh in Time magazine entitled *What the West Can Do,* dated September 2, 1991, speaks of bringing other countries "under the wing" of the EC and granting them "associate membership."

"The new front-line Central European democracies, meanwhile, argued with some trepidation that bringing them under the Western wing was of the highest importance. The European Community seemed to agree, offering to step up negotiations toward admitting Poland, Czechoslovakia and Hungary as associate members."

A report in The Gospel Truth by N. W. Hutchings entitled *Who Will Rule The New World Order,* dated January 1992, says,

> "While the membership of the Common Market is at present 12 members, there are now 30 associate members, and we can be sure that when this new empire gains commercial power and strength, most nations will rush to join as trading partners."

Keep in mind the fact that the Revived Roman Empire will be "partly strong and partly broken" and the fact that it will lack unity because the iron and the clay will not mix as you read this excerpt from the Boston Globe newspaper. It was printed on December 31, 1990 and it reads just like it was taken "right out of the Bible." It says,

> "Still reeling from the changes that have reshaped the map of Europe, France, Germany, Italy, Britain, and their neighbors are accelerating toward another goal that once seemed unthinkable: a United States of Europe. From summit meetings of leaders to the way students decide where to go to college, Western Europe is beginning to fuse together and exert a magnetic attraction on the countries of the former Eastern bloc, who are clamoring to enter. Last week Sweden voted to apply for membership in the 12-nation European Community, joining a line that already includes Austria and Turkey. Switzerland, Norway, Iceland, and Finland are expected to follow soon. Hungary, Czechoslovakia, and Poland have served notice they'll apply by 1995. . . . A United States of Europe would be **more decentralized than the United States (of America). Countries would retain their own languages and many of their own institutions.** National governments would still meet and elect prime ministers and presidents. But in fundamental and far-reaching ways, Europe is on its way to becoming a united continent."

What do we see? An unusual kingdom coming together with two feet containing a tightly integrated group of strong, wealthy iron nations called EC members and a more loosely connected group of weaker clay nations, referred to as associate members, who are hoping to become full members at a later date. We see "a rich men's club" led by Germany and France and a second-class carriage" led by Britain—a group of nations that will be partly united with a common currency, a common military, a common pay scale and a common passport. But they will be partly divided because they will speak different languages, retain their own institutions, cultures, etc. The fact is, we see the fat lady standing in the wings and she wants to sing.

A New World Leader

The news media does not report the news from a Biblical point of view, but much of the news about the EC fits what Hal Lindsey, David Wilkerson and Dr. LaHaye wrote. An Article by Philip Revzin in The Wall Street Journal entitled, *Europeans Foresee Era Of Prosperity, Unity And Growing Power,* dated July 5, 1990, states,

> "A new world leader is being forged in a cauldron of political change: a Europe bigger, more united and more powerful than seemed possible six months ago. . . . 'Before the end of the century there will be a single currency in Europe,' Cornelis van der Klugt, former chairman of N.V. Philips of Holland, recently told a lecture hall jammed with business students in St. Gallen, Switzerland. 'Much of Eastern Europe will be in the EC,' he continued, 'and 20 years from now there will be a Europe of 700 million people able to be equal partners with the U.S., Japan and the rest of the world.' "

The downfall of British Prime Minister, Margaret Thatcher was directly related to her opposition to the merging of Europe. In its article by Barbara Toman and Tim Carrington entitled, *How Britain's Thatcher Got in Serious Trouble With Her Own Party,* dated December 21, 1990, The Wall Street Journal states,

> "After being forced into an embarrassing run-off vote for the leadership of her own party, Prime Minister Margaret Thatcher faces the toughest and very possibly the last great battle of her long political career. What brought her to this humiliating position was the prospect of a united Europe-and her intransigence against it."

Margaret Thatcher fell because she did not realize the strength and determination of the forces behind the uniting of Europe. The "ten-toed kingdom"of iron and clay is quickly becoming a force to be reckoned with.

An Economic Superpower

The Revived Roman Empire will never control the entire world, but it will become the economic superpower of the world. And the vile Antichrist will use Europe's massive economy to force support for his global ambitions; to forge a juggernaut whose purpose is to steamroll every nation on earth (Revelation 13:16,17).

On April 25, 1988, Forbes magazine quoted French President Giscard d'Estaing as saying, "By the year 2010, the entity that is Europe will be number one in the world's economy." And in April 1992, Rev. Noah Hutchings wrote, "When the 12 nations of the Common Market form a national federation, it will immediately be in control of 46 percent of the world's trade and commerce."

This all amounts to something that should curl anyone's toes; the EC is transforming itself into a two-pronged world economic superpower with individual nations no longer being allowed to go their own way. It is bringing several countries under one governing body, with a central bank, a single currency—the European Currency Unit (ECU), common citizenship, a joint foreign policy, joint defense compatible with NATO, joint diplomacy, unified rules with regard to industry, health, education, immigration and more. These blind nations are surrendering their sovereignty to a global giant that Bible prophecy warns will become the empire of a leader in cahoots with the devil.

An article in Time magazine by Jill Smolowe entitled, *Blueprint for the Dream,* dated December 23, 1991, outlines "The Road Ahead." The following dates are important:

Jan. 1, 1994:
The European Monetary Institute, precursor of a European Central Bank, begins coordinating policy.

June 1994:
Election for the next European Parliament, which will assume some added powers.

Jan. 1, 1997:
If seven members meet the ECs tough economic criteria, they will adopt a single currency. Britain will have the choice of opting in or out

at this stage, while Denmark will hold a referendum before joining.

Jan. 1, 1999
The single currency, if not already in force, will be invoked automatically.

The President of Europe

The Antichrist rises to power over a unified Europe after its two main divisions have organized into ten kingdoms. He ascends as a man of peace, but forcefully subdues three of the ten kingdoms. This spellbinding, muscle-flexing, silver-tongued devil will be very intelligent, very impressive and very persuasive. He will prosper and gain the admiration of the whole world (Daniel 7:8, 20, 24; 8:23-25; 11:36; Revelation 13:8).

But how can he do that? The United States is "the world's only superpower." The United States is called "the world's policeman." Consider the following statement by Karen Elliott House. It comes from a February 21, 1989 article in The Wall Street Journal entitled, *As Power Is Dispersed Among Nations, Need For Leadership Grows.*

"The bipolar era dominated by the American and Soviet super-powers is dead . . . . So, debt-ridden old Uncle Sam no longer has the ability—or even the need—to bear the burden of world leadership . . . . The need, then is all the greater for a global leader to protect peace and promote prosperity."

So much for the United States. Let's go back to Europe. In a Wall Street Journal article entitled, *Europe Will Become Economic Superpower As Barriers Crumble,* dated December 29, 1988, Philip Revzin says, "A majority of Europeans want to elect a president of Europe." In an article called, *Europe prepares for the Antichrist,* dated January 1990, Countdown magazine says, "So close is Western Europe to unification that pollsters have already begun surveying the population about whom they would prefer to see as president of Europe."

The problem is EC leaders now realize they may not be capable of defending member nations in a sudden crisis without a strong central government. They learned this when they acted with ambivalence during the Persian Gulf flare-up. Several leaders were slow to respond to the invasion of Kuwait. Member nations disagreed about what to do. Some wanted to negotiate with Saddam Hussein. Others wanted to help Turkey and Jordan, but not the United States. Some did the bare minimum or nothing at all. The problem reared its ugly head again over the break up of Yugoslavia. With the EC divided over the recognition of Croatia, Slovenia and Macedonia, Germany acted alone and forced its will on the EC by recognizing Croatia and Slovenia. And Greece had its way by blocking recognition of Macedonia. The political feuds continued and the EC was paralyzed over the situation in Bosnia. The group needed a unified response, but couldn't get it. So the EC now understands that agreement may not be possible on many important issues unless there is a powerful president who has the authority to force his will on reluctant member states. It will opt for pooled sovereignty and wind up with a leader who has unbridled Satanic ambitions.

A Military Superpower

Europe will become a military superpower and the beastly Antichrist will direct his massive military in a futile attempt to take over the world. This terrible leader will claim to be bringing peace to the world, but in reality he will be taking peace from the world (Daniel 8:24, 38; Revelation 6:2, 13:4). His sweet sounding words should be weighed against what he is; the voice of darkness transformed into an angel of light. The Wall Street Journal published an article by Philip Revzin entitled, *Europe Will Rely Less On U.S. for Security, More on Own Devices,* dated May 4, 1990, which says,

> "A new vision of European security is taking shape, one that heralds an altered-and diminished-role for the U.S. . . . Europe is more ambivalent about the American presence here than at any time since World War II. It is both more willing and more able to pay for and manage its own defense. With a united Germany at its heart, Europe will naturally shift its political attention to European-dominated institutions. The EC recently took a significant step by endorsing a French and German initiative that could lead to joint decision-making on political and defense matters within three years, and

could even lead to a Pan-European army of sorts in the next century."

Another article by Philip Revzin in The Wall Street Journal enti-tled, *EC Leaders Adopt 2-Year Plan to Forge Political, Monetary Unity in Europe,* dated December 17, 1990, reads,

> "The European Community embarked on ambitious plans to transform itself into a political, economic and monetary superpower able to speak with one powerful voice on the world stage about everything from interest rates to defense.

> "In a historic step that could change the political shape of Europe well into the next century, EC leaders, at a summit meeting here, gave themselves two years to negotiate, write and ratify two new treaties that would extend the community's powers from its present largely economic role to foreign and security policy, monetary affairs, and eventually defense.

> " 'This is a major turning point, a U-turn almost for Europe,' said an Italian government spokesman. 'Many of the countries are going to have to give up major parts of their sovereignty.' "

It is much too early for "the world's finest maker of swords to become the world's finest maker of plowshares." A European mili-tary force is in the making. The EC is speaking of a joint "defensive" force, but the Bible plainly teaches it will be used in an offensive manner for unjust causes. The EC will have the money and the mus-cle to try to transform the world according to the desires of its coun-terfeit Christ.

The New World Order

The new world order is not the same thing as the EC. But the EC is the model intellectuals and world leaders are using. They want to divide the world into trading blocks. The EC, NAFTA and the Pacific Rim nations are examples. If they succeed, the EC will become the dominant force in the new world order. And cause it to take on devilish overtones. The implications are so horrendous, Christians are wise to be wary.

President Bush was one of the chief spokesmen for the modern day promoters of this concept. He seemed to be fronting for such institutions as the World Bank, the United Nations, the Trilateral Commission, the Council on Foreign Relations, the Bilderberg Group, the international bankers, the international corporations, the global organizations and such. These people want to standardize things. They promote a one world monetary system, a uniform measuring system, one set of laws and one set of values (apart from Christ). They want a world charter, the United Nations to have a standing military, the United Nations to have authority to cross borders and attack nations, a world income tax and much more. They use buzz words like "collective security, interdependence, global harmony, integration, a democratic world, a new civilization, global citizenship, a world perspective" and "the international community."

They think in terms of human rights, eliminating war, promoting world peace, establishing a fair and benevolent government, eliminating famine, sharing wealth, stopping the proliferation of nuclear weapons, protecting the environment and such. They would find the idea of a new Hitler (Antichrist) repulsive and would shun any kind of political process they thought would lead to that. They are not evil. They are just naive because it has not dawned on them the rapture of the Church will leave unregenerate men in control of every government on earth. Even if they were told, they probably would not believe it.

The promoters of the new world order will claim to be "broadminded" and "liberal." They will establish a new social order including lesbians, homosexuals, socialists, New-Agers and the like. In their formative stages, they will claim to be tolerant of everyone's beliefs, but they will progress into persecutors and brutalizers of Christians and Jews.

The new world order will not be based upon what the people want. It will be based upon what the global power brokers want and people will be forced to accept it. Influential entities will gain control of legislatures, militaries, banks, food, the police and everything they need to dictate their desires. Dishonest men will control religion, morality, business and every other institution.

Don't think it won't happen. Right now, powerful forces are trying to control who can buy and sell chemical, nuclear and biological weapons in the Middle East. The deployment of multi-national troops to Somalia, ostensibly to feed the starving, has turned into an effort to establish a United Nations approved government. United States warships have surrounded Haiti to bring down a renegade military general and set up a United Nations approved leader. Several nations are discussing the deployment of troops to Bosnia to stop "ethnic cleansing" and other atrocities. And the United Nations has threatened to disqualify leaders in Cambodia if they are found guilty of disrupting elections there. Some of this may sound good, but when monstrous men are in charge, and they tell us who can lead our nation, we will regret it.

Some thought the election of President Clinton would slow the march toward a new world order. But they didn't take a close look because he picked up where his predecessor left off. Most of his cabinet and foreign policy advisors are members of, or have strong ties with, groups working for a global government. And now he wants an Assistant Secretary of Defense for Democracy and Peacekeeping appointed to push it.

How close is the new world order? There are reports a world parliament has already held at least three meetings and a world constitution has already been drafted. And when Mikhail Gorbachev traveled to the United States in May of 1992, he called on the nations of the world to surrender their sovereignty by the year 2000. He said, "Even now many countries are morbidly jealous of their sovereignty and many peoples of their national independence and identity. This is one of the newest global contradictions, one which must be overcome."

The Smiting Stone
The new world order is a futile attempt to create an ideal world government without Jesus. But nations cannot forget God's beloved

Son, ignore His excellent Word, cry to the wrong God, support evil practices, persecute Christians and attack Israel without incurring His terrible wrath.

That is why Jesus is coming back. He is returning to purge the world of wickedness; to establish a kingdom of righteousness; not to destroy the world. He has promised to establish a wonderful kingdom where the "wolf can dwell with the lamb," the "calf can lie down with the young lion," and "the earth shall be full of the knowledge of the Lord;" a kingdom of real justice, truth and peace on earth.

Nebuchadnezzar's Dream Can Not be Changed

Several years passed and Nebuchadnezzar still had that dream on his mind. He probably did not want his kingdom to come to an end. He most surely hoped Daniel's interpretation was wrong. He would have chosen Babylon to be the kingdom that will not be destroyed.

So Nebuchadnezzar decided to make his own great statue. He could have made it out of gold, silver, brass, iron and clay like the statue in his dream, but he did not want to do that. He did not want Babylon to be overthrown. He did not want those other kingdoms to appear. And he did not want Jesus to come and set up His own kingdom.

Gold represented Nebuchadnezzar and Babylon in the dream so the king made his statue out of gold, from "head-to-foot." He refused to use silver, brass, iron and clay in his statue. His creation contradicted the dream. It signified that Babylon would last forever and God's view of history would not come to pass.

Then he called all his public officials together for a dedication service. Everyone was told music would sound and they should bow down and worship the great golden image. Those who did not were told they would be cast into a fiery furnace.

When three young Hebrews refused, they were thrown into the fire. But they were not burned. The Lord Jesus Christ miraculously preserved them. Nebuchadnezzar interpreted this to mean God would not accept what he was doing. He realized there is no god like the Shield of Israel (Daniel 3:1-30).

His statue had no effect on history and it disappeared. The Medes and Persians conquered Babylon. The Greeks came; then the Romans; now the Revived Romans. The dream can not be changed.

We are not the owners of this world. We are the tenants. We may desire for things to turn out a certain way, but we can not make it happen. God knows the future as well as He knows the past. He has told us what will happen. The kingdom of iron and clay is forming. Be ready. The great crushing Rock will soon return.

Chapter 5

Babylon

In 1940, World War II was going on and many people thought the Battle of Armageddon had arrived. That was when Rev. Arthur E. Bloomfield wrote a booklet for The Gospel Truth Series entitled, *Armageddon.* He was commenting on The Time of The Battle when he said,

> "The Jews will return to Palestine by the power of God . . . Jerusalem will be a Jewish city . . . Germany is usually thought of as being allied with Russia . . . In Daniel's prophecy, the Roman Empire is the last world empire. It will be revived and be a world force at that time . . . . The city of Babylon is mentioned in connection with Armageddon. There is every indication that the ancient city will be rebuilt."[1]

He was saying "will" because Jerusalem was not a Jewish city and there was no nation of Israel in 1940. He was saying, "Since the holy city is in the wrong hands and the nation of Israel has not been re-established, World War II cannot be the Battle of Armageddon." He was using his knowledge of Bible prophecy to calm the situation and he had many Bible-based reasons for saying what he did. Rev. Bloomfield was doing the same thing the apostle Paul did at Thessalonica. The Thessalonian believers were enduring severe persecution and someone was preaching or circulating a letter, in the name of Paul, saying, *The day of Christ is at hand.* Paul responded, *Let*

no man deceive you by any means: for that day shall not come,
except there come a falling away first, and that man of sin be
revealed, the son of perdition (II Thessalonians 2:2, 3). Both men used
their prophetic knowledge to still the peoples anxieties.

The statement, "Germany is usually thought of as being allied
with Russia," shows great awareness. Rev. Bloomfield wrote that at
a time when Germany was on the verge of invading Russia. The two
nations were bitter enemies, but the good preacher predicted an
alliance between them. They would fight a bitter war and kill millions of each others citizens, but he understood they would be on
the same side during the Battle of Armageddon.

Babylon is another reason why Rev. Bloomfield knew W W II
was not Armageddon. Bible prophecy indicates the city of Babylon
will come back into existence prior to the great conflict, but it did
not exist in 1940. Rev. Bloomfield said,

> "The city of Babylon is mentioned in connection with Armageddon.
> There is every indication that the ancient city will be rebuilt. Many
> of the prophecies concerning Babylon were never fulfilled literally.
> They must, therefore, refer to a future Babylon."[2]

Reasons Why Babylon Will Be Rebuilt

There are several reasons why prophecy buffs expect Babylon
to be rebuilt. Five of them are as follows:

(1) The Nature of Babylon's Final Destruction

Babylon's final end will be very similar to the sudden destruction of Sodom and Gomorrah. The city's ruin will be so swift and
complete it will never be inhabited again. Arabs will not set up tents
there anymore. And shepherds will abandon their folds and stay
away forever.

That did not happen to ancient Babylon. The Medes and Persians went under the wall of the city and captured it intact. They
kept it up and it still existed several hundred years later when the
Apostle Peter wrote his first epistle (I Peter 5:13). It gradually met its
demise when the Euphrates River changed its course and buried it

under sand. Archaeology reveals Arab villages were built on top of the covered ruins and squatters often inhabited the site.

✦ *And Babylon, the glory of kingdoms, the beauty of the Chaldees excellency, shall be as when God overthrew Sodom and Gomorrah.*
(Isaiah 13:19)

✦ *It shall never be inhabited, neither shall it be dwelt in from generation to generation: neither shall the Arabian pitch tent there; neither shall the shepherds make their fold there.*
(Isaiah 13:20)

(2) A Future Attack

Babylon must come back into existence for a future attack. But it will not be a two-nation assault like that of the Medes and Persians who went under the wall of the ancient city. It will be a multi-nation battle using "the weapons of his (God's) indignation," and it will occur when "the day of the Lord is at hand." The *indignation* and the *day of the Lord* are Old Testament terms associated with the tribulation period.

✦ *A tumultuous noise of the kingdoms of nations.*
(Isaiah 13:4)

✦ *They come from a far country, from the end of heaven, even the Lord, and the weapons of his indignation, to destroy the whole land.*
(Isaiah 13:5)

✦ *Howl ye; for the day of the Lord is at hand.*
(Isaiah 13:6)

(3) The Existence of Israel

The permanent ruin of Babylon occurs while Israel is in the land. That was not the case when the Medes and Persians attacked Babylon because Nebuchadnezzar had destroyed Israel. This tells us Israel and Babylon will both have to come back into existence for Israel to be a nation when Babylon is overthrown for the last time.

✦ *The Lord will have mercy on Jacob, and will yet choose Israel, and set them in their own land.*
(Isaiah 14:1)

✦ *I will rise up against them, saith the Lord of hosts, and cut off*
   from Babylon the name, and remnant, and son, and nephew,
   saith the Lord.
   (Isaiah 14:22)

(4) The Bricks and Stones

When Babylon is finally destroyed, the bricks and stones will
never be used again. But that was not the case in ancient Babylon
because those bricks and stones were re-used. History and archaeology verify Babylon straddled the Euphrates River when the great
stream started changing its course. At that time, many of the buildings and walls of ancient Babylon were torn down and transported
to such places as Seleucia, Kufa and Baghdad for re-use in other
structures. Other bricks and stones were buried, but people went
back and mined them after the river changed its course again. We
know this to be fact because the re-used bricks and stones bearing
the old Babylonian stamp have been found in other archaeological
sites. Since this is contrary to the prophecy, and because God fulfills
every jot and tittle of His Word, we can expect another city of Babylon.

✦ *And they shall not take of thee a stone for a corner, nor a stone*
   for foundations; but thou shalt be desolate for ever, saith the
   Lord.
   (Jeremiah 51:26)

(5) A Big Fire

New Babylon is to be utterly burned with fire in one hour of
time (Revelation 18:8–10). But old Babylon was not the victim of a fiery
destruction. It was the victim of a changing river, atrophy and decay.
It was slowly torn down and buried under sand.

The point is easy to see. The fall of Babylon to the Medes and
Persians and its eventual burial by the Euphrates river did not meet
the requirements for Babylon's final destruction. Therefore, a future
restoration of Babylon is essential to the performance of the remaining prophecies.

✦ *I will stretch out mine hand upon thee, and roll thee down from the rocks, and make thee a burnt mountain.*
(Jeremiah 51:25)

Babylon is Rising

For hundreds of years, it seemed unlikely Babylon would never be the end-time city the Bible speaks of. Many liberal Bible scholars even refused to believe it would ever exist again. Some of these blind guides espoused the idea the prophecies were nothing more than prophetic imagery. Some refused to admit there were any unfulfilled prophecies. Others said the prophecies were symbolic. Some, of little faith, loudly criticized those who interpret the prophecies literally. Many tried to explain the Scriptures away because they could not accept the idea Babylon would rise again. Well, Babylon is rising and it is being propelled down the road to Armageddon by an idea called Baathism.

Baathism

Baathism is an Arab concept of a new world order. To be sure, it is different from the concept held by former President Bush, but nonetheless, its purpose is to produce a new world order more favorable to the Arabs and less favorable to the West.

In 1940–41, a small group of intellectuals founded the Baath Party in Damascus, Syria. Arab nationalism was its major ingredient. The Party envisioned a large united Arab nation. It would have power and prestige in the world. It would create a grand and glorious Arab future. Arab society would be greatly improved and citizens would be free and equal. The united Arab nation would bring forth a powerful Arab leadership that could influence and perhaps even control world events.

The idea got off to a slow start because it made many Arabs uneasy. They were fearful because existing nations would have to transfer their sovereignty to a united Arab nation. It meant existing governments and leaders would have to be absorbed or toppled. There could be only one ruling family or one ruling central government. Many Arab leaders were not prepared for that and some apprehensive leaders openly opposed it.

The situation changed considerably when the Baath Party merged with a group of socialists in the late 1940s. The combined group called itself the Arab Baath Socialist Party. Its merger of nationalism and socialism proved to be a step forward. It started attracting the poorer class of people who wanted to share in the wealth of the land.

The group began trying to take over Syria. It was a long struggle, but a series of coups took them to the top in 1963. One of its more famous members is Hafez al-Assad, who seized control in 1970. He rules the country today.

The Baathist idea of a united Arab nation was also picked up by a small group of intellectuals in Iraq. A young, 19 year old, Saddam Hussein joined the militant group in 1956 and helped with a coup in 1959. That failed and he was forced to flee the country. He was still away when another coup occurred in 1963. That one succeeded and the Baathists gained strength, but not total control of the government.

That same year, Saddam Hussein was elected to the Regional Command of the Baath Party in Iraq and he decided to return to his country. His decision cost him his freedom because he ended up in prison. He was still there in 1965 when he was elected to the National Command, but he escaped one year later.

The Baath Party finally took control of the government of Iraq in 1968, and one of Saddam Hussein's cousins, Ahmad Hasan al-Bakr, became president. He chose the aggressive Saddam for his deputy and Saddam's brother-in-law for his minister of defense. He ruled until 1979 and Saddam took over. Six days later, Saddam had 22 of his top opponents executed, and he immediately became the undisputed leader of Iraq.

Two other attempts to spread Baathism failed. Syria and Egypt formed the United Arab Republic in 1958, but a coup in Syria produced a new government that broke it off in 1961. Egypt continued to use the name United Arab Republic and attempted to merge with Syria and Iraq in 1963, but political problems doomed the effort.

An Arab World Leader

A united Arab nation needs a leader. He must be one who is acceptable to all the Arabs, but that is a major problem. In fact, leadership is the main issue that ultimately broke up the United Arab Republic. Gamal Abdel Nasser refused to cede the sovereignty of Egypt to the leaders of Syria and the Syrian leaders refused to accept Nasser's rule.

When Saddam Hussein took over Iraq in 1979, he immediately set out to become the Arab world ruler. His goal was to dominate all his neighbors and to mold them into one nation under his leadership. He did not have to worry about Gamal Abdel Nasser because he had been assassinated. However, Hafez al-Assad was still on the scene and another player had entered the picture, the Ayatollah Khomeini.

Hafez al-Assad

Hafez al-Assad and Saddam Hussein are two of a kind and there is no love lost between them. Both belong to the Baath Party and both came to power through coups. Both hold absolute authority in their respective countries. Both have executed their internal enemies. Both want the same position, Arab world leader. They are natural enemies and each one considers the other a threat to be dealt with.

Their animosity toward each other played a big part in the Persian Gulf War. Hafez al-Assad became a fair-weather friend to the United States. He did not co-operate with the United States because he likes America. He co-operated because he wanted to bring his old enemy, Saddam Hussein, down. Saddam's fall would put him in the driver's seat to rule the Arab new world order.

The Ayatollah Khomeini

The Ayatollah Khomeini also had some ideas about a new world order. He wanted to unite the people under the banner of Islamic fundamentalism. In his system of government, the supreme leader is a scholar in Islamic law and most of the other leaders are members of the Islamic clergy. Saddam Hussein would not qualify because of his religious, cultural and ethnic views. Moreover, the Ayatollah had already installed himself as the head of the Islamic faith.

He took control of Iran in February 1979. The following year, his government was in turmoil. Some of his new leaders had been assassinated. Others had been dismissed or jailed for supposedly working against the new Islamic republic. The economy was in a crisis, the military was demoralized and there was widespread discontent.

Saddam Hussein could never hope to get the Ayatollah to support him or his idea of a united Arab nation. He looked at Iran's problems and assumed the nation was an easy target. He believed his powerful military could invade Iran and win a quick victory. He attacked in 1980.

But Iran was not the paper tiger he expected to encounter. The nation was competitive and he reaped the bitter fruits of a long standstill.

A Revived Babylon

The war painfully and tediously dragged on. Iraqi soldiers were shoved back. Iranian missiles struck Iraqi cities including Baghdad. Iraqi trade was disrupted. Oil production dropped. Shipping ports were closed. Multitudes of young Iraqi soldiers were wounded or killed. Civilian pain, suffering and death increased. Saddam's popularity slipped. His image was tarnished and people wondered if he really was a glorious Arab leader. Why couldn't he win the war? Why were Arabs killing Arabs? How could Saddam lead all Arabs if he could not successfully lead Iraq?

Saddam was embarrassed and he began to seek a way to muster support against the growing tide of discontent. He needed a cause to help sustain the war effort. If he failed to find it, he might be toppled. He searched for something that would mobilize the Iraqis and discredit the Iranians. He found it about 55 miles south of Baghdad.

Iraq had started to rebuild the ancient city of Babylon as a tourist attraction. In times past, beautiful Babylon was one of the Seven Wonders of the World. It was a "special place." The Iraqi people proudly called it "the cradle of civilization."

There was another very important consideration. Babylon had pre-Islamic roots so it preceded Islamic fundamentalism. Its government was older than the Ayatollah's form of government. Its religion was even older than the Islamic religion. Saddam could show other Arabs the Ayatollah had deserted the old ways. He could prove the Ayatollah had abandoned the real government and the true religion.

Saddam thought of something else. Babylon was overthrown by the Medes and Persians (Iranians). That made Iran a former invading enemy. Arabs could kill Arabs in such cases. Iraq had the right to seek revenge and to kill Iranians for what they did to ancient Babylon.

Saddam decided old Babylon was very important. It could be used to motivate Iraqi nationalism by reminding the people of their former greatness. It could become a tool for pointing out Iran was a long-time enemy. If Saddam worked fast, he could accelerate construction and Babylon could play an important role in the war effort.

At that time, the Iraqi government was spending about $6 million a year on archaeological work and construction. Saddam quickly pledged $100 million to the project. It was not long until he vastly increased expenditures again by giving the builders an open checkbook. They received anything they wanted for the project. Supplies and labor were unlimited. Hundreds of workers were moved in. Construction shifted to 16 hour days and it went to seven days a week.

By 1987, hundreds of millions of dollars had been spent and magnificent Babylon was ready for the First Annual International Babylonian Festival. By 1990, 60 million bricks had been laid and grandiose plans were formed to complete the entire project in just four more years. The 1990 World Book Encyclopedia has this to say about it:

"The area included the ziggurat, a monument known in later times
as the Tower of Babel . . . . The government of Iraq has begun to
restore a number of structures, including the ziggurat,
Nebuchadnezzar's main palace, a temple, the Processional
Street, and the city's Greek Theater."[3]

A Revived Nebuchadnezzar

A secondary purpose for rebuilding Babylon was to portray Saddam Hussein as an Arab world leader. Saddam compared himself to Nebuchadnezzar, the greatest leader in Arab history. He reminded the Iraqi people Nebuchadnezzar built Babylon and he rebuilt it. He pointed out Nebuchadnezzar brought all Arabs under his leadership and he promised to do the same. Babylon, and the images it conjured up, were props Saddam Hussein used to promote his leadership in the Arab world. He was a "second Nebuchadnezzar" who would lead the Arab world to all-time greatness.

Turning Evil Into Good

The Book of Genesis tells us the story of Joseph and his jealous brothers. The brothers took Joseph and cast him into an empty pit. They intended to murder him, but they wound up selling him into slavery instead. It was an evil thing they did.

The Most High God protected Joseph and he ended up in a place of leadership in Egypt. He became wealthy and influential. He instituted policies that saved multitudes during the famine. He provided food to his father and brothers. The little shepherd boy from Israel became a great man in the land of Egypt.

After Joseph became famous, his brothers recognized who he was and what he could do. They realized his great power and they feared him. They sought his forgiveness. They even asked to be his servants. Joseph replied, *Ye thought evil against me; but God meant it unto good, to bring to pass, as it is this day, to save much people alive* (Genesis 50:20). He meant, "You had evil intentions, but God used it to bring about the good you now see."

Many times bad things happen, but good things come out of them. Evil deeds occur, but God overrules them. His Word assures us all things can work together for good. It certainly did in Joseph's case. His slavery was bad, but it caused him to wind up in Egypt, where he became rich, famous and the saviour of multitudes. The evil intentions of his brothers produced much good in his life and brought great honor and glory to God.

That is the story behind the rebuilding of Babylon. Saddam Hussein spent millions of dollars to do one thing, but something else happened while he was doing it. His efforts to glorify himself literally fulfilled the Word of God. He intended to create a symbol to rally his people, but he actually created a prophetic sign of the soon return of Jesus. He intended to show he is a great Arab leader, but he really demonstrated God is in control. He had evil intentions, but he proved God knows the end from the beginning.

Praise God! We can see the prophecies of Isaiah, Jeremiah and John coming to pass just as they were written. Pray for those liberal lamps without oil who call themselves scholars.

Babylon's Future

Babylon's future is best understood by looking at its sordid past. The place was permeated with Satanic activity. It wreaked with false religions and corrupt religious practices; was infected with false deities and misplaced loyalties; was the home of escalating corruption and spiritual warfare. It was a loathsome, decadent place that often repeated its age-old mistakes. The Lord God Almighty has always renounced her infidels and ultimately He will ravage her for allowing them to abide there.

Past

The garden of Eden was in the land of Babylon and Satan came there to corrupt Adam and Eve. He continued to work until his fiendish activity provoked The Almighty into destroying the human race with a flood (except for Noah and his family).

Following the flood, Noah and his family moved back to the land of Babylon. Three generations later, his great-grandson Nimrod, began to rule there. It was God's intention for men to spread out and populate the earth, but the rebellious Nimrod had other ideas.

He wanted to keep the people clustered together. He wanted to build the city of Babel (Babylon) to keep them in his shadow. He decided to unite the people and start a world government.

Nimrod built the city of Babel and then he began construction on the Tower of Babel. It was God's intention for men to worship Him, but archaeology tells us the Tower of Babel was used to worship false gods and goddesses. Archaeology also reveals astrology was a main focus there. This was the work of the self-exalting Satan.

The living and true God confounded the language of Nimrod's people and scattered them abroad. He instantly stopped the construction of Babel, but only temporarily. Nebuchadnezzar came along in the spirit of Nimrod and rebuilt the city under the name of Babylon. He began taking conquered people (Daniel, Shadrach, etc.) back to Babylon which was the reverse of the scattering the everlasting God had done. Like his ancestors before him, he delved into astrology and Satanism. When he had his famous dream, his first act was to call in the magicians, astrologers and sorcerers (Daniel 2:2). When he took captives, he tried to reverse the confusion of languages by requiring Daniel and the others to learn the tongue of the Chaldeans (Daniel 1:4). Nebuchadnezzar came very close to accomplishing the things Nimrod was prevented from doing.

Present

Babylon was overthrown by the Medes and Persians and the city withered away. One day, Saddam Hussein came along posing as a "second Nebuchadnezzar" and he started rebuilding it. He even revived the worship of false gods. Rev. Joseph Chambers attended the Second Annual Babylonian International Festival in 1988 and he reported the Iraqis were worshipping such pagan deities as Inanna, Astarte, Ishtar and Marduk. On one occasion, he wrote,

> "Ishtar, the famous goddess of Babylon, was the star of the 'Babylonian Festival.' I heard such words as 'Ishtar has come again to Baghdad.' She was worshipped in the dramas and extolled in music. The mood was such as to suggest that an Ishtar cult was developing . . . .
> After a brief statement in Arabic, the mystic-sounding event begins. Background music with a mythological ring heralds the drama of a

returning monarch. King Nebuchadnezzar enters with great fanfare. Paganistic incense fills the air as the worshipers of this godlike king march to his tune. The ceremonial dress is the ancient Babylonian attire. Other than the amplification, strobe lights, and fireworks, it is very authentic. The air is pregnant with excitement (or evil, depending on your perspective) . . . . I am surprised when this drama by the Iraqi House of Fashion becomes a mythological presentation of everything from the Babylonian epic of creation to a breathtaking picture of Ishtar, the goddess of fertility. Incense and worship are dramatically blended into a glowing history of Iraq's past. The cradle of creation is evident, but the God of creation was missing. I am so glad I have Him in my heart!"[4]

Saddam Hussein publicly embraces the Moslem faith, but he appears to do it as a matter of necessity. He publicly kneels towards Mecca because most Arabs would not follow him if he did not. But Saddam has cast Allah aside in favor of other famous false deities in rebuilt Babylon. The primeval mistakes continue unabated in that area.

Future

Babylon will go through several wars before it reaches the end of the road. It is difficult to say how many wars, but there will be at least three. The nation will have to fight the Medes (probably the Kurds), an assembly of great nations from the north country (probably the United Nations or Antichrist) and God's battle ax (Israel).

At some point, before the city's ultimate destruction, foreigners will take over and turn it into a center for religion and trade. It is unrealistic to believe they will worship or invest much money there under the present conditions so they are likely to use war to clear out the Iraqis and secure the area before they move in. We learn this from a vision the prophet Zechariah had. He saw a wicked woman, in an ephah, being transported to the land of Babylon (Zechariah 5:5-11).

A woman often symbolizes the Church in the Bible. A good woman stands for the true Church and a wicked woman represents the false Church. The woman in Zechariah's vision is a wicked woman. She is the opposite of the bride of Christ. She is the mystery harlot of Revelation chapter 17. She represents the false church (apostate Christendom; Protestantism as well as Roman Catholicism).

In Old Testament times, an ephah was a basket. It was similar to a bushel basket and the Israelis used it to measure flour and grain (Ezekiel 45:10-11). It became the standard symbol of commerce and trade, and represents the world economic system.

The wicked woman (false church) will be led by the false prophet during the tribulation period. She will be trapped in the ephah (world economic system) and transported to the land of Shinar (Babylon). This happens because the false prophet will take his orders from the head of the world economic system (the charismatic Antichrist) and he will want the misguided church to move to "the city of Satan."

When that happens, Babylon will no longer be a tourist attraction. The Antichrist will make it his seat of power. World leaders will love this eloquent man and his city. They will make Babylon the capital of global commerce. Big business will move in and set up shop. Big corporations will control who buys and sells. They will cut unholy deals; make each other rich and have their own way in the world. They will trade gold, silver, jewels, clothing, perfumes, food, building materials, liquor and more. Their merchandise will cover every type of goods known to man. If it exists, it will be controlled out of Babylon.

Babylon will become the home of demons. Satan came near there to Adam and Eve's garden of Eden. Astrology and false worship flourished in Nimrod's Babel. Astrology and sorcery were prevalent in Nebuchadnezzar's Babylon. False gods and goddesses are being worshipped in Saddam's rebuilt Babylon. The Antichrist will demand to be worshipped there during the tribulation period. And when Babylon is finally destroyed, it will be the dwelling place of demons. The prophet Isaiah tells us satyrs (demons) shall dance there and the Apostle John tells us Babylon will become the habitation of devils and foul spirits (Isaiah 13:21; Revelation 18:2).

This appalling place is the city world leaders will choose for their headquarters during the indignation. It is referred to as the "city of Satan" because it has always been the home of deplorable demonic activity. It will be the final seat of rebellion against the God of heaven. It will be a good place to avoid because it will become the recipient of His unstoppable wrath. When it is demolished, in one hour, this future inferno will be permanently unfit for human habitation.

✦ *Behold, I will stir up the Medes against them.*
(Isaiah 13:17)

✦ *I will raise and cause to come up against Babylon an assembly of great nations from the north country.*
(Jeremiah 50:9)

✦ *Thou (Israel) art my battle axe and weapons of war . . . . And I will render unto Babylon and to all the inhabitants of Chaldea all their evil that they have done in Zion in your sight, saith the Lord.*
(Jeremiah 51:20, 24)

✦ *To build it an house in the land of Shinar.*
(Zechariah 5:5–11)

✦ Babylon will become a wealthy city.
(Revelation 18:1–24)

✦ Babylon will become the home of demons.
(Isaiah 13:19-22; Revelation 18:1–2)

Bible Billboards

Billboards are large signs used to display messages. Rev. Bloomfield knew World War II was not Armageddon because he did not see the Bible billboards God said would be erected. He did not see the nation of Israel, Jews controlling Jerusalem, the city of Babylon, or any of the other signs that God said would be displayed. So he knew Armageddon had not arrived.

Times have changed and the Bible billboards are appearing. God is allowing them to be erected because He loves His creation. Those who pay attention and seek a relationship with Him through Jesus will not be here when Armageddon arrives. Those who ignore them will surely face His swift and ruthless judgment. This is a message the Church must get out.

Some people do not want to believe this. Some worry they will appear foolish for believing remarkable things in the Bible. Some do not want to be thought unkind, unloving or unintelligent for believing in the judgment of God. A few do not believe in watching for Bible billboards. Let me tell you something about this.

Two men were traveling down the road to Emmaus shortly after the resurrection of Jesus. They were talking about His death and resurrection when He approached them. They were greatly disappointed. They had believed the good things in the Scriptures, but ignored what they thought was bad. They hoped Jesus was the Redeemer, but had not counted on Him being delivered up, condemned and crucified (even though Gabriel told Daniel Messiah would be cut off). They heard a report Jesus was risen, but some of their friends went to the grave and could not find Him. All of this bad did not fit their interpretation of things. Jesus replied, *O, fools, and slow of heart to believe **all that the prophets have spoken*** (Luke 24:13-25).

All that the prophets have spoken is important. It includes the bad as well as the good—the judgments as well as the promises. The Bible billboards are designed to get our attention. They are God's way of opening our eyes and it is both intelligent and loving to heed them and to point them out to others, especially our loved ones.

Chapter 6

The Rapture

All who honestly take a hard look at end-time prophecies in concert with current events are bound to see many troubling similarities. Just a quick glance often reveals obvious parallels with vast and disturbing implications. But it is not enough to show only the looming desolation of the tribulation period.

Our loving God has brighter days than that in store for His Church. No one has ever loved as He loves. He sincerely delights in the well-being of His children. So in spite of the blackness of its own sin, the Church will not be here when the 70th week of Daniel arrives. It will miss the non-stop disasters of that day because of a mysterious event Christians call "the rapture."

Definition

Perhaps someone has told you the word "rapture" is not in the Bible. They are right, but only to a point. It is not in the English translations of the Bible, but "rapture" is the Anglicized version of a word that appears in the Latin translations. Notice what The New King James Prophecy Bible says,

> "The term rapture is an expression for the Greek word harpazo. Rapture comes from the Latin word rapere, meaning 'to snatch or carry off.' Harpazo is the word used to describe the action of the Holy Spirit when He took (caught away) Philip from the environs of Gaza and deposited him in Caesarea (Acts 8:39). It conveys the

idea of being taken away in a sudden swoop by a force that cannot be resisted. This word is used by Paul in I Thessalonians 4:15–17 to describe the event which is called the Rapture."[1]

The first New Testament Bible texts were written in the Greek language. When they were compiled, the writers used the Greek word "harpazo." Next, the Greek texts were translated into Latin and the translators used the Latin word "rapere." After that, the Latin texts were translated into English, but a problem developed at that point. "Harpazo"and "rapere" could not be translated into just one English word. They required a combination of English words to relay their true meaning. One of the combinations is "caught away" (Acts 8:39).

This is what we have. The Bible contains prophecies which teach there will be a "rapere" at the end of the Church age. Christians have Anglicized the word "rapere" into the word "rapture." And it means the Church will be "caught away" into heaven in the last days of this present age.

Bible Descriptions

Several passages in the Bible translate the words "harpazo," "rapere" and their derivations. These Scriptures clearly describe the words. Notice how they have been translated in the following verses:

✦ *And from the days of John the Baptist until now the kingdom of heaven suffereth violence, and the violent take it by force.* (Matthew 11:12)

✦ *When any one heareth the word of the kingdom, and understandeth it not, then cometh the wicked one, and catcheth away that which was sown in his heart.* (Mathew 13:19)

✦ *And I give unto them eternal life; and they shall never perish, neither shall any man pluck them out of my hand.* (John 10:28)

✦ *And when there arose a great dissension, the chief captain, fearing lest Paul should have been pulled in pieces of them, commanded the soldiers to go down, and to take him by force from among them, and to bring him into the castle.* (Acts 23:10)

✦ *Then we which are alive and remain shall be <u>caught up</u> together with them in the clouds to meet the Lord in the air; and so shall we ever be with the Lord.*
(I Thessalonians 4:17)

These statements leave no doubt about what the rapture is. It is a "taking by force, catching away, plucking out," or "catching up" of the Church. It is the sudden seizure of God's special people. God takes His Church to its heavenly home; its hiding place; its place of refuge.

We do not want to miss this because Planet Earth will be in a blood bath. The forces of heaven and hell will lock horns. Demonic powers will be unleashed. The laws of nature will be suspended. Madness and depravity will reign. Cruelty and deception will prevail. Crime and war will rage. Disease and chaos will flourish.

Examples of the Rapture

The Bible contains several examples of the rapture. It even includes the writings of some who went to heaven and returned to talk about it. Seven of them are as follows:

(1) Enoch

Moses records the generations of Adam in the fifth chapter of Genesis. He says, Adam died, Seth died, Enos died, Cainan died, Mahalaleel died, Jared died and Enoch "was not." He tells how long each one of these men lived and, except for Enoch, he says each one died. Oddly enough, he does not say Enoch died. He simply says, *Enoch was not; for God took him.*

The Apostle Paul explains what happened. He writes, *Enoch was translated that he should not see death* (Hebrews 11:5). Since "translated" means he was moved from one place to another, Paul is saying, "Enoch was moved from where he was to a different place to prevent his death." He was translated from earth to paradise to keep him from dying. Adam died, Seth died, Enos died, Cainan died, Mahalaleel died, Jared died, but Enoch did not die. He "was not" means he was raptured into paradise.

✦ *Enoch walked with God: and he was not; for God took him.*
(Genesis 5:24)

(2) Elijah

The Bible does not say Elijah was raptured, but many preachers and teachers say he was raptured because he was here one minute and gone the next. He suddenly "went up" into heaven without dying.

✦ *Elijah went up by a whirlwind into heaven.*
  (II Kings 2:11)

(3) Jesus

While the Apostles were watching, Jesus ascended into heaven. After talking to His disciples, He was "taken up" into the clouds. And now He is seated at the right hand of God.

✦ *He was taken up.*
  (Acts 1:9)

(4) Philip

Philip was witnessing to the Ethiopian eunuch when the Holy Spirit suddenly took him away and the eunuch could see him no more. He disappeared and was transported to another location where he continued his ministry. This miracle is unusual because Philip did not go to heaven. According to the Scriptures, he reappeared in Azotus (Ashdod).

✦ *The Spirit of the Lord caught away Philip.*
  (Acts 8:39)

(5) Paul

Something mysterious happened to the Apostle Paul and he kept it a secret for more than fourteen years. It was a private matter between God and him. He could not explain exactly what happened, but he knew it took place.

His incredible experience was different from that of Enoch and Elijah. They went to heaven and stayed. Paul went to heaven and came back to give an eyewitness report. Was he raptured? Many outstanding Bible scholars and preachers say yes because he was "caught up" into paradise.

✦ *Such an one was caught up into paradise.*
  (II Corinthians 12:1–4)

(6) John

The Apostle John was on the Isle of Patmos when he looked and a door was opened in heaven. He heard a trumpet-sounding voice speaking to him saying, *Come up hither.* He immediately went to heaven in the spirit. And he saw many wonderful things before he was returned to share his amazing experience with us.

✦ *Immediately I was in the spirit.*
(Revelation 4:1-2)

(7) The Two Witnesses

In the Old Testament, the Most High God required two witnesses to give testimony in matters of law and religion. He will continue that practice during the tribulation period by sending two witnesses to bear testimony to the truth of the Gospel. Under His hand, they will bring a message of mercy and grace that God will enforce with a series of powerful miracles.

The Antichrist will be displeased and try to deal with it by having them killed. He will even leave their dead bodies lying in the street for everyone to see. Suddenly, while the whole world is watching, these two witnesses will be raised from the dead and they will ascend into heaven.

✦ *They ascended up to heaven in a cloud.*
(Revelation 11:3-12)

The Church

It is apparent to those who interpret the Scriptures literally Jesus, Paul, John and the others are not alone when it comes to this matter of being raptured. Several Scriptures teach the day will come when God will abruptly seize His Church and take it into heaven. His people will meet Jesus in the air before He allows the worst tragedies to strike this wicked, sinful, God-forsaking world. It is an act of grace, love, hope, mercy, comfort, protection, healing, resurrection, reunion, blessing and reward. The blessed hope of the Church is, *The glorious appearing of the great God and our Saviour Jesus Christ* (Titus 2:13).

We Go Together

Those who believe the Bible have God's promise that Jesus Himself will return to raise Christians from the dead. There will be living believers when that occurs, but the Scriptures say they will not go to heaven first. The living Christians will be required to wait on the resurrection of the departed saints.

There is more

After the dead are raised, those Christians who are alive will be "caught up" with them. The dead will be raised first. Then all Christians will go to heaven together. The rapture follows the resurrection of the dead in Christ so all Christians can go to heaven together as one body.

> ✦ *The dead in Christ shall rise first: Then we which are alive and remain shall be caught up together with them in the clouds to meet the Lord.*
> (I Thessalonians 4:13–18)

Our Glorious Body

Every Christian will receive a new glorified body when the rapture occurs. It will not matter whether we have died or not. We will be changed. And this change will happen instantaneously. It will take place as soon as the dead have been raised. The dead will be raised and the bodies of the living will be changed in a split-second. Our current bodies are perishable. But God intends to give us new bodies that are immortal.

The Shepherd and Bishop of our souls will not allow death to defeat His people. He will not allow mortal bodies to prevent His children from achieving immortality. Be thankful. Continue to serve Him. The rapture guarantees believers in God's only begotten Son a great victory. The sting of death is not permanent. And the victory of the grave is only temporary. Yes, thanks be unto God because He makes us more than conquerors through our loving Lord Jesus Christ.

> ✦ *We shall not all sleep, but we shall all be changed . . . . The dead shall be raised incorruptible, and we shall be changed.*
> (I Corinthians 15:51–57)

A Great Gathering

The rapture is a great gathering of Christians unto Jesus. A powerful force will raise the dead and gather the Church unto the Friend of sinners.It will not matter where Christians have been buried or where they live in the world. The Father of Eternity knows where each believer is.

✦ *The coming of our Lord Jesus is a gathering unto him.*
  (II Thessalonians 2:2)

A Wonderful Promise

One of the most loved passages in the entire Bible is found in John chapter 14. No Scripture, poem or writing of any kind surpasses it for comfort and encouragement. If you are depressed, discouraged or cast down, this is the remedy. If you are despondent, perplexed or anxious, read this passage. It is doubtful if any is read more often or in more places. It is read in hospital rooms, at funerals and beside graves all over the world.

Notwithstanding, few people associate it with the rapture. Many connect it with illness and death, but not with the rapture. Many can even quote it from memory, but they do not realize what it actually refers to.

Jesus was going away, but He asked that we not worry. He urged us to believe in Him. He said there are many mansions in heaven and He was going to prepare a place for us. He promised He would return and receive us unto Himself.

When the believer dies, there is no doubt his soul and spirit go to be with God. However, this promise to return and receive us is to be distinguished from that. The wonderful Jesus is not personally operating a shuttle back and forth between heaven and earth to pick up dying believers. He is in heaven with the Father, preparing a place for His Church. Angels usher the dying into the presence of God (Luke 16:22).

This passage is also to be distinguished from the return of the King of Kings and Lord of Lords at the end of the tribulation period. At that time, He returns with His Church. Here, He comes for His Church. Hence, we see this great passage of comfort and love actually refers to the rapture.

✦ *I will come again, and receive you unto myself.*
  (John 14:1-3)

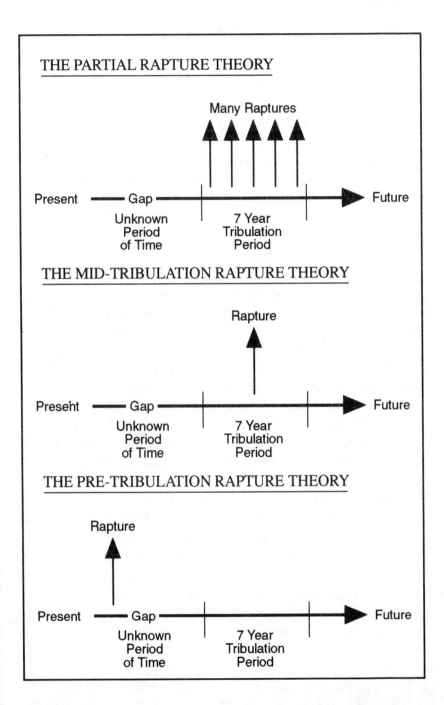

THE PARTIAL RAPTURE THEORY

Many Raptures

Present — Gap — | 7 Year | Future
Unknown   Tribulation
Period   Period
of Time

THE MID-TRIBULATION RAPTURE THEORY

Rapture

Preseht — Gap — | 7 Year | Future
Unknown   Tribulation
Period   Period
of Time

THE PRE-TRIBULATION RAPTURE THEORY

Rapture

Present — Gap — | 7 Year | Future
Unknown   Tribulation
Period   Period
of Time

The Partial Rapture Theory

A few very sincere Christians honestly believe in a partial rapture. They teach that those who do not "watch," or "expect" the soon return of Jesus, will be left behind to go through some or all of the tribulation period. They believe you can "run out of oil," so to speak, and not make it on the first go around. In their view, the rapture is for "spiritual" Christians. Carnal believers will be left behind for one of several later raptures.

But what does the Bible say? The Apostle Paul told the Corinthian believers, *We shall all be changed.* "All" includes every member of the Body of Christ whether we are spiritual or carnal and no one is left out. And he said it will happen, *In a moment, in the twinkling of an eye, at the last trump.* It cannot be spread out over seven years because everyone will be gone in the blink of an eye. The Church is one body (I Corinthians 12:12-13). The Head of the Body is not coming for a dismembered body. He is not coming to gather the arms, but not the hands; to gather the legs, but not the feet. He will not leave some Christians in their graves and wed a partial bride. There are no Bible reasons to believe He will resurrect the "good" Christians and leave the "poor" Christians in their graves. The partial rapture theory must be rejected because it does not reconcile with other Scriptures. The chart on the preceding page will help clarify the different rapture theories.

✦ *We shall not all sleep, but we shall all be changed.*
   (I Corinthians 15:51)

✦ *In a moment, in the twinkling of an eye, at the last trump.*
   (I Corinthians 15:52)

The Mid-Tribulation Rapture Theory

A minority of Christians subscribe to the theory the rapture will take place at the middle of the tribulation period. They give assent to the idea the Church will endure the events of the first three and one-half years. These believers teach the rapture will happen when the two witnesses of Revelation chapter 11 are caught up.

The arguments in favor of this theory are weak, but the arguments against it are many and strong. Some of them are as follows:

+ I Corinthians 15:52 teaches the trumpet sounds *before* the dead are raised. In Revelation 11:15, the trumpet sounds after the two witnesses are raised.

+ I Corinthians 15:52 teaches a trumpet will sound *before* the rapture. The seventh trumpet of Revelation 11:15 sounds after the two witnesses have already *ascended* into heaven.

+ I Corinthians 15:52 teaches the rapture occurs *in the twinkling of an eye*. In Revelation 11:11, the two witnesses stand on their feet and people who see them are afraid.

+ The I Corinthians 15 passage teaches the dead come out of their graves. In Revelation 11:9, we learn the witnesses are refused burial.

+ In I Thessalonians 4:16, Jesus descends from heaven with a shout. There is no mention of this in Revelation 11.

+ In I Thessalonians 4:16, the archangel speaks *before* the dead are raised. In Revelation 11:12, a voice speaks *after* the two witnesses are raised.

These are not all of the arguments by any means, but an examination of them reveals why only a minority of Christians believe in the mid-tribulation rapture. The theory does not stand when put in the light of other Scriptures so most Christians discard it.

The Pre-Tribulation Rapture Theory

The majority of Christians believe the rapture will occur prior to the tribulation period. They believe Jesus died to redeem the Church and His death guarantees its deliverance from the day of wrath and vengeance. God's family is in this world, but it is not of this world and it will not suffer with this world. The precious atoning blood of Jesus guarantees all Christians a different future from that of Israel, the false church and those who have not heard the Word of God.

The arguments for the pre-tribulation rapture are all based on Scripture. It can even be said they are based on the literal interpretation of Scripture. They are many and, in this writer's view, positively overwhelming. Dr. John Walvoord has published a list of fifty.[2]

Dr. Raymond Ludwigson has published a list of thirty-one.[3] Seven arguments for this position are as follows:

(1) Deuteronomy 4:1-2

First, there are several passages in the Bible that instruct us not to tamper with the Word of God (Proverbs. 30:6,7; Revelation 22:18,19). The Word of God is perfect, incapable of error and eternal. We should accept it just the way it is.

This is the point. There are many passages in the Old Testament on the tribulation period, but none of them place the Church on earth. There are many more passages in the New Testament, including most of the Book of Revelation, but none of them place the Church on earth during the tribulation period either. The conclusion is, the Church will not be on earth when the seventieth week occurs and we should not take it upon ourselves to say it will be.

✦ *Ye shall not add unto the word which I command you, neither shall ye diminish ought from it.*
(vs. 2)

(2) Isaiah 26:19–21

Second, there is an interesting passage in Isaiah that predicts the dead shall live. It says they shall arise and be summoned into God's chambers until the indignation (tribulation period) passes. The saved are called to hide because *The Lord cometh out of his place to punish the inhabitants of the earth for their iniquity.* Notice the sequence of events. The resurrection occurs first; the rapture second; and the indignation last (See Isaiah 34:1-8; Jeremiah 10:10; Zephaniah 3:8; Habbakuk 3:12).

✦ Thy dead men shall live, together with my dead body shall they arise.
(vs. 19)

✦ Come, my people, enter thou into thy chambers, and shut thy doors about thee: hide thyself as it were for a little moment, until the indignation be overpast.
(vs. 20)

(3) Psalms 145:18–21

Third, one of the great doctrines of Christianity says the God of heaven takes care of all them that love Him. That is His nature and what makes Him happy. It is His promise to the saved of the Lord. Many in the Church will point out God has always protected His people. For example, He sent Noah into the ark before He caused the flood (Genesis 7:23). Again, He refused to destroy Sodom until His angels removed Lot (Genesis 19:16). By analogy, the believers Defense will rapture His redeemed before He sends the tribulation period.

✦ *The Lord preserveth all them that love Him.*
   (vs. 20)

(4) Luke 21:34–36

Fourth, Christians have always believed in the power of prayer. When you get on your knees and get serious, it works. James, the half brother of Jesus, said, *The effectual fervent prayer of a righteous man availeth much* (James 5:16). And the Apostle Paul said, God is *Able to do exceeding abundantly above all that we ask or think* (Ephesians 3:20).

The point is Jesus advised us to pray that we would be accounted worthy to escape the terrible events of the tribulation period. And we do not believe He would instruct us to do that unless He is willing to grant it. The right kind of prayer gets results even if it means something as powerful as the rapture.

✦ *Pray always, that ye may be accounted worthy to escape all these things that shall come to pass.*
   (vs. 36)

(5) I Thessalonians 5:1–11

Fifth, the Apostle Paul revealed the rapture in the last six verses of I Thessalonians chapter four. Chapter five begins with a discussion of the day of the Lord and gets directly at the question at hand. It discusses what will signal the destruction, who it will come upon, who will not escape and who will not be overtaken. Paul says, *God hath not appointed us to wrath* and the word "wrath" is a reference to the tribulation period (Zephaniah 1:14–15; Revelation 6:17). Clearly, the meaning of this passage is the wrath of God will fall upon the lost, but not upon the saved. It comes upon them, but not us.

The pronouns in the passage are very significant. Who does the sudden destruction come upon? The answer is "them (the lost)." Who is not in darkness and not overtaken? The answer is "ye, bretheren (the Church)." Who is not appointed unto wrath? The answer is "us (the Church)." Sudden destruction comes upon the lost, but the Church will not be overtaken and it is not appointed unto wrath.

+ *Sudden destruction cometh upon them.*
  (vs. 3)

+ *But ye, bretheren, are not in darkness, that that day should overtake you as a thief.*
  (vs. 4)

+ *For God hath not appointed us to wrath.*
  (vs. 9)

(6) II Thessalonians 2:1–12

Sixth, the Apostle Paul revealed the sequence of events to the Thessalonian church. He did not want the believers there to be troubled by thinking the day of the Lord had come. He reminded them that the man of sin will be revealed before the tribulation period begins.

He taught that a lawless spirit, called the *mystery of iniquity* is already working in the world. This lawless spirit is partially restrained and will remain in this suppressed condition until the Holy Spirit is taken out of the way. Then the wicked and deceptive Antichrist will be revealed.

Look at it like this. The Holy Spirit indwells the Church (the Temple of the Holy Ghost—I Corinthians 6:19) and works through this Temple to restrain iniquity in the world. The presence of the Church in the world means the presence of the Holy Spirit and this is preventing the appearance of the Antichrist. Hence, the Church must leave before the man of sin can come on the scene.

+ *He who now letteth will let, until he be taken out of the way.*
  (vs. 7)

✦ *Then shall that Wicked be revealed.*
  (vs. 8)

(7) Revelation 3:10

Seventh, in the Book of Revelation, Jesus promised to keep those who have *kept the word . . . from the hour of temptation which shall come upon all the world.* Those who have "kept the Word" refers to the Church. "The hour of temptation" refers to the tribulation period. Jesus will use the rapture to keep the Church out of the 70th week.

✦ *Because thou hast kept the word of my patience, I also will keep thee from the hour of temptation, which shall come upon all the world, to try them that dwell upon the earth.*
  (vs. 10)

Other Theories

This is only a sampling of the theories. A few scholars believe in a post-tribulation rapture. Some have a post-millennial view of the second coming and others hold to what is called the amillennial view. Simply stated, my opinion on these theories is this. They stretch the imagination and are Scripturally unsound.

Between the Rapture and the Tribulation Period

How much time will pass between the rapture and the tribulation period? Will the Antichrist sign the covenant with Israel immediately following the rapture or will there be a delay? The New King James Version Prophecy Bible says this:

"Sometime after the Rapture, a seven-year period will begin which is called the Tribulation. It is nowhere specified that the Tribulation will immediately follow the Rapture, and so there may be some interval between the two events."[4]

Hal Lindsey writes:

"The Roman Antichrist must have time to be revealed, take over the ten-nation European confederacy and establish himself as a world leader before he can have a power base from which to make the covenant with the Israeli leader.

"Such momentous events necessitate an interlude between the revelation of the Antichrist and the official beginning of the Day of the Lord."[5]

Dr. David Hocking teaches:

"We may be in heaven for many years until the tribulation actually starts . . . . The rapture could happen many years ahead of that."[6]

"From my perspective, the rapture could happen tonight and it still may be 20 years until the tribulation."[7]

The questions are answered. The Church is raptured before the Antichrist is divulged. After the rapture, this counterfeit Christ will rise to power and negotiate a covenant pertaining to Israel. That will take time. But the Bible does not say how much. It could be a few weeks and it may be several years.

Signs of the Rapture

And now we come to something very important and everyone should be aware of it. Some want to know, "What are the signs of the rapture?" None! The Bible gives many signs of the last days, the tribulation period, the Battle of Armageddon, etc., but it does not provide us with any signs of the rapture. Many things must happen before the tribulation period can begin and before the second coming can happen, but nothing is required for the rapture to take place.

A Failure to Divide the Word

Unfortunately, there is a lot of darkness and confusion surrounding this issue of signs. Most of it centers around the failure of people to rightly divide the Word of God. Many writers, preachers and teachers tend to lump all the end-time events together. They do not divide them up, but refer to all of them as the second coming of Jesus. When they speak of Jesus coming *for* His Church, they call it the second coming. When they speak of Jesus coming *with* His Church, they call it the second coming. When they speak of the tribulation period, they speak of the second coming. It matters not what they are speaking of, they call it the second coming. This practice muddles the whole issue of signs. It confuses people and shows these writers, preachers and teachers are not as informed as they seem to want people to believe.

A Misapplication of Scriptures.

Another unfortunate habit is the practice of taking verses out of context. For example, most prophecy buffs will tell you the events of Matthew chapter 24 do not refer to the rapture. The disciples came to the great Teacher privately and asked three questions, none of which pertained to the rapture. Yet, when one speaks of the rapture, many Christians will quote Matthew 24:36 (which does not refer to the rapture) and say, *Of that day and hour knoweth no man, no, not the angels of heaven, but my Father only.* Some will quote Mark 13:32 (which also does not refer to the rapture) and say, "Jesus does not even know." Many preachers are guilty of this practice.

Another example of this sloppy exegesis concerns the question the disciples asked the Master in Acts chapter one. They were naturally concerned about the nation of Israel and they asked, *Lord wilt thou at this time restore again the kingdom to Israel* (Acts 1:6)? In other words, they were asking, "Will you restore the throne of David to Israel at this time." Jesus replied, *It is not for you to know the times or the seasons, which the Father hath put in his own power.* The point is, this question has nothing to do with the rapture or with signs of the rapture. And to be true to the context, it should not be applied to the rapture. Many make the mistake of doing that.

Let me be clear. This writer is not saying "people can know when the rapture will occur." Date-setting is not Scriptural. And no date is being set. This author is simply pointing out that many Christians are failing to rightly divide the end-time events. Some are taking Scriptures out of context. And some are misapplying them. These practices are causing confusion. They are impeding a proper understanding of the prophetic scenario and they need to be corrected.

A Lack of Balance

A third unfortunate situation, is the practice of going overboard. This two-edged sword cuts both ways. On one side are those who become so preoccupied with signs they predict dates. They do not care what the Scriptures say or that every person who ever predicted a date was wrong. They still do it. Edgar C. Whisenant did it when he wrote his book *88 Reasons Why The Rapture Could Be In 1988*. Elizabeth Clare Prophet did it when she talked members of the Church Universal and Triumphant into selling their homes and moving into underground bunkers. Mission for the Coming Days (MCD) did it in South Korea when they predicted both the date and the hour; on October 28, 1992 at 10:00 a.m. in New York City; 5:00 p.m. in Jerusalem; midnight in Seoul, South Korea.

On the other side, and just as bad as the date-setters, are those who bristle and boil with righteous indignation every time the rapture is mentioned. They do not care that Christians are told to "watch" (I Thessalonians 5:6). They ignore the Scriptures that say we can see the day approaching (Luke 21:28; I Thessalonians 5:4; Hebrews 10:25). They go out-of-bounds by choosing an extreme position on the opposite side of the signs issue.

The point is, all Christians need to strike a balance. The true Scriptural position is not that someone can know the date. And it *is not* that someone cannot know when the rapture is close. *The true Scriptural position on signs is in between those who set dates and those who scoff at people for watching.* It is wrong to set a date and withdraw to bunkers. And it is equally wrong to close your eyes and go to sleep.

We do not know the day or the hour of the rapture. But that does not mean we will not know when it is getting close (unless we are lost or not watching). Consider this example. A young woman is expecting a baby in a few weeks. She does not know the day or the hour her baby will arrive. Nevertheless, she will know when it is getting close. She will recognize the signs. And that is the way it is with the rapture.

The Doctrine of Imminence

At first glance, some of this seems contradictory. We have said there are no signs of the rapture, but we have also said watch. Are we sending up mixed signals? No. The doctrine of imminence explains what we are saying.

The word "imminent" denotes something can happen at any moment and without any warning. Concerning the rapture, the doctrine of imminence means the "catching away" can occur at any time and without any advance notice. The Bible does not say anything precedes the rapture. Nothing is required to happen before it can take place.

The Church has lived under the doctrine of imminence for almost 2000 years. It teaches that there are no signs of the rapture and no warning will occur. It tells us to live like our days are numbered and to be ready to go at any time.

This doctrine has characterized the Church since its very beginning. Both Peter and Paul rightfully looked for the rapture in their lifetime. The earliest believers correctly expected it before they died. And for almost 2000 years, preachers have properly said, "Our Lord could come this afternoon," or "Our Lord could come tonight." They have been accused of scaring people, being false prophets and a whole lot of other things, but the fact is, they were telling the truth. The rapture could have occurred 2000 years ago, or 200 years ago, or 2 years ago, or it could take place in the next 2 seconds. This brings up a question. What do we watch for? If there are no signs of the rapture, then how will we know when it is close? How will we see the day approaching? Do we have any plausible grounds for believing the rapture could, in fact, occur very soon? Believe it or not, there are answers to these questions.

It is true that no signs precede the rapture, but we know what follows the rapture. We are sure the Antichrist follows the rapture. We are sure the tribulation period and the Battle of Armageddon comes after the rapture. And we have signs to warn us when they are approaching. We know Israel will be back in the land, Europe will come back together, Babylon will be rebuilt and so on. Logic tells us the rapture is getting close because some of the things that must occur after the rapture are now coming on the scene. We know the rapture is approaching because it occurs prior to the tribulation period and we can see that is getting near.

Look at it like this. A friend calls you and says, "I was traveling from my house to the mall and my car broke down. I will be standing on the side of the road. Will you come and pick me up?" You start traveling the same route. You do not know where your friend is, so you start watching immediately. You do not know when you will get to your friend, but you know it will be before you get to the mall. You know the closer you get to the mall, the closer you are to your friend. And when you get very close to the mall, you know you are very close to your friend.

We do not have any literal signs of the rapture. We only know it will happen before the tribulation period and the closer we get to that, the nearer we are to the rapture. The signs of Antichrist, the tribulation period, the Battle of Armageddon and so forth are showing up. They are clear indicators of an impending rapture. They are how we can have no signs, but still see it coming.

Why God Revealed the Rapture

Some people seem to think those who talk about the rapture are trying to scare people. Did the gentle Jesus reveal the rapture to scare people? Absolutely not! Our Lord unveiled the rapture to comfort those who were worrying about their deceased loved ones. He did it to assure us. The rapture means the resurrection of dead believers, the reuniting of families, blessings, healing, new bodies and going to heaven. It is a cause for Christians to rejoice and it should not scare anyone unless they are poorly informed or lost.

Chapter 7

New Testament Signs Of His Coming

Many misinformed or misguided people write and speak on the subject of signs. Some of what they say is ridiculous. Some of it leads to a lot of confusion. The confusion in turn causes more than a few to become lukewarm. And it causes others to question everything they hear out of the Bible.

Let's consider some of the signs that herald our Lord's return. But before we do, it is necessary to add that we are not talking about signs of the rapture. As already stated, there are no signs of that event. The Bible clearly teaches the "catching away" is imminent which means it could occur anytime. And there will be no warning. The return of Jesus at the end of the 70th week is an entirely different matter. There are many prophetic indicators for the great day of the Lord and the second coming of Jesus. We will not attempt to identify or study all of them. But it is our purpose to examine some of the more important references found in the New Testament. A large number of them were given by our Lord Himself. And they all point to the fact the world is steadily and very rapidly moving toward His return.

Matthew

Matthew was a publican before Jesus called him to be one of the Twelve. He wrote in Hebrew and his primary audience was the Jews. This probably explains why he quoted so many Old Testament Scriptures. He understood many of the events of his day were fulfillments of prophecy.

He recorded one of the most famous end-time prophecies ever given. Because it was delivered on the Mount of Olives, it is called the Olivet Discourse. Jesus was the speaker. And if we want to understand it, we must keep in mind four things:

1. It is best understood in connection with Old Testament prophecies;
2. The angel Gabriel's revelation to Daniel is a major key (Daniel 9:24–27);
3. It has nothing to do with the rapture;
4. It begins with a caring message designed to ease our fears.

Let us recall part of what Gabriel revealed to Daniel in Babylon. He predicted Jerusalem and the temple would be rebuilt; the first coming of Messiah would occur 69 weeks (483 years) from the commandment to rebuild Jerusalem; Messiah would be cut off; Jerusalem and the temple would be destroyed again; and the end would come with a flood.

The Olivet Discourse occurred in the middle of the events Gabriel had predicted. The city and the temple had been rebuilt just as Gabriel said. Jesus arrived right on schedule. He made His triumphal entry into the city on the exact day Gabriel prophesied. He went to the rebuilt temple and drove the money-changers away. He left and spent the night at Bethany.

The next day, He went to the temple for the last time. He revealed that He would soon be cut off. He pronounced a series of "woes" upon the religious rulers and began to leave the temple. He would never return; never speak or teach there again (Matthew 21-23; John 12:12-50).

While He was exiting, His disciples approached Him to point out the buildings of the temple. They were built with huge white granite stones. They were very expensive and they made a magnificent structure. Jesus may have recalled Gabriel's prophecy. He answered and said, *There shall not be left here one stone upon another.*

The disciples were shocked. Why would God Almighty allow such a thing happen to His temple? What kind of incredible events would bring it to pass? They must have remembered Gabriel's message to Daniel and they wanted a date and some signs. They were curious to know more.

Jesus stopped at the Mount of Olives and sat down. Four of His followers joined Him. They had three questions.

✦ *When shall these things be?*
(Matthew 24:3)

✦ *What shall be the sign of thy coming?*
(Matthew 24:3)

✦ *What shall be the sign of the end of the world?*
(Matthew 24:3)

These queries have nothing to do with the rapture. At this time, the Twelve probably did not even know about the rapture. That mystery would not be revealed until the Apostle Paul came along. These questions refer to the time and the signs of the events in Gabriel's message to Daniel.

The Beginning of Sorrows (Before the 70th Week)

As Jesus talked about the signs of the end, He grouped false Christs, wars, famines, pestilences and earthquakes into a special category. The King James version calls it *the beginning of sorrows.* The Modern Language version calls it *the early pains of childbirth* and the Revised Standard Version calls it *the beginning of the birthpangs.*

The beginning of sorrows covers the period from when Jesus was speaking to the end of the age. During that time, there are five signs that will be similar to an expectant mother's birth pangs. We know that labor pains get closer together, harder and more painful, as the birth of a child nears. By analogy, Jesus was saying, "False Christs, wars, famines, pestilences and earthquakes will increase in frequency and intensity as you approach the second coming and the end of the age."

Why did Jesus identify these particular signs? The answer is Gabriel told Daniel about the 70th week, the Antichrist, the end of the war and desolations. And these five signs are all characteristics of that. But there is more. There is a loving word of caution here to keep us from being frightened; to keep us from going off the deep end. These are signs of the 70th week. But they will also happen to a lesser degree before that time. And we should expect it.

(1) False Christs

The ultimate false Christ is called the Antichrist. According to Gabriel, the tribulation period begins when he signs a seven year covenant to protect Israel (Daniel 9:27). He is the false Christ who is the rider on the white horse (Revelation 6:2). He will rise to power as a man of peace; be lavished with praise; speak marvelous things; be backed by Satan with power, signs and lying wonders; and multitudes will be deceived (Daniel 7:20; II Thessalonians 2:9-11). He will gain dominion over much of the earth after the rapture. But this bloody and deceitful man will turn on those who accept Jesus in his day; and have them killed (Revelation 13:7, 15).

In recent years, the Church has seen "Sweet Daddy Grace," "Father Divine," Jim Jones, Charles Manson and others who claimed to be the Christ. In the late '80s and early '90s, a Korean Messiah, Rev. Sun Myung Moon, appeared. At the same time, a British Messiah, Lord Maitreya, showed up in London. In 1990, a black Messiah, Hulon Mitchell, Jr., otherwise known as "Yahweh ben Yahweh," turned up in Florida and an Arab Messiah, Saddam Hussein appeared in Iraq. In 1992, the followers of Rabbi Menachem Mendel Schneerson of Brooklyn, N.Y. claimed he is the Jewish Messiah and newspapers dubbed Marcos Antonio Bonilla of Nicaragua "Jesus of the poor." In 1993, David Koresh, leader of the Branch Davidians in

Waco, Texas, called himself the Lamb of God. We could go on. But altogether, there have been at least fifty men and two women in the United States alone who have claimed to be the Christ. This is the beginning of sorrows and they have deceived many.

But Jesus does not want us to get upset or make others nervous because this is happening. The appearance of false Christs does not mean the Antichrist has arrived. Keep in mind the Church will be raptured before he can be revealed. The only Christians who need worry about this devilish man are those who get saved after the rapture.

> ✦ *Take heed that no man deceive you. For many shall come in my name, saying, I am Christ; and shall deceive many.* (Matthew 24:4,5)

(2) Wars and rumors of wars

The ultimate war and real "mother of all battles" is called the Battle of Armageddon. It begins when the fiery rider on the red horse of blood snatches peace from the earth; embroiling the whole world in war and causing the bloodshed and slaughter of multiplied millions (Revelation 6:4). The Prophets Zechariah, Zephaniah and Joel foretold this catastrophic event (Zechariah 14:1-3; Zephaniah 3:8; Joel 3:2).

Historians tell us the world has experienced more than 4,000 wars in the last 5,000 years. During the last 3,000 years, war has raged somewhere in the world fourteen out of every fifteen years. And the average annual death from war is drastically increasing every century reminding us of the labor pains of a mother as she approaches the birth of her child. Many of the living today have seen World War I, World War II, the Korean War, the Vietnam War, the Persian Gulf War and others. We also see nations all around us armed to the teeth.

But Jesus does not want us to be deceived by these wars and rumors of war. They are not a sign the 70th week of Daniel has arrived. The fiery rider on the red horse cannot charge forth with his hatred, conflict and bloodshed until the Church is raptured and the Antichrist revealed. *The Lord shall preserve thee from all evil: he shall preserve thy soul* (Psalms 121:7).

✦ *Ye shall hear of wars and rumors of wars: see that ye be not troubled: for all these things must come to pass, but the end is not yet.*
(Matthew 24:6)

(3) Famines

The 70th week of Daniel will be marked by famine on a scale the world has never seen. It will be greater than the "Great Starvation Exodus" from Ethiopia in the 1980s; greater than the "World's Worst Human Disaster" in Somalia in the 1990s.

Following the rapture, many of the earth's farmers will be gone. The fruited plains will be barren. The pastures will not be clothed with flocks. The valleys will not be covered with corn. Groups of governments, loyal to the Antichrist, will blockade food shipments; confiscate food supplies. Social, political and physical structures will collapse. The morbid rider on the black horse will go forth spreading rationing and famine (Revelation 6:5, 6). The False Prophet will require everyone who buys and sells to take the mark of the Beast (Revelation 13:16, 17). Many will refuse. Others will have no money. Famine will become a deadly reality and multitudes will cease to exist.

In the '30s and '40s, it is estimated 10 million troops and 10 million civilians were killed in World War I; another 20 million died from famine and disease. In the late '60s, the Nigerian Civil War created a famine that killed more than 500,000. In the early '90s Kurds, fleeing Saddam Hussein's army, following the Persian Gulf War, died at the rate of 1,000 a day. Today, famine has come to Angola, Ethiopia, Mozambique, Somalia and Sudan; and 26 million people are threatened with malnutrition and starvation. Furthermore, it is estimated almost one-half the world's population is underfed. These disasters are a shadow of things to come, but they do not mean the tribulation period is near.

✦ *Nation shall rise against nation, and kingdom against kingdom: and there shall be famines.*
(Matthew 24:7)

(4) Pestilences

The 70th week of Daniel will be a week of death when plagues strike in epic proportions on a worldwide scale. The skeleton of death will don his graveclothes; grasp the great scythe with his bony fingers; mount the pale horse; and gallop forth to harvest the lives of the poor, the diseased and the starving. Hell will tag along to gather the littered souls of the lost. One-fourth of the earth's citizens will be decimated by war, famine, pestilence and beasts. And Zechariah predicted a plague will strike all who fight against Jerusalem (Revelation 6:7, 8; Zechariah 14:12).

The National Jewish Center for Immunology and Respiratory Medicine is reporting dramatic increases in the mortality rate among those stricken with emphysema, chronic bronchitis and asthma. The American Lung Association recently reported a new and dangerous type of tuberculosis that is "out of control." Strains have been found that "drugs can't stop." This decade has experienced an AIDS epidemic in Africa, a cholera epidemic in Latin America and outbreaks of cholera, typhoid and polio in Iraq following the Persian Gulf War. And look at the toll of new and old killers given by Dr. Billy Graham in Storm Warning. It seems prophetic when he says,

> "Worldwide there are 5 million malaria deaths per year and 3 million from tuberculosis; 2.8 million children die annually from vaccine-preventable diseases, while infectious diseases kill 4 million unimmunized children. There are 5 million diarrhea deaths of children under age 5; 4 million die of pneumonia . . . . Add to these numbers the estimated 16.8 million who die from parasitic diseases, 13.3 million from circulatory disease, 5 million cardiovascular deaths, 4.3 million cancer deaths, 3.3 million perinatal deaths, 2.6 million tobacco-related deaths, and 401,000 suicides every year."[1]

Jesus said pestilences would occur and He indicated they will worsen as we near the end of the age. These rapidly spreading diseases are a symptom that the 70th week of Daniel is approaching, but they do not mean it has arrived. They represent only a fraction of what the world will experience in that day.

✦ *There shall be pestilences.*
(Matthew 24:7)

(5) Earthquakes

Strong quakes have rumbled across the world in diverse places. But "the big one" will not occur until the tribulation period. The Apostle John speaks of major quakes at that time and *a great earthquake, such as was not since men were upon the earth, so mighty an earthquake, and so great* (Revelation 8:5; 11:19; 16:18).

The prophet Joel says the Lord will shake the heavens and the earth (Joel 3:16). And the prophet Zechariah tells us a massive earthquake will split the mount of Olives when Jesus returns (Zechariah 14:1-5).

Collapsed buildings and crushed people are becoming familiar sights in the world today. Hard quakes are more frequent, more powerful and more destructive than ever before. An article in the 3rd Quarter 1992 *Dispatch From Jerusalem* reports there were 157 major earthquakes in the 14th century; 174 in the 15th century; 253 in the 16th century; 278 in the 17th century; 640 in the 18th century; 2,119 in the 19th century; and nearly 900,000 thus far in the 20th century. This birth-pang type increase is a jolting reminder that the great day of wrath is really approaching. But take heed because thousands of bone rattling tremors are not the sign it has arrived.

✦ *There shall be earthquakes in diverse places.*
(Matthew 24:7)

Signs of the Tribulation Period

Now Jesus answers the question, *What shall be the sign of thy coming, and of the end of the world (age)?* This has reference to His return at the end of the tribulation period.

(1) Persecution and betrayal

The first sign mentioned is the persecution, murder and betrayal of believers. The book of Revelation teaches the martyrdom of those who believe in Christ during the seventieth week. And Zechariah teaches the nations of the earth will hate and kill two-thirds of the

Jews during that time. The World War II concentration camps of Hitler are just a sample of things to come as the mistreatment of believers and anti-Semitism reaches its peak (Revelation 6:11; 13:7, 15, 20:4; Zechariah 12:1-3; 13:8).

In the United States, Christians are being persecuted for speaking out against homosexuality, demonstrating against abortion, praying at school, distributing Bibles, boycotting stores for selling pornography and so on. Believers are being fined, jailed, sued and sent to "sensitivity training."

The American Civil Liberties Union (ACLU) has filed hundreds of lawsuits to promote "separation of church and state." It seeks to remove prayer, the Ten Commandments, crosses and Bibles from schools. It wants Christian symbols and paintings taken out of public buildings. And it wants to rid public parks and lands of religious (especially Christmas and Easter) displays.

Inceasingly, Hollywood and the media are demonstrating an anti-Christian bias. Movies are used to assault the Church and to attack the divinity of Jesus. TV programs are used to stereotype Christians as bigots, buffoons, hypocrites and adulterers. Cartoons are used to ridicule Christians and promote false religions.

On the Jewish front, the United States media is showing a pro-Arab bias. Reporters are taking great pains to show "the Jewish mistreatment of Palestinians." But they rarely explain why the Israelis have to use force. Broadcasters keep talking about the "occupied territories." But they ignore why the area is occupied. The media keeps talking about "swapping land for peace." It almost never points out that the Arabs have 600 times more land than the Israelis or that the Jews bought much of the land they possess.

The Christian-bashers and anti-Semites are waxing worse and worse. This is setting the stage for greater persecution and murder. It is a forerunner of things to come when the Antichrist will decide what is "politically correct."

✦ *Then shall they deliver you up to be afflicted, and shall kill you.*
(Matthew 24:9)

✦ *And then shall many be offended, and shall betray one another, and shall hate.*
(Matthew 24:10)

(2) False prophets and falling away.

There is nothing more dangerous than corrupt religious leaders. Morally unsound priests led the Jews into spiritual blindness. Depraved clergy plotted the death of Messiah. Wicked scribes and Pharisees stirred the wrath of God and brought destruction upon the rebuilt city and its temple. Almost without exception they claimed to speak for God while their well-turned words led their own people astray (Matthew 23:36).

When the true Church is raptured, the false church will be left behind. Wolves, in sheep's clothing, will pace back and forth in the pulpits making the 70th week a time of great deception. False prophets, in robes of godliness and piety, will mingle a sprinkling of Scripture with the wisdom of the world and the doctrines of other religions. Split-tongued artists will distort most of what the Scriptures really teach; speak against Christ; and confuse the masses.

Many will stumble, stagger and fall away. *How then shall they call on Him in whom they have not believed? And how shall they believe in him of whom they have not heard? And how shall they hear without a preacher? And how shall they preach, except they be sent* (Roman 10:14, 15)?

✦ *And many false prophets shall rise, and shall deceive many.*
(Matthew 24:11)

✦ *And because iniquity shall abound, the love of many shall wax cold.*
(Matthew 24:12)

(3) The Gospel

In spite of the false prophets, the Gospel of Christ will go all over the world during the tribulation period. God will give the world one last chance to be saved before Jesus returns. After He raptures the Church, He will seal a remnant of 144,000 Jews to evangelize the planet (Revelation 7:1-7). He will call two witnesses and empower them to preach the Gospel (Revelation 11:3-12). And He will send an angel through the air to preach to everyone on earth in their own language (Revelation 14:6).

It is not necessary to the fulfillment of this prophecy, but the Gospel has been going all over the world by short wave radio since 1989. Strategically located transmitters and space satellites are carrying the Gospel in ninety different languages. Trans World Radio is even broadcasting the Gospel to the Middle East over its huge 500,000-watt Monte Carlo transmitter. The Gideons distribute Bibles in most of the world. The Billy Graham Evangelistic Association, Campus Crusade for Christ and others are training pastors and evangelists inside the former Soviet Union. Nations that once closed their doors to the Gospel are now wide open and even seeking missionaries and evangelists. Bible prophecy does not require it, but the Gospel is going all over the world right now.

✦ *This gospel of the kingdom shall be preached in all the world for a witness unto all nations; and then shall the end come.* (Matthew 24:14)

(4) The temple

Clues are found in a sign Jesus referred to as *the abomination of desolation.* This abomination will be so offensive it will cause the Jews to abandon the temple. The prophet Daniel spoke of it at least three different times. He said,

And he shall confirm the covenant with many for one week: and in the midst of the week he shall cause the sacrifice and the oblation to cease, and for the overspreading of abominations he shall make it desolate, even until the consummation, and that determined shall be poured upon the desolate (Daniel 9:27).

And arms shall stand on his part, and they shall pollute the sanctuary of strength, and shall take away the daily sacrifice, and they shall place the abomination that maketh desolate (Daniel 11:31).

And from the time that the daily sacrifice shall be taken away, and the abomination that maketh desolate set up, there shall be a thousand two hundred and ninety days (Daniel 12:11).

"The abomination of desolation" refers to a statue (or an image) of the Antichrist that will be placed in the temple at the mid-point of the 70th week. Idols are forbidden in Israel and polluting the temple with an idol will be especially offensive to the Jews. They will flee and leave it desolate.

Several things are implied by this. Israel must be back in the land and the Antichrist will have to be on the scene. Israel must control the Temple Mount and the temple will have to be rebuilt. Priests will have to be anointed, clothing made, equipment manufactured, animal sacrifices reinstituted and so on. And all of this must be done before the middle of the tribulation period.

In 1948, Israel became a nation. In 1967, the Temple Mount was captured, but control was turned over to the Moslems. In 1989, a group called the Temple Mount Faithful attempted to start construction of the temple by laying the cornerstone, but they were stopped. That same year, the Temple Institute completed a robe for the High Priest and an unknown number of robes for other members of the priesthood. They also completed most of the equipment needed for the animal sacrifices and the musical instruments necessary for the worship services. One year later, the Temple Mount Faithful attempted to lay the cornerstone a second time, but construction was prevented again. Today, Arabs administer the Temple Mount, but it is surrounded by Jews and they can take control anytime they desire. I believe it is time to wake up. Events that do not have to happen before the rapture are taking place right now and events that only need to come to pass by the middle of the tribulation period are already reality. These events mean the day of the Lord's vengeance is approaching and the closer we get to that, the closer we are to the rapture.

> ✦ *When ye therefore shall see the abomination of desolation, spoken by Daniel the prophet, stand in the holy place . . . flee into the mountains.*
> (Matthew 24:15,16)

(5) The great tribulation

After the temple is defiled, indescribable disasters will paralyze the planet. The laws of nature will be suspended and this crippled world will crawl and stagger under the awful events of the last three and one-half years. Suffering will be unlike anything registered in history.

The Apostle John recorded some of the details. One-third of the earth's plant life will be killed, one-third of the sea will become polluted, one-third of the creatures in the sea will die, one-third of the ships will sink, one-third of the waters of the earth will be poisoned, one-third of the sun will be put out, one-third of the moonlight will be gone, one-third of the stars will go out, locusts will plague the earth and demons will persecute the people (Revelation 8:1-9:21). Crisis will follow crisis like a raging storm that cannot be stopped. It would destroy the whole world without the intervention of the King of kings and Lord of lords. But thank God, He will intervene and shorten the relentless flood of desolations.

The prophet Isaiah said that God will "shake terribly the earth" in the last days (Isaiah 2:1-19). Most of the inhabitants of the earth will be destroyed (Isaiah. 24:1-6).

The Word of God teaches the world is not getting better. It is getting worse. Great tribulation is coming. It is coming because people, even religious people, refuse to heed what the Almighty has said. Read Jeremiah 30:7, Daniel 12:1, Joel 2:1-2 and Amos 5:18-20.

✦ *For then shall be great tribulation, such as was not since the beginning of the world to this time, no, nor ever shall be.* (Matthew 24:21)

(6) Miracles

Some ask, "Why would anyone follow the Antichrist, false Messiahs or false prophets?" When the man Christ Jesus walked upon this earth He performed great signs and wonders. He walked on water; cast out demons; healed the sick; raised the dead. He performed miracles that attracted great multitudes. *Many believed in His name, when they saw the miracles which He did* (John 2:22-23).

During the tribulation period, powerful personalities will perform great signs and wonders. They will use those signs and wonders to deceive and convince people they are the Christ. They will quickly gather a following and multitudes will wrongly believe the Messiah has arrived. Most of the world's leaders will even be fooled.

The Apostle Paul warned the Antichrist will come, *After the working of Satan with all power and signs and lying wonders* (II Thessalonians 2:9). The Apostle John said the False Prophet will have all the power of the Antichrist, *And he doeth great wonders, so that he maketh fire come down from heaven on the earth in the sight of men* (Revelation 13:12,13). John prophesied unclean spirits will go forth from Satan, the Antichrist and the False Prophet. They will *work miracles* and gather the leaders of the world for the Battle of Armageddon (Revelation 16:13-14).

> ✦ *There shall arise false Christs, and false prophets, and shall shew great signs and wonders.*
> (Matthew 24:24)

(7) Heavenly signs

The prophet Joel predicted there will be wonders in the heavens with the sun turning into darkness and the moon into blood (Joel 2:30-31). The prophet Isaiah said the stars will not give their light, the sun will be darkened, the moon will not shine and the earth will remove out of its place (Isaiah 13:9-13). The Apostle John confirmed it and the Apostle Peter preached it on the first Day of Pentecost (Revelation 6:12,13; Acts 2:19,20).

There will be universal upheavals during the tribulation period. Conditions will become intolerable. People will pray to die. The world will be unable to cope.

> ✦ *The sun shall be darkened, and the moon shall not give her light, and the stars shall fall from heaven, and the powers of the heavens shall be shaken.*
> (Matthew 24:29)

(8) The fig tree

The Parable of the Fig Tree is something the Teacher used to answer the questions His disciples asked about the second coming and the end of the age. What is a parable? A parable is a simple story used to illustrate a more complex matter; an easily understood story designed to relay a deeper truth.

What is the fig tree? The prophet Jeremiah had a vision several years after the children of Israel were taken to Babylon. God showed him two baskets of figs. One basket contained very good figs; newly ripe and edible. The other basket contained very bad figs; overripe and inedible. And God asked, *What seest thou, Jeremiah? And I said, Figs; the good figs, very good; and the evil, very evil, that cannot be eaten, they are so evil* (Jeremiah 24:1-10).

Concerning the good figs, God said, *I will set mine eyes upon them for good, and I will bring them again to this land: and I will build them, and not pull them down; and I will plant them, and not pluck them up. And I will give them a heart to know me, that I am the Lord: and they shall be my people, and I will be their God: for they shall return unto me with their whole heart.*

We see that the figs represented people. The good figs represented Jews who had been taken captive to Babylon. And the bad figs represented those who escaped the Babylonian captivity.

The immutable God chose the fig as a symbol for Israel on another occasion. In reference to Abraham, Isaac and Jacob, He said, *I found Israel like grapes in the wilderness; I saw your fathers as the firstripe in the fig tree at her first time* (Hosea 9:10). In God's eyes, Abraham, Isaac and Jacob were the first figs in the fig tree. That is, they were the beginning of the nation of Israel.

Israel is the Bible "fig tree." Jesus was saying, *When you see a fig tree budding, you know summer is near and it will soon bear fruit. In like manner, when you see the regathering and re-establishment of Israel, you know the end of the age is close and Israel will soon be saved.*

This is happening. The Jews have been revived as a nation. God is preparing to start the 70th week. He is getting ready to complete the curse and bring Israel's punishment to an end. I believe Jesus is even saying some who are alive today will witness these events.

✦ *Now learn a parable of the fig tree; When his branch is yet tender, and putteth forth leaves, ye know that summer is nigh: So likewise ye, when ye shall see all these things, know that it is near, even at the doors. Verily I say unto you, This generation shall not pass, till all these things be fulfilled.*
(Matthew 24:32-34)

(9) Days of Noah

Noah was a preacher of righteousness. But when he preached, people scoffed at his message from the Mighty God. He preached, but they paid no attention; foretold the flood, but they refused to listen. They lived as they pleased right up until the day the flood began. That day started just like every other day, but when the torrential rains fell and the flood waters rose, the people were unprepared. And they all drowned.

People will be making the same mistake when Jesus returns. Many will ignore the preachers who speak on the second coming; live the way they want to live; do what they want to do right up until the final day. That day will begin like most other days. Multitudes will not walk in the Lord's ways. Some will sit down to eat. Some will stagger up to a bottle of alcohol. Others will run to a wedding. And when Jesus suddenly appears, they will be unprepared. And their doom will be sealed.

Consider these sobering facts about alcohol use by United States students. More than half in grades seven through twelve occasionally drink a small amount. More than one-third drink at least once a week. More than two percent drink five or more drinks in one sitting. And when they get to college, four percent drink daily and seventy-five percent drink regularly.

And the United States divorce rate has doubled since 1965. People are marrying and divorcing; marrying and divorcing. Some are repeating this cycle so often, it can be said they are marrying wives (Luke 17:27). This is precisely what the Scriptures predict for the endtimes.

✦ *As the days of No'e were, so shall also the coming of the Son of man be. For as in the days that were before the flood they were eating and drinking, marrying and giving in marriage, until the day that No'e entered into the ark. And knew not until the flood came, and took them all away; so shall also the coming of the Son of man be.*
(Matthew 24:37-39)

(10) Population growth

The days of Noah were also marked by a multiplication of men (Genesis 6:1). Some estimate there may have been several billion people upon the earth. Earth's population has now reached 5 billion. And some forecasters are predicting it may increase at the rate of 1 billion per year soon after 2000 A.D. Now you know why so many governments support euthanasia, homosexuality, lesbianism, abortion, same-sex marriages, etc.

✦ *As the days of No'e were, so shall also the coming of the Son of man.*
(Matthew 24:37)

Luke

Many Bible scholars believe Luke was a Gentile. He traveled with the Apostle Paul on his Second Missionary Journey and again on the latter part of his Third Missionary Journey. He was "the beloved physician" who investigated "all things." And even the secular world recognizes him as an accurate historian.

His writings verify much of what Matthew recorded about the Olivet Discourse. And some verses provide extra information not found in Matthew or Mark.

Distress of Nations

Jesus was commenting on the tribulation period when He said there will be, "upon the earth distress of nations, with perplexity." Some think we are about to usher in an era of peace and harmony, but when the peaceful, honest and all-wise Jesus read the signs of history, He predicted the fires of distress will burn among nations. And a steady succession of problems will blaze around the world. Many thought the breakup of Russia would douse the flames. But it fueled revolution, ethnic cleansing, great religious struggles, the sale of nuclear weapons and the rise of nationalism. That roared across the border into other nations, including Yugoslavia. There people, whose ancestors were Catholic citizens of the old Holy Roman Empire, are trying to stave off Moslem encroachment. And powerful European leaders, such as the Hapsburg family and their royal relatives, are trying to keep those areas for the new Revived Roman Empire. If you want to know what is going on in Bosnia, Serbia and Hercegovina, it is a struggle for religious and political domination. If you want to know who will win, those who are trying to Revive the Roman Empire will gain a temporary victory. But Jesus has won the war.

✦ *And upon the earth distress of nations, with perplexity.*
(Luke 21:25)

The Sea and the Waves (The Weather)

Another sign of the tribulation period foretold by Jesus is the roaring of the sea and the waves. We find more than one interpretation, but the literal view means Jesus was predicting a period of violent weather; great storms that upset the normal patterns and cause terrible convulsions of nature; unbelievable storms that churn and stir the sea and the waves.

What do we see? In the September 1993 issue of Life magazine, Stephen Petranek says;

"This is how weird our weather has been: The three most powerful damaging climatic disasters in United States history happened in the past 12 months. First, Hurricane Andrew devastated south Florida last September. Then, on March 12, a giant blizzard–which the National Weather Service calls 'the single biggest storm of the century'–swept from Florida to Maine, releasing more snow, hail, rain and sleet than any other storm since 1888. Finally, the relentless rain flooding the Midwest brought on what may be the costliest weather disaster of all."

✦ *The sea and the waves roaring.*
(Luke 21:25)

Acts

The Book of Acts was probably written by Luke. It bridges several years of early Church history and its main emphasis is on the Holy Spirit's work in the Body of Christ. One must not overlook the commitment of the early Christians–their love, faith, sacrifices, giving, worship, emphasis on the resurrection and so forth. But there is something else. The newborn Church also expected Israel to have a kingdom.

The Kingdom of Israel

The disciples grew up on the Old Testament prophecies. All their life, they expected the Messiah to come and establish an earthly kingdom in Israel. It was the desire of their hearts. They thought Jesus was their king and were terribly disappointed when He was nailed to the cross. They even scattered when that happened. But the Son of God was raised from the dead and He began to appear unto them. Once when He came back, they asked a question which shows they were wondering, "Is this your second coming? Have you returned to bring in the kingdom?"

Jesus did not deny the kingdom will be restored. In fact, His answer implies it will be, but we will not be given a date. But date or no, this is what the return of Israel is all about. It is a preparation for the second coming of Jesus and His earthly kingdom in the promised land. God is not through with this planet or the Jews. He intends to clean up this globe and set up the house of David (Romans 11:26-27).

> ✦ *Lord, wilt thou at this time restore again the kingdom to Israel? And he said unto them, It is not for you to know the times or the seasons, which the Father hath put in his own power.*
> (Acts 1:6,7)

I & II Thessalonians

The Apostle Paul established a church at Thessalonica on his second missionary journey. He spent three Sabbaths there and was forced to flee. Shortly after that, he received word the believers had many questions about the return of Jesus. He sought to comfort them with a letter. His first letter sparked more questions so he wrote them a second time.

Peace and Safety

Jesus told His disciples, *And ye shall hear of wars and rumors of wars . . . but the end is not yet* (Matthew 24:6). The Apostle Paul said, *For when they shall say, Peace and safety; then sudden de-*

struction cometh (I Thessalonians 5:3). So war is not a sign, but a global declaration of peace and safety is. War does not mean the end of the age is hanging over the earth. But when the governments of the world declare they have achieved peace and safety, the end will hang like the sword of Damocles ready to fall; ready to abruptly and unexpectedly cut off the enemies of Christ.

Shortly after the rapture, the hideous Antichrist will make his appearance. He will rise to power over the EC proclaiming peace. Many Jews will think he is the Messiah. Many will allow him to force a seven year false covenant on Israel. He will announce to the world he has achieved peace and safety for all men. The media will go wild. World leaders will proclaim an end to bloodshed and war. A brief period of euphoria and false security will follow. But suddenly and unexpectedly, like a great flash of unbearable pain, the greatest war the world has ever seen will break loose. It will end only when the Lion of the tribe of Judah returns.

The current Middle East peace talks represent a significant step in this direction. An agreement has been signed giving the Palestinians interim self-rule over the Gaza Strip and Jerico; giving Israel security positions and full recognition; and committing the parties to produce a permanent settlement within two years. All Christians should know diplomats are working toward peace on several levels. And the EC is involved.

Christians should also be aware of the growing ties between Israel and the European Community (EC). These growing ties equate to a growing EC influence that will eventually evolve into the EC forcing a peace treaty on Israel. Then the world will shout "peace and safety," but the tribulation period will have begun and the Second Advent of Jesus will be closing in.

The possibility of the EC and its Antichrist leader becoming involved in peace negotiations in the Middle East raises questions about relations between Israel and the EC. It is unlikely Israel would respond to EC peace initiatives without motivating circumstances. We should understand many incentives do exist.

In an article in Israel Scene magazine, dated January 1991, entitled *Uneasy Partnership—Israel and the European Community,* Leopold Yehuda Laufer wrote,

> "When David Levy took over Israel's Foreign Ministry in the Likud-led government, his first overseas visit was to western Europe, specifically, to the principle countries of the twelve-nation European Community (EC). It was confirmation that except for the United States, the EC countries were at the top of Israel's priority list. The reasons for this are not hard to understand. They fall into both the political and economic realm of Israel's international relations.

> "On the economic side, the countries of the EC make up Israel's largest trading partners, with a current annual turnover of about $10 billion, and an Israeli trade deficit of some $3 billion. The EC countries account for nearly 40 percent of Israel's total imports and exports. In terms of both needed imports and the potential for Israeli exports, the EC countries are Israel's most promising long-term market. In light of the EC decision to unite into a single economically integrated bloc by 1992, the economic policies which this powerful bloc of countries is likely to pursue in the Middle East, and toward Israel in particular, must be of paramount concern to any Israeli government.

> "It is not surprising that ever since the establishment of the European Economic Community in 1958, Israel has maintained close official contacts with it."

> ✦ *For when they shall say, Peace and safety; then sudden destruction cometh upon them, as travail upon a woman with child; and they shall not escape.*
> (I Thessalonians 5:2)

A Falling Away

The Apostle Paul said there would be a "falling away" before the day of the Lord arrives. But there is a problem. The word translated "falling away" in the King James Version is translated "departing" in several earlier versions. Those who use the King James Version believe "falling away" refers to apostasy. And those who use the earlier versions believe "departing" refers to the rapture.

We could debate whether Paul was speaking of an apostasy or the rapture, but it would be pointless. Both views are correct. The

Bible plainly teaches that many will abandon the faith before the church age comes to an end. And it also teaches the rapture will occur before the Day of the Lord arrives.

Apostasy is not new, but the strength of those who are corrupting today's mainline denominations is. Compromise is not new, but the number and power of pastors and theologians who have departed from the faith is. Satan's angels of light easily cast away the "primacy of Scripture." Lucifer's ministers of righteousness receive standing ovations for teaching unsound doctrines and misguided concepts. Many no longer consider the Bible authoritative on such things as homosexuality, lesbianism, capital punishment, abortion and the right to bear arms; and they harvest great praise. Worldliness, humanism, feminism and secularism have poisoned their beliefs, but they stand tall in the Church. Their Jesus is not the Jesus of the Bible, but the elite of the Church won't speak out. This is the beginning of what Jesus said, *And because iniquity shall abound, the love of many shall wax cold* (Matthew 24:12).

In an article in The Wall Street Journal entitled, *The Episcopalian Goes the Way of the Dodo,* Wade Clark Roof said,

> "The Religious makeup of the American population is changing-slowly but discernibly. By the year 2000, the United States will be a far more pluralistic country than anyone would have imagined in 1950-and vastly more pluralistic than it was in 1783, when Yale President Ezra Stiles pictured a future America divided about equally among Congregationalists, Presbyterians and Episcopalians.

> "The big story is the continuing, long-time decline of the Protestant majority, to 57% in 1987 from 67% in 1952. At the present rate of decline, Protestants will be barely a numerical majority of the American population by the year 2000. . . .

> "The religiously non-affiliated have grown to 9% today from 2% in the early 1950s. As their numbers have increased, their cultural characteristics have changed: No longer a small marginal group of theists and social dissidents, non-affiliates today are predominately young, white, well-educated and socially mobile."

An article by Helen Parmley in The Dallas Morning News, on December 2, 1989, entitled, *New Gallup Book Looks at Decade Of Religious Trends,* says,

> "Among Christian groups, Methodists have the most unchurched (32 percent), followed by Episcopalians and Baptists (28 percent each), Lutherans (27 percent), Catholics (21 percent), Southern Baptists and Mormons (20 percent each) and Presbyterians (17 percent)."

Boil it all down and you will see the nations churches are in trouble for casting aside traditional Christian beliefs and time-honored Biblical texts. Many are losing former members faster than they can take in new ones. Consider these words of Jesus, *Abide in me, and I in you. As the branch cannot bear fruit of itself, except it abide in the vine; no more can ye, except ye abide in me* (John 15:4).

> ✦ *Let no man deceive you by any means: for that day shall not come, except there come a falling away first.*
> (II Thessalonians 2:3)

The Man of Sin

"Man of sin" is a name for "the son of perdition." The Bible gives him some thirty different titles. He is the amazing Antichrist; the sinister character who rises to power over the EC; the one who signs the seven year covenant to protect Israel.

He will be full of self-admiration, self-confidence, self-sufficiency and self-satisfaction. His picture will be on all the TV sets, in all the magazines and on all of the front pages. He will persuade the world of his greatness. He will brag on those in the false church and they will brag on him. He will be anti-God, anti-Bible, pro-self and the world will love to gloat over his charismatic, self-exalting deceptions.

He will visit the temple. This is one reason why it must be rebuilt. He will enter the temple, erect a statue (or an image) of himself, sit down and declare he is God. Some teach he will even sacrifice a pig on the altar while he is there.

The spirit of Antichrist is already in the world, but the Holy Spirit has been preventing him from coming forth as a man. When the Habitation of God is raptured, the Holy Spirit will be removed and the time will be right for the only wise God to allow this evil man to take charge.

He will be Satan's man. The Tempter will send him with power, signs and lying wonders. The masses of mankind will be amazed. And their ignorance of the Word of God will leave them exposed to this demonic miracle worker.

What is his fate? He will meet his doom when Jesus comes to end his terrible reign. The Lord will put a stop to his deception, war and false worship. He will not be able to survive the brightness of His second coming.

Today, the world wants a leader, but it does not want the Holy One of Israel. It wants a man who can bring peace, settle disputes, stop bloodshed, increase prosperity and solve problems, but it does not want Jesus. The Holy Spirit will allow one to appear, but he will cause more problems than he solves. And he will meet a fearful fate.

+ *For that day shall not come except there come a falling away first, and that man of sin be revealed, the son of perdition.*
(II Thessalonians 2:3)

+ *Who opposeth and exalteth himself.*
(II Thessalonians 2:4)

+ *He as God sitteth in the temple of God.*
(II Thessalonians 2:4)

+ *Now ye know what withholdeth that he might be revealed in his time.*
(II Thessalonians 2:6)

+ *Even him, whose coming is after the working of Satan with all power and signs and lying wonders.*
(II Thessalonians 2:9)

+ *Whom the Lord shall consume with the spirit of his mouth and destroy with the brightness of his coming.*
(II Thessalonians 2:8)

I & II Timothy

Timothy was a young pastor in the early Church. The Apostle Paul sent him two letters. Among other things, they address the identifying characteristics of the true Church. They talk about faith-fulness, allegiance, apostasy and the like. Paul was saying a church is not *the* Church unless it meets the requirements of the *true* God. This seems relevant to the "New Age Movement" today. New Agers are involved in contacting spirit guides, channeling, transcendental meditation, shamanism, numerology, astrology, reincarnation, sor-cery, developing psychic powers, cosmic consciousness and other "consciousness raising" techniques. These are not things for church members to be involved in, but many are.

Seducing Spirits & Doctrines of Devils

The Holy Spirit has an explicit message for Timothy and the Church. It concerns something foreboding; something that will happen to the organized church in "the latter times." Some will listen to unseen sinister spirits and abandon the fundamentals of the faith. They will become unwitting agents of dark forces in the spirit world and permit those unseen demonic powers to lure them into the doctrines of Satan.

The Presbyterian Layman published an article entitled, *Witch Addresses San Francisco Seminary,* in the July/August 1989 issue, which says;

> "On March 3, 1989, Starhawk, a West Coast woman who calls herself a witch, addressed students and faculty members of San Francisco Presbyterian Theological Seminary. Speaking from the pulpit in Stewart Chapel, the witch addressed her seminary congregation under the auspices of the Feminist Perspectives Committee, a campus group composed of students and faculty advisors. . . .

> "Who is Starhawk? Starhawk is the founder of two covens in San Francisco, and a licensed minister of the Covenant of the Goddess, a legally recognized church. She calls herself a 'priestess of the Old Religion,' and claims that her faith pre-dates Christianity."

In an article entitled, *UM Seminary Charged with Allowing Witchcraft Ritual,* that appeared in The United Methodist Reporter on August 17, 1990, M. Garlinda Burton wrote:

"A United Methodist congregation in Oklahoma is seeking action against Perkins School of Theology for allowing an educational forum of witchcraft during its annual "Women's Week" symposium. . . .

"According to information mailed to several southwestern churches by Mr. Wise, the workshop leader involved the 30 participants in a 'ceremony.' A small altar set in front of the meeting room held candles and a statue of the mythical goddess Diana, he said. . . .

'Most of our presenters for the week were Christian, and none of the workshops was mandatory,' said Ms. Latham.

"She said charges against Perkins filed with the University Senate were 'based on misstatements and half-truths.'

"The Rev. Stanley J. Menking, associate dean at Perkins, said he and Perkins Dean James E. Kirby met earlier this year with several Dallas Area pastors who also received Mr. Wise's mailings.

'We told them it is an issue of academic freedom,' said Dr. Menking, a United Methodist clergyman."

An article by Richard N. Ostling, in Time magazine, dated May 6, 1991, entitled, *When God Was a Woman,* says,

"The ceremonies were part of a growing United States spiritual movement: Goddess worship, the effort to create a female-centered focus for spiritual expression. Most participants are women who seek a deity other than God the Father, and a faith less patriarchal than the Judeo-Christian tradition seems to offer. Adherents claim the movement involves as many as 100,000 women. . . .

"Despite Christianity's centuries of opposition to paganism, some old-line churches are opening up to the Goddess. A witch teaches in an institute at the Roman Catholic Holy Names College in California. A book by two United Methodist pastors proposes experimental Bible readings about the crucifixion that replace Jesus with Sophia (Wisdom), a name for the divine personality used by Goddess-minded Christians."

This should not surprise us. We should not suppose this New Age nonsense will go on just outside the Church. The spread of occultic practices, Satanism, demonism, spirit guides and the like is a preparation for Satan's rule on earth. It is one of the sins of the tribulation period (Revelation 9:20, 21); the making of the false church that will be headed by the False Prophet during the tribulation period. It will lead to a One-World Harlot Religion that will move to Babylon and support the son of perdition (Revelation 17:1-18). Now the Spirit speaketh expressly, that in the latter times some shall depart from the faith, giving heed to seducing spirits, and doctrines of devils (I Timothy 4:1).

Perilous Times (When The Spirit of Antichrist Prevails)

All that God has and does is good. And Satan tries to counterfeit every bit of it. God has the Trinity: Father, Son and Holy Ghost. And Satan has his trinity: the Dragon, the Antichrist and the False Prophet. God has the True Church. And Satan has the False Church. God calls preachers and teachers to give out the pure Word. And Satan calls false prophets and false teachers to give out the poisoned word.

This all combines to make the last days very dangerous. The great organization that calls itself a church will drink the wine of fornication; and not be the Church at all. What will it be? It will be an apostate organization that reflects the spirit of Antichrist; a huge conglomeration dominated by pagan religions, cults, faulty doctrines and unchristian attitudes. The Word of God calls it "the mother of harlots." Many preachers call it the False Church. Because it will carry inclusiveness too far, these 21 characteristics of Antichrist will prevail.

(1) Self-lovers

Loving Christ and others will take a back seat to self-love. And the self-aggrandizing Antichrist will lead the pack as one, Who opposeth and exalteth himself above all that is called God, or that is worshipped; so that he as God sitteth in the temple of God, shewing himself that he is God (II Thessalonians 2:4). This is the lie Satan told Eve in the Garden of Eden, For God doth know that in the day ye eat therof, then your eyes shall be opened, and ye shall be as gods (Genesis 3:5). This is the sin that caused the fall of all mankind. It was committed in the beginning and it will become prevalent in the last

days. Society will move from self-denial to self-affection. It will gloat
on self-affirmation, self-exaltation and self-glorification. Listen to
what Dr. Robert Lindsted has written about today's New Age Movement. He says,

> "Seventeen magazine tells young girls how to mellow out, meditate,
> and say softly to themselves, "I am, I am." These are the exact words
> of God to Moses. Cartoons, television, and even our education
> system tries to tell our children that they are gods, that they are
> perfect beings. Dear friends, these things are a set-up for the New
> Age thinking.[2]

> "Among the things that the New Age advocates is that Jesus Christ
> was not and is not the only Christ, nor was He God. They say that
> God is an impersonal, cosmic god of energy forces. They say that
> man is himself God . . . .[3]

> "I know of places that now use Sunday school material that no
> longer teaches against sin, but elevates man. They are more
> concerned with our self-image than that we are sinners. I really
> believe that one of the detriments of the Gospel today is that
> people are no longer willing to say: "I am a sinner. I need God's
> forgiveness."[4]

Self-lovers are listening to the hiss of a serpent when they say,
"Jesus is not God, but I am." Who is a liar but he that denieth that
Jesus is the Christ? He is Antichrist, that denieth the Father and the
Son (I John 2:22).

✦ *In the last days, men shall be lovers of their own selves.*
  (II Timothy 3:2)

(2) Covetous

Why would preachers depart from the faith? Because they are
covetous. And through covetousness shall they with feigned words
make merchandise of you (II Peter 2:3). This was the sin of Balaam the
son of Beor; a type of the Antichrist who *l*oved the wages of unrighteousness and taught error for reward (Numbers 23, 24; II Peter 2:15;
Jude 11). It is the condemnation Jesus wrote in His letter to the church
in Pergamos (Revelation 2:14). And it is one reason why the last days
will be perilous; the parsonages will be occupied by men and
women whose main desire is filthy lucre.

✦ *In the last days, people will be covetous.*
(II Timothy 3:2)

(3) Boasters

Bragging and railing will be a way of life in the last days. A lofty view of oneself and not knowing that one can only do what the invisible God allows him to do will be prevalent. It was the boastful Philistine Goliath, a type of the Antichrist, whose self-vaunting dismayed God's people and made them greatly afraid. And the Antichrist will exalt himself, and magnify himself above every god (Daniel 11:36).

✦ *In the last days, people will be boasters.*
(II Timothy 3:2)

(4) Proud

This was a sin of Nebuchadnezzar. He suffered greatly because his heart was lifted up and his mind was hardened in pride (Daniel 5:20). He also did what the False Prophet will do. He built a great statue for people to worship (Daniel 3:1-7; Revelation 13:14,15).

And in the end-time church, a God-renouncing haughtiness will prevail. Many will take great pleasure and satisfaction in exalting themselves instead of the Lord God Almighty; credit themselves for all their successes; and falsely assume they are in control.

✦ *In the last days, people will be proud.*
(II Timothy 3:2)

(5) Blasphemers

Antichrist shall come and upon his heads the name of blasphemy (Revelation 13:1). And there was given unto him a mouth speaking great things and blasphemies (Revelation 13:5). And he opened his mouth in blasphemy against God, to blaspheme his name, and his tabernacle, and them that dwell in heaven (Revelation 13:6). He will scream out unbelievable blasphemies against God, his temple and the True Church in heaven.

Ungodly men and women in the False Church will also mock His holy name and show contempt for sacred things. They will ridicule Jesus, the Scriptures, the Church, the Sacraments, Christian behavior and everything pertaining to the one true God; take His name in vain; deny the Bible is the Word of God; and deny the virgin birth of Jesus. Consider these words of J. R. Church:

> "The movie version of "The Last Temptation of Christ," released by Universal Studios in 1988, is the most vile and wicked bit of blasphemy ever to be shown on the silver screen. In 1984, Paramount Pictures attempted to film it, but because of public pressure, the movie was shelved. Now, probably due to a greater potential for public acceptance, Universal Studios released it. It tells a sordid story about Jesus Christ and a so-called 'love affair' with Mary Magdalene. Christians across America are furious and have every right to be."[5]

U.S. News & World Report carried an article by John Leo on April 1, 1991, entitled, *The Gay Tide of Catholic-bashing*. It says,

> "Savage mockery of Christianity is now a conventional part of the public gay culture. A ridiculous-looking Jesus figure carrying a cross is always featured in the gay Halloween parade in New York, along with the usual throng of hairy guys dressed as nuns. Some gay clubs and at least one gay movie feature a tableau of Jesus being sodomized. Gays in L.A. have dressed as angels with coat-hanger halos when disrupting masses, and gays in Boston as silly-looking bishops in red miters. Producers of "The Cardinal Detoxes," a poisonously anti-Catholic monologue that ran off-Broadway, invited nightly mockery of the church by offering free admission to patrons dressed as nuns or priests. This "Rocky Horror" side of gay culture is ever more virulently anti-Catholic"

Time magazine carried an article by Nancy Gibbs, on December 9, 1991, entitled, *America's Holy War,* which says,

> "In this nation of spiritual paradoxes, it is legal to hang a picture in a public exhibit of a crucifix submerged in urine, or to utter virtually any conceivable blasphemy in a public place; it is not legal, the federal courts have ruled, to mention God reverently in a classroom, on a football field or at a commencement ceremony as a part of a public prayer."

This kind of contempt and mockery of the things of God is dangerous. Scurrilous behavior like this will help provoke God. It will bring forth great tribulation. *In the last days, people will be blasphemers* (II Timothy 3:2).

(6) Disobedient to parents

Jesus said, *Now the brother shall betray the brother to death, and the father the son; and children shall rise up against their parents, and shall cause them to be put to death* (Mark 13:12). And Daniel said the Antichrist will not regard the God of His fathers (Daniel 11:37). The desires of his parents and ancestors will be meaningless to him.

In the United States today, the two-income home is almost a necessity. Double-career marriages are quite normal. Much of the parental responsibility is left to the preschool, the day care center, the school, the counselors and others. This is not working. Children are disobedient. Parents are abusive. As many as one million children become "runaways" or "throwaways" every year. Cities need hotlines to help them communicate.

Hillary Rodham Clinton, U.S. First Lady, supports the right of children to sue their parents; Janet Reno, U.S. attorney general, wants to make violence in the family a major focus of her department; and Kimberly Mays and Shawn Russ (Gregory K) have "divorced" their biological parents. According to William J. Bennett, secretary of education from 1985 to 1988, the last 30 years has seen "a 560% increase in violent crimes; a 419% increase in illegitimate births; a quadrupling in divorce rates; a tripling of the percentage of children in single-parent homes; more than a 200% increase in the teenage suicide rate; and a drop of almost 80 points in SAT scores."

✦ *In the last days, children will be disobedient to parents.*
   (II Timothy 3:2)

(7) Unthankful

The Antichrist should humbly bow down before the Lord Jesus with thanksgiving and praise. But he will not thank or praise God. He will oppose God, fight God, magnify himself and stand up against the Prince of princes (Daniel 8:25). On the whole, we have become a thankless society; no blessing before meals, no prayer in the home; no prayer in the schools; and no tithing at church.

According to information in Newsweek magazine on January 22, 1990, the Gallup organization has found that church members contribute substantially less than 10 percent of their income to religious groups. They found Catholics contribute 1.0%, Methodists 1.3%, Jews 1.4%, Lutherans 1.6%, Presbyterians 2.2% and all other Protestants 2.5%. In the last days, people will be unthankful (II Timothy 3:2).

(8) Unholy

The Antichrist will destroy the holy people; defile the holy place; violate the Holy Scriptures; and establish a harlot church. He will commit idolatry, kill and lie (Daniel 8:24; 8:11; Matthew 24:15; Daniel 7:25; Matthew 24:9; II Thesselonians 2:9; Revelation 17:4). His False Church will not conform to the image of Christ; not be indwelt by the Holy Spirit; and not be a holy nation (I Peter 2:9). His false prophets and teachers will not consider the Bible to be holy, the Lord's Supper to be holy, matrimony to be holy or the Sabbath to be holy. It will be an ordinary thing to commit offenses against the holy God and to profane things consecrated unto Him.

Holy is a forgotten word today. Preachers and teachers seldom stress holy living. Many say, "Bible" instead of "Holy Bible," "Communion" instead of "Holy Communion," "Church" instead of "holy nation" and "marriage" instead of "holy matrimony." Church buildings are looted, damaged and burned. Few things are considered holy.

✦ *In the last days, people will be unholy.*
   (II Timothy 3:2)

(9) Without natural affection

The Antichrist will not regard the desire of women (Daniel 11:37). One interpretation says he will not have a natural desire for love, sex or marriage. This may seem to be a strange interpretation, but the fact is, false teachers will actually forbid people to marry in the last days (I Timothy 4:3).

Let's delve a little deeper. We know that natural affection is affection between male and female or husband and wife. The opposite is true of "without natural affection." That refers to abnormal relationships such as male affection for males and female affection for females. It clearly covers homosexuals and lesbians.

Heterosexual marriage signifies the mystical union which exists between Christ and His Church. Perverted relationships between men and men do not symbolize this union. Neither do unnatural relationships between women and women. God's will on this is written in brightly glowing neon lights. But the Episcopal Diocese ordains lesbians. The Lutheran Church permits homosexual ministers. And many mainline denominations refuse to condemn this sin.

Gays are incredibly strong in the United States today. It is a naked truth they are the darlings of the media; have stripped many of our sodomy laws; are disrobing the Biblical concept of marriage; are destroying the traditional two-parent family; have uncovered our society; and exposed it to a dark storm of unnatural behavior.

✦ *In the last days, people will be without natural affection.*
(II Timothy 3:3)

(10) Trucebreakers

We have seen that the war-mongering Antichrist will appear as a man of peace, sign a seven year covenant to protect Israel and break it three and one-half years later (Revelation 6:2; Daniel 9:27). Then he will persecute and try to destroy Israel (Revelation 12). His agreements will be meaningless. He will break his truces, abrogate his security agreements and abolish his peace treaties.

One modern example concerns the EC diplomatic efforts in Yugoslavia.Dozens of agreements have been broken. Some within hours because combatants will not keep their promises. Another example concerns agreements Iraq made following the Persian Gulf War. The country agreed to co-operate with United Nations inspection teams, but it did just the opposite. It interfered with inspectors and attempted to hide information and weapons. A third example is Haiti. There Lt. Gen. Raoul Cedras broke his agreement to step down and pave the way for the United Nations approved government of President Jean-Bertrand Aristide.

✦ *In the last days, people will be trucebreakers.*
(II Timothy 3:3)

(11) False accusers

During the tribulation period, the Antichrist will falsely speak against God; believers will be betrayed by parents, bretheren, kinfolks and friends; and the accuser of the bretheren will be cast down to earth (Daniel 11:36; Luke 21:16; Revelation 12:10). The "seriousness of the charges" will carry more weight than the supporting evidence.

The nomination of Judge Robert Bork to the U.S. Supreme Court was defeated primarily with accusations. The practice was so successful someone coined the phrase "Bork him." Later, some pledged to defeat the nomination of Judge Clarence Thomas in the same way. The accusations were terrible, but the effort failed for a lack of evidence. This same practice is common in the media and rampant in politics and law. Unfortunately, it will get worse.

✦ *In the last days, people will be false accusers.*
(II Timothy 3:3)

(12) Incontinent

Webster's New World Dictionary defines incontinent as "without self-restraint, especially in regard to sexual activity." It refers to members of the False Church who will not restrain their passions and sexual desires; members shackled by-and enslaved to-the lusts of the flesh; men who creep into houses and involve captive silly women in sin; and women burning with all kinds of lusts (II Timothy 3:6).

In hearings before the U.S. Senate Judiciary Committee, in April of 1991, it was reported, "A woman is raped every six minutes in the United States." Each year, 1 million teen-age girls get pregnant; 36 percent abort their babies; and 25 percent of all births are to unwed mothers. And Rock Hudson, Tony Perkins, Liberace, Robert Maplethorpe and many others will never see the light of day again because of the HIV virus. Our society has lowered its standard of personal conduct and we are reaping the bad fruit of incontinence.

✦ *In the last days, people will be incontinent.*
(II Timothy 3:3)

(13) Fierce

Fierce describes the Antichrist. He is the one Daniel was speaking of when he said, *In the latter time . . . a king of fierce counte-*

nance, and understanding dark sentences, shall stand up. And his power shall be mighty, but not by his own power: and he shall destroy wonderfully, and shall prosper, and practise, and shall destroy the mighty and the holy people (Daniel 8:23, 24). The Antichrist will be the master of evil; the power of Satan in the flesh. He and his False Church will practice witchcraft (Revelation 9:20, 21; 18:2). And it will lead to the slaughter of God's people.

Believe what you want, but Satanic cults that gather in dark places to torture and sacrifice animals are real. Cults that perform late-night sacrifices to the tune of ritual chants are a growing menace. Does the name Matamoros, Mexico ring a bell? That is where a 21-year old University of Texas student was found dead along with pots of human brains and blood; and decapitated animal bodies. Does the name Richard Ramirez sound familiar? He is the "Night Stalker" who admitted to worshipping Satan and killing 14 people. Do you recall "Gina?" She is the demon possessed Florida teen-ager who was exorcised on ABC's "20/20" in 1991. Have you heard of Anton La Vey? He heads the Church of Satan and has written the Satanic Bible. This is real and the situation is rapidly growing worse. (Refer back to the comments in this chapter on I Timothy 4:1).

✦ *In the last days, people will be fierce.*
(II Timothy 3:3)

(14) Despisers of those that are good

The False Church will get falling down drunk; drunk with the blood of the saints, and with the blood of the martyrs of Jesus (Revelation 17:6). Its demon possessed members will hate things that are good. Its Satan worshipers will hate true believers, righteousness, godliness, decency, honesty, integrity and morality. Its witches will show animosity toward the Christian lifestyle and rules of moral conduct. Its false prophets and false teachers will attempt to reorder the institutions, lives and characters of almost everyone by substituting their values for God's values. They will be like those the Prophet Isaiah spoke of who, *Call evil good, and good evil; that put darkness for light, and light for darkness; that put bitter for sweet, and sweet for bitter* (Isaiah 5:20)!

This sounds very much like Political Correctness (PC). PC is the latest attempt to abolish free speech. If we criticize the feminist movement, condemn homosexuals, say anything against blacks, speak out against welfare or even welfare fraud, we are not PC. The only way we can be PC is to support the views of the radical feminists, the gays, the black leadership, the liberal agenda and the educated elite. And we have to practice intellectual fraud to do that.

Humanists use PC to try to silence pastors and religious leaders. With the help of a biased liberal media, they label conservative Christians as "bigots," "fundamentalists" and "the religious right." They are trying to brand or stigmatize them. They want people to believe the views of these members of Christ's Body are disgraceful and shameful. They want to establish the idea that some Christians should not be listened to. This is blatant censorship and it will move from attempts to silence conservative believers to attempts to deliver them up for persecution and death.

✦ *In the last days, people will despise those that are good.*
(II Timothy 3:3)

(15) Traitors

The Antichrist will be the master traitor. His promise to protect Israel will be broken (Daniel 9:27). His promise of peace will be a campaign to conquer (Revelation 6:2). And his love affair with the False Church will only last until he gets what he wants. The False Church will miss the rapture; never make it to heaven; never find itself in the presence of Christ. It will not even be loved by the heinous Antichrist or his ten puppet kings. They will betray and destroy it (Revelation 17:16, 17).

✦ *In the last days, people will be traitors.*
(II Timothy 3:4)

(16) Heady

The False Prophet will be a scientific genius.

And he doeth great wonders, so that he maketh fire come down from heaven on the earth in the sight of men, And deceiveth them that dwell on the earth by the means of those miracles which he had power to do in the sight of the beast; saying to them that dwell on the earth, that they should make an image to the beast, which had the wound by a sword, and did live. And he had power to give life unto the image of the beast, that the image of the beast should both speak, and cause that as many as would not worship the image of the beast should be killed (Revelation 13:13-15).

Like Pentecost, when tongues as of fire came from heaven, he will bring fire down from heaven. Like Nebuchadnezzar of Babylon, he will build a statue for people to worship. And like Pentecost, when people received eternal life and spoke in other tongues, he will give his statue life and cause it to speak.

It is said that 90 percent of the world's scientists are alive today. They have split the atom, manufactured nuclear weapons and walked on the moon. Men have walked in space "faster than a speeding bullet," started the life of babies in a test tube, put life histories on objects smaller than the head of a pin and stored them in computers. These are heady things. And their knowledge is doubling every two and one-half years.

✦ *In the last days, people will be heady.*
(II Timothy 3:4)

(17) Highminded

The Antichrist will come forth with "a mouth speaking great things (Daniel 7:8); "a mouth speaking great things and blasphemies" (Revelation 13:5); a mouth speaking "marvellous things against the God of gods" (Daniel 11:36). No doubt he will be the most eloquent speaker on earth. He will be very popular because he will stand for all the ungodly principles embraced by an ungodly world; a Christ-rejecting world that will extol his great education, laud his intelligence, praise his lofty oratory and admire his low-down blasphemy. He will be educated beyond his ability to make wise decisions; make quantum leaps in ear-tickling; and backward steps in God-pleasing.

In March of 1991, a group of self-proclaimed "religious scholars," called the Jesus Seminar, concluded a six-year study of what the historical Jesus probably said. These highminded individuals, from universities and divinity schools around the world, even decided they know more about it than those who wrote the Bible. They decided Jesus did not speak the Lord's Prayer, that He did not predict His death and resurrection, that the Apostles made up the story about His promise to return, and that He did not say anything while He was hanging on the cross. These "scholars" eliminated 80 percent of the words attributed to Jesus.They studied Mark's Gospel and found only one verse they believe Jesus probably said (Mark 12:17). It is highminded people who think they know more than the greatest book ever written. They will help bring the judgment of God on this world.

    ✦ *In the last days, people will be highminded.*
    (II Timothy 3:4)

(18) Lovers of pleasure more than lovers of God

The false prophets and false teachers of the last days will have "eyes full of adultery, and that cannot cease from sin" (II Peter 2:1, 14). Many will give "themselves over to fornication" (Jude 7). They will be sensual, having not the Spirit" (Jude 19).

In a special report, in U.S. News & World Report, April 22, 1991, Gerald Parshall wrote, "The belief that moral decency required a girl to remain a virgin until marriage (or at least engagement) held sway in the middle class for much of United States history. Then, in the 1960s and 1970s, chastity all but died as a mainstream ideal."

An article by Jeffery L Sheler with Joannie M. Schrof and Gary Cohen, in U.S. News & World Report on June 10, 1991, says,

> "This week in Baltimore, a task force of the 2.9 million-member Presbyterian Church (U.S.A.) will ask the denomination's general assembly to consider abandoning traditional sanctions against sex outside of marriage, including homosexuality, and replacing rigid sexual taboos with a vaguely defined but certainly less restrictive ethic of 'justice-love.' Later this summer, the Episcopal Church will consider a hotly contested plan to permit the ordination of active gays and lesbians. Meanwhile, study groups in the United Methodist and Evangelical Lutheran churches are preparing similar proposals to be debated in the next two years. And last fall the nation's Roman Catholic bishops for the first time approved guidelines for sex education in Catholic schools, though they held fast to the church's

traditional stands against abortion, contraception and sex outside marriage.

"In each case, the moves toward a more liberal sexual ethic face strong opposition. Yet voices calling for change within the churches are growing louder, signaling an increasing and perhaps unavoidable conflict between traditional standards and changing mores. . . .

"Declining membership in mainline Protestant denominations is one of the driving forces behind the current debate. . . . Evans (Rev. Louis Evans Jr.) and others see the membership decline more as a result of the churches' earlier shifts from 'biblical pre-eminence' to a more political and social agenda."

Fortunately, the Presbyterian Church (U.S.A.) rejected these recommendations. But this shows the strong odor of pleasure-seeking. It has the rotten smell of spiritual decline. And regrettably, some want to mask this pursuit of pleasure by defining Biblical morality down.

+ *In the last days, people will be lovers of pleasure more than lovers of God.*
(II Timothy 3:4)

(19) Having a form of godliness, but denying the power thereof

The Antichrist will simulate Christ by coming forth on a white horse (Revelation 6:2); pretend to be the Prince of Peace with his false peace program (Daniel 8:25); and give the appearance of Christ with a fake resurrection (Revelation 13:3, 12). He will have a form of godliness, but it will be simulation, pretense and fakery.

Today, the Church is more organized and formal and less free and spiritual than ever before. It has committees for everything. It has the National Council of Churches, the World Council of Churches and efforts to merge all of the denominations into a one-world super-church. It is very well organized, but many have abandoned the power of God-denying even the inerrancy of Scripture, the deity of Christ and the bodily resurrection of Christ. Many have abandoned true worship; are embarrassed to say, "Amen," "Hallelujah," or "Praise God." Too many church services are "cut and dried."

And it is not unusual for members to be bored at church. Too many have a form of godliness and the power is gone.

> ✦ In the last days, people will have a form of godliness,
>   but deny the power thereof.
>   (II Timothy 3:5)

(20) Ever learning, and never able to come to the knowledge of the truth

The Antichrist will come forth understanding dark sentences, but he will never be able to learn it is God that allows him to prosper (Daniel 8:23; 11:36). He will do according to his own will, but never understand the removal of the Holy Spirit made it possible (Daniel 11:36; II Thessalonian 2:6,7). His false prophets and teachers will have college degrees; some will have multiple degrees; and some will study and learn all their life. But they will never know the true God. And their church members won't be any better off.

In an article in the Baptist and Reflector, Newsjournal of The Tennessee Baptist Convention, dated May 29, 1991, George Gallup Jr. is quoted as saying, "I doubt if more than five to ten percent of Christians are prepared to defend their faith. Many don't know what it means to be a Christian." He says, "Only 4 out of 10 Christians know who delivered the Sermon on the Mount" and "Many people who say they are Christians subscribe to New Age beliefs."

> ✦ In the last days, people will be ever learning, and never able to
>   come to the knowledge of the truth.
>   (II Timothy 3:7)

(21) Evil men and seducers shall wax worse and worse, deceiving and being deceived

The truth about the Antichrist is he will gather his political cronies and come forth jogging the path of lying deception (II Thessalonian 2:10). Jesus said, *Many false prophets shall rise, and shall deceive many* (Matthew 24:11). He said, *There shall arise false Christs, and false prophets, and shall shew great signs and wonders; insomuch that, if it were possible, they shall deceive the very elect* (Matthew 24:24).

Many in the United States today are spinning a web of deceit. University professors will not speak the truth because they want to be politically correct. The evening news is using word twisters, rigged accidents and phony exposés. Congress deceives its own people in order to promote partisan political programs. Every time society tears down a guardrail of truth more people go over the cliff of deception.

✦ *In the last days, evil people and seducers shall wax worse and worse, deceiving and being deceived.*
(II Timothy 3:13)

The Pope's Visit

Here is something else to watch for. Watch for the appearance of religious people intolerant of the true Word of God; people who object to messages right out of the Bible; people who object to sermons that step on their toes; people who prefer preachers and teachers who approve of their ungodly deeds. Doesn't this sound a lot like our contemporary society?

When Pope John Paul II visited Denver, Colorado for World Youth Day in August 1993, there was an outcry from many within the church who wanted him to change church teachings on such issues as abortion, birth control, homosexuality, premarital sex and women priests. They questioned the church's authority on these matters and harshly criticized the Pope for reaffirming traditional teachings. They want theologians with new doctrines. This is backwards. The true church should be Biblically correct not politically correct (BC not PC). It should change the world not allow the world to squeeze it into its mold.

For the time will come when they will not endure sound doctrine; but after their own lusts shall they heap to themselves teachers, having itching ears (II Timothy 4:3).

II Peter

Peter was an impetuous young man. The three years he spent with Jesus profoundly changed his life. He dearly loved the Lord.

And his unquestioning belief in the risen Savior resulted in his being persecuted, jailed and crucified.

Peter became known as the Apostle of hope for trying to help despairing and suffering believers keep the faith. He reminded troubled Christians we are never without hope. We have the power of prayer, fellowship with Christ, the help of other believers, the promise of the resurrection and the hope of the second coming. Concerning the return of Jesus, he once said, *We have not followed cunningly devised fables, when we made known unto you the power and coming of our Lord Jesus Christ, but were eyewitnesses of his majesty* (II Peter 1:16). He was saying, *The second coming is not a myth or a cleverly contrived story. It is a real incident the Lord Jesus revealed to us on the Mount of Transfiguration.* That is what the early Church believed.

False Teachers and Damnable Heresies.

How do you recognize a false teacher? Not by his vocation or occupation, because he is a pretender. But by his message. He always contradicts an essential of the Christian faith. The false teacher always spins a web of false doctrines. He always integrates false beliefs and destructive doctrines into his message. He can't resist blending secular and pagan philosophy with Bible teachings. He always teaches as doctrine "the precepts of men."

On July 1, 1991, Joseph Lowery, president of the Southern Christian Leadership Conference, spoke in Memphis, Tennessee at the dedication of the National Civil Rights Museum. Among other things, he said, "We are on holy ground. The site of Martin Luther King's death is the new Calvary." Perhaps he really believes that, but he is mixing his personal beliefs with Christian teachings. Dr. King's death was tragic, but there will never be "a new Calvary."

John Spong is a Bishop in the Episcopal Church and has written a book entitled, *Rescuing The Bible From Fundamentalism.* In his view, the New Testament portrays Jesus as "narrow-minded" and "vindictive." He believes the Gospel writers "twisted" the facts of our Lord's resurrection, contends the doctrine of the virgin birth is unthinkable, the doctrine of the Trinity is not worth very much and the Apostle Paul was a "self-loathing" homosexual. He is a perfect example of someone entering the Church with secular teachings that are inconsistent with the Bible.

✦ *There shall be false teachers among you, who privily shall bring in damnable heresies, even denying the Lord that bought them.* (II Peter 2:1)

Scoffers

According to the Apostle Peter, the last days will be marked by social decay and scoffers ridiculing the second coming. Evildoers will establish their own morality and show contempt for the return of Christ. They will ask a question and make a statement. They will ask, "Where is the promise of His coming?" And they will say, *"for since the fathers fell asleep, all things continue as they were from the beginning of creation* (II Peter 3:3, 4).

Peter dealt with these in reverse order. He calls the statement ignorance. And reminds us all things are not the same since the beginning of creation. The Flood of Noah's day changed much of the creation. Where are the dinosaurs? Did they have computers, catalogs or CAT-scans back then; public address systems, pet rocks or pasteurized milk; telephones, televisions or tennis balls? Did the nation of Israel exist 100 years ago? Was Russia and Germany friendly to each other during W W II? Was there an Israeli-PLO peace treaty 10 years ago? Surely we must admit that many things have changed since the creation.

Now let's look at how Peter answers those who question our Lord's promise to return. He says, "The Lord is not slack concerning his promise, as some men count slackness; but is longsuffering to usward, not willing that any should perish, but that all should come to repentance" (II Peter 3:9). God doesn't break His promises. He is a very patient God. He is delaying His return for two reasons: He will not enjoy sending judgment upon this world and He wants everyone to be saved.

On March 18, 1991, Newsweek magazine carried an article by Kenneth L. Woodward entitled, *The Final Days Are Here Again*. He seems to be scoffing at those who believe the end-times are here when he writes, Jesus, of course, warned that "you know not the day or the hour of his return. And for orthodox Scripture scholars, treating the Bible like tea leaves is no way to get at the truth." We should be very concerned about anyone who tries to "read tea leaves" and also anyone who does not know the difference between "treating the Bible like tea leaves" and studying Bible prophecy. The Word tells us to "watch" and it says we "can see the day approaching" (Matthew 24:42; Hebrew 10:25). Our "poverty of values" and the existence of taunters serves to verify the truth of Peter's prediction

✦ *There shall come in the last days scoffers.*
   (II Peter 3:3, 4)

I John

The Apostle John is generally credited with writing five books in the New Testament. He spent three years with his beloved Jesus and was a member of the inner circle. He served as pastor of the congregation the Apostle Paul established in Ephesus and dedicated his whole life to serving Christ. He suffered many things for his faith.

Antichrist

John made it plain there were many antichrists in his day. And many were yet to come. But there will be an especially evil one who is called the Antichrist. Anyone who denies the deity of Christ, that He is the Son of God, that He is the Messiah, or that He died for our sins is an antichrist. But Satan's abomination of desolation will not only deny the deity of Jesus, he will actually claim to be the Christ. John calls this demagogue "the angel of the bottomless pit" (Revelation 9:11).

✦ *He is antichrist, that denieth the Father and the Son.*
   (I John 2:22)

Revelation

The Book of Revelation was written by the Apostle John, but it refers to itself as "The Revelation of Jesus Christ." Its stated purpose is to shew unto his servants things which must shortly come to pass (Revelation 1:1). According to the book, a terrible time is coming when everything will be thrown into disarray and billions of people will die. But it contains good news too–those who serve the merciful God will be the ultimate winners in life. Revelation 6:17 through 19:21 is a commentary on the 70th week of Daniel.

Food Prices

When the black horse of famine gallops across the earth, there will be a worldwide shortage of foodstuff. Food prices will sky-rocket. A measure of wheat (one quart), or three measures of barley (three quarts) will cost a day's wages. Can you imagine working all day for four cups of wheat? Some will have to. And they will feel lucky to have the job.

Oil and wine were luxury foods in the Apostle John's day. Foods of extravagance will be available during the tribulation period, but the average man will be unable to afford them. He literally will not have the money.

We have seen this happen in Russia. On January 2, 1992, food prices were deregulated as the former Soviet republics took their first steps toward a market economy. That night, the Cable News Network (CNN) reported Russian citizens will have to pay "two days wages for a quart of milk," and "three days wages for a pound of meat."

In an article entitled "Higher prices, but Moscow wonders where's the beef," that appeared in the Jackson Sun newspaper on January 2, 1992, AP writer Larry Ryckman wrote,

> "Among the eye-popping new prices: boiled sausages cost five times more; mandarin oranges more than tripled, carrots shot up more than fivefold-as did the cost of a slice of pizza with pepperoni.
>
> "At Food Store No. 2 next to the Foreign Ministry, refrigerated cases were filled with sausage, frankfurters, chickens and spiced bologna, but there was no beef. Despite windows that advertised milk, none was to be found; only displays of champagne for 156 rubles, more than 20 times its state-controlled price just a few days ago.
>
> "Bread prices, although still regulated, more than doubled.
>
> "Although wages also are expected to rise, the average salary last year was about 350 rubles per month."

Things may change, but beef and milk were not available. Champagne was, but the price of a bottle approached two weeks wages.

✦ *A measure of wheat for a penny, and three measures of barley*
   for a penny; and see thou hurt not the oil and the wine.
   (Revelation 6:6)

The 200 Million Man Army

Now we come to an incredible prophecy. Where could an army of 200 million men come from when the population of the world did not even come up to this figure in the Apostle John's day? How could he foresee a 200 million man army?

Many say he didn't. A few say this is an army of demons instead of men because horsemen do not wear "breastplates of fire, and of jacinth and brimstone" and horses do not have mouths that issue "fire and smoke and brimstone." A small number say the figure of 200 million is not literal, but an expression meaning "a very large army." Some contend these are tanks, or a future weapon of some type. Others say the size of the army is literal and the tribulation period cannot occur until someone can assemble an army of 200 million men. Each individual will have to come to his own conclusion.

But prophecy buffs were amazed when an Associated Press article by John H. Hightower was printed on April 28, 1964, saying Red Chinese leaders estimate they have "200 million armed and organized militiamen." The fact that one nation could field this tribulation size army was seen as both significant and terrifying. After all, this means the population of the world has probably reached tribulation period proportions and an army now exists that is large enough to kill one-third of our population.

✦ *The number of the army of the horsemen were two hundred*
   thousand thousand: and I heard the number of them.
   (Revelation 9:16)

Tribulation Period Sins

During the tribulation period, the true Church will be in heaven and the vast majority of earth's inhabitants will not walk in the blood-sprinkled way. The Apostle John identified six sins that will prevail.

The first tribulation period sin is devil worship. Who would believe our modern enlightened society would worship the devil? And yet, we have the Satanic Bible, the Church of Satan, goddess worship, witches and the like. And when the Antichrist begins to utter his dark sayings, and his false church spreads the table with poison meat, the number who will flatter the devil with their mouths and lie with their tongues will greatly increase.

The second tribulation period sin is idolatry. Many do not think they would worship an idol, but when the False Prophet sets up his statue of the Antichrist, the word will go out that anyone who refuses will be killed. Multitudes will bow down and worship the image.

The third tribulation period sin is murder. Unlawful killing is skyrocketing in the United States today with several cities setting new records every year. On January 13, 1992, David Ellis wrote, in Time magazine, "Every 22 minutes, another American is shot, stabbed, beaten or strangled to death." Washington, D.C. is now known as "the murder capitol of the world" and the United States as "the culture of death."

The fourth tribulation period sin is sorceries. The Greek word is "pharmakeion." This is where we get the English word "pharmacy." It means "drugs." Drug-abuse is ravaging our society. We have periodic attempts to legalize marijuana and have learned such words as "rocks," "ice," and "crack cocaine."

The fifth tribulation period sin is fornication. The Greek word is "porneia" and it refers to illicit sexual activity, pornography and such. The "sexual revolution" in the United States has made our nation a cesspool of immorality. Most advertising exploits sex. X-rated movies appear on TV. Condoms are advertised on TV and distributed in schools. Pornographic books and videos, including child pornography, are available in most communities; and nude dancing is widespread.

The sixth tribulation period sin is theft. Burglaries and robberies have become a way of life for a growing number of citizens. Our moral collapse is costing government, business and individuals billions of dollars each year.

When we read this list of sins, we see a similarity to the current daily newspaper. The all-knowing God accurately foretold what our society would come down to and America has arrived. This moral meltdown has a price-God's mercy, patience and protection.

> ✦ *They will refuse to repent of their devil worship, idolatry, murders, sorceries, fornication and thefts.*
> (Revelation 9:20, 21)

The Two Witnesses

Most people want to know who the two witnesses are. We will deal with their identity. But that is not the main point of this passage.

Their identity– All we can do is speculate about who they are. They are not identified in the Bible.

Elijah seems to be the most popular choice. Here are five reasons:

1. He will appear before "the great and dreadful day of the Lord" (Malachi 4:5).

2. He called down fire out of heaven (I Kings 18:38). The two witnesses will destroy their enemies with fire (Revelation 11:5).

3. He stopped the rain (I Kings 17:5). The two witnesses will shut up heaven that it rain not (Revelation 11:6).

4. He did not die (II Kings 2:11). But it is appointed unto men once to die (Hebrew 9:27).

5. He appeared with Jesus when the second coming was revealed on the Mount of Transfiguration (Matthew 17;3; II Peter 1:16–18).

Moses is a favorite choice of many. The three main reasons are as follows:

1. He had the power to smite the earth with plagues (Exodus 7:17–12:30). The two witnesses will have that power (Revelation 11:6).

2. He had the power to turn water into blood (Exodus 7:20). The two witnesses will have that power (Revelation 11:6).

3. He appeared with Jesus and Elijah on the Mount of Transfiguration (Matthew 17:3).

Enoch is commonly named. There are at least three reasons for that. They are:

1. He did not die (Genesis 5:24; Hebrew 11:5). But it is appointed unto men once to die (Hebrew 9:27).

2. He prophesied the second coming (Jude 14). And the two witnesses will prophesy (Revelation 11:3).

3. He prophesied judgment (Jude 15).

The main points— Many points can be made. But the central teaching concerns the ministry, authority, death, non-burial, resurrection and ascension of the two witnesses.

1. Jesus could not die until His hour had come (John 2:4). And the two witnesses cannot die until they complete their mission (Revelation 11:3-5).

2. Jesus had the authority to execute judgment (John 5:26, 27) And the two witnesses will have that same authority (Revelation 11:6).

3. The mission of Jesus included His death (John 3:14). And the mission of the two witnesses includes their death (Revelation 11:7).

4. Jesus was buried. But the two witnesses will not be buried (Revelation 11:8).

5. Jesus rose from the dead. And the two witnesses will rise from the dead (Revelation 11:11).

6. Jesus ascended into heaven. And the two witnesses will ascend into heaven (Revelation 11:12).

Following the death, burial and resurrection of Jesus, some said, "His disciples took Him off the cross before He died." Others said, "His disciples came by night, and stole Him away while we slept" (Matthew 28:13). Still others said, "There is no resurrection of the dead" (I Corinthians 5:12). They did not believe the things they were told.

The world will know the two witnesses are dead. Their bodies will lie in the street for three and one-half days. Multitudes will see their corpses and rejoice over that gruesome sight. But suddenly, God will show the world He can raise the dead. Isn't this exciting! Our loving God will allow the world to witness the resurrection of two people from the dead. All questions will be fully answered. Death was defeated at the cross.

Jesus ascended into heaven, but many do not believe. When the Church is raptured, people will say, "They didn't go to heaven; God removed them because they stood in the way of peace; God got rid of them because they wouldn't accept the new beliefs; they opposed our world ruler, etc." Then the two witnesses will rise, stand upon their feet, and ascend up to heaven. Many will believe Jesus was raised and the Church was raptured.

There is another thing too. The Antichrist will require people to take the Mark of the Beast or be killed. But our loving God will show people not to be afraid of death. Those who the Antichrist slays will not stay dead. Those who know the power of His resurrection will have nothing to fear. "Yea, though I walk through the valley of the shadow of death, I will fear no evil" (Psalm 23:4).

Some expositors think this prophecy presents significant proof that the second coming is near. There was a time when men did not believe most of the world could see the corpses of these two men lying in the street. They said it was humanly impossible. But now that we have satellites and worldwide TV, many nations can view this great event. So even the "boob tube" is a sign.

+ *And I will give power unto my two witnesses, and they shall prophesy a thousand two hundred and threescore days, clothed in sackcloth.*
   (Revelation 11:3)

+ *And they of the people and kindreds and tongues and nations shall see their dead bodies.*
   (Revelation 11:9)

The Great Red Dragon

Many people do not understand the Book of Revelation because they do not recognize the symbols John used. He used difficult symbols. But most of the time, they are explained in the context, or someplace else in the Bible. That is what Peter meant when he said, "no prophecy of the scripture is of any private interpretation" (II Peter 1:20). The Bible interprets itself. When we have a difficult verse, we should look for another verse to explain it. When we have a difficult prophetic symbol we should look for a Bible interpretation.

It is also helpful to keep in mind the fact that John's visions switch back and forth between heaven and earth. Things will be happening in heaven while the tribulation period is taking place on earth. One of those things is a war with Satan. Revelation chapter 12 gives us some of the details.

John saw *a woman clothed with the sun, and the moon under her feet, and upon her head a crown of twelve stars.* This is one of the dreams Joseph had. It is recorded in the Old Testament (Genesis 37:9-11). And Jacob interpreted the dream like this: the sun is Jacob (Israel); the moon is Rachel (Israel's wife); and the twelve stars are Joseph and his eleven brothers (the twelve tribes of Israel).

This woman, who symbolizes Jacob, Rachel and the twelve tribes of Israel, was "with child." She is a mother-to-be. And her unborn child is Jesus. He is identified in verse 5 as "a man child, who was to rule all nations with a rod of iron." Psalm 2:5,9 tells us the one who will break the nations with a rod of iron is the Lord. His ascension is seen in verse 6 which says, "her child was caught up unto God."

A great red dragon is standing before the woman waiting to devour her child. He is identified in verse 9 *as that old serpent, called the Devil, and Satan.* He wants to rule the nations too. In fact, he offered Jesus the nations of the world if He would just worship him (Matthew 4:8, 9).

The crowning achievement of this dragon is the EC. He has "seven heads and ten horns, and seven crowns upon his heads." Satan will be the unseen force behind the Revived Roman Empire;

the unseen power behind the Antichrist and his ten (or seven) puppet kings; the ruler of darkness behind the covenant the Antichrist makes with regard to Israel.

Some time after the woman's (Israel's) child (Jesus) is caught up (ascended) unto God, there will be war in heaven. It will come because God will decree that Satan can no longer have access to His throne. Satan will not be allowed to appear before God anymore. God will give the order and there will be war. Michael and his angels will cast Satan and his angels out. Where to? They will be "cast out into the earth." And there will be rejoicing in heaven. But woe to the inhabitants of earth.

When this happens, the great red dragon (Satan) will persecute the woman (Israel) because she brought forth the man child (Jesus). So the woman will flee into the wilderness. God will feed and protect her there for three and one-half years. Many believe she will flee to an ancient rock fortress called Petra. But who knows?

But this is a clue to when Satan will be cast out of heaven. Jesus told the Jews, "When ye therefore shall see the abomination of desolation, spoken by Daniel the prophet, stand in the holy place . . . Then let them which be in Judaea flee into the mountains" (Matthew 24:15, 16). That occurs at the tribulation period mid-point. When the Antichrist sets up his statue, or image, Satan will be cast from heaven to earth. And there will be great persecution of Christians and Jews on earth.

What does all of this mean? Notice the connection of Christ with Israel; and Satan with the Revived Roman Empire. It reveals that Satan is behind the covenant of Antichrist and his Revived Roman Empire. Notice the connection between evil on earth and evil forces with access to God's throne. Notice those evil forces are destined for defeat. And Israel is destined for salvation. This is a message of hope. The rulers of the darkness of this world will ultimately be defeated. And God's people will ultimately be saved.

✦ *And there appeared another wonder in heaven; and behold a great red dragon, having seven heads and ten horns, and seven*

crowns upon his heads.
(Revelation 12:3)

The Mark of the Beast

During the tribulation period, the black horse of hunger, rationing, suffering and famine will gallop to and fro across the earth. It will do so because the Antichrist, and those groups of nations who support him, will use trade (especially food) as a weapon. This is why large trading blocks of nations are so dangerous. Their wicked leaders will control the distribution of food and decide who can buy and sell the small amount available. And the son of perdition will not choose his customers on the basis of their status or wealth. He will make the determining factor a mark that will identify those who are willing to worship him.

In former times, masters branded their slaves, commanders branded their troops and farmers branded their cattle. It may seem far-fetched, but the Bible says the insidious Antichrist will renew this practice during the tribulation period. It even tells us exactly where the man of sin will want the brands to be placed (on either the right hand or the forehead).

In addition to the two different brand locations, there will be three different brand types: the mark of the Antichrist, his name, or the number of his name (His number not my number or yours). Any of his three brand types will suffice.

What is his mark and his name? The Bible does not say. But it does say the number of his name is 666. When the correct numerical value is assigned to each letter of his name, the total value will be 666. We must leave it there until a beastly man comes to power in Europe with a peace treaty to protect Israel.

More important than his mark or name is the fact that everyone should refuse to be branded. For those who take the mark are receiving the brand of Antichrist. And the sovereign God says they will be eternally damned. On the other hand, it is true that those who refuse the mark will be killed, but they will not be condemned. The God of life will raise them from the dead. And they will reign with Him (Revelation 20:4). Still more important is the fact that all who sincerely accept Christ before the rapture will not have to worry about it. We will not be here.

At one time, the control of all buying and selling, and the marking and tracking of every individual seemed remote, but that is no longer true. The development of supercomputers, microchips, large data banks, "stealth" bar codes and satellite tracking systems have made this possible.

We already have computers to authorize or reject credit card sales; computers to track transactions in a split second; bar code printers and scanners to read marks and numbers placed on anything; "stealth" codes with invisible ink that do not leave unsightly marks on things like hands and foreheads; microchips that can be implanted under the skin with a hypodermic needle so they cannot be seen; computers to read them; and receivers that work with satellites to track an individual anywhere he moves. Government officials are already confining criminals to their homes and attaching devices that sound an alarm if they leave. Technology is already available to know who is buying and selling, who has taken or rejected the mark and where they are.

> ✦ *And he causeth all, both small and great, rich and poor, free and bond, to receive a mark in their right hand, or in their foreheads: And that no man might buy or sell, save he that had the mark, or the name of the beast, or the number of his name. Here is wisdom. Let him that hath understanding count the number of the beast: for it is the number of a man; and his number is Six hundred threescore and six.*
> (Revelation 13:16–18)

The Battle of Armageddon

"Armageddon" is Hebrew and it is the name of a place. When translated, it means "Mount of Megiddo." This mount is a large hill located west of the Jordan River, in the Plain of Esdraelon. The Bible contains several references to it, but the only verse that calls it "Armageddon" is found in Revelation 16:16

The Euphrates River will dry up so a great army can approach from the east (Revelation 16:12). Demon spirits will go forth from the dragon (Satan), the beast (Antichrist) and the False Prophet to gather armies from all over the world (Revelation 16:13, 14). They will approach Armageddon (the Mount of Megiddo). A war will begin that will rage over the last three and one-half years of the tribulation period. It will end with the second coming of the One who is "far above all principality, and power, and might, and dominion, and every name that is named, not only in this world, but also in that which is to come" (Ephesians 1:22).

A study of the Scriptures reveals certain conditions must exist before this lengthy war can take place. For example, the Jews must have their own nation, be in control of the land, possess the city of Jerusalem, rebuild the temple, and be a problem for the entire world. Europe must be united, the "prince that shall come" must be in power, and he must sign the seven year covenant pertaining to Israel. The city of Babylon must exist and be an important religious center. It must also be a wealthy trading center.

When these conditions are examined in light of history, it is obvious people should not have worried that World War I, World War II, the Korean War, the Persian Gulf War or any other war might be the Battle of Armageddon. If the Battle of Armageddon is taken as a literal battle, the conditions should be accepted as literal conditions. These conditions did not exist in their entirety when those wars were fought, but the stage is obviously being set.

✦ *And he gathered them together into a place called in the Hebrew tongue Armageddon.*
(Revelation 16:16)

The Mother of Harlots

Now we come to a very difficult and disturbing subject. It is important because it will affect millions of people; unpopular because it reflects on the Church; and sensitive because it reflects on some of our Church leadership. Our subject is the false church.

It is helpful to keep in mind some things Jesus taught about the Church. For example, His parable of The Wheat and The Tares tells us an evil force is working to produce religious apostates in the world (Matthew 13:24-30, 36-43). His parable of The Mustard Seed tells us these religious apostates will use Christendom as a resting place (Matthew 13:30-32). And His parable of The Leaven tells us about an evil woman who will introduce corruption and false doctrines into the Church (Matthew 13:33). As a whole, these teachings produce a picture of progressive corruption in the Church.

It is also helpful to remember the true Church is depicted in the Bible as a good woman. It is the Bride of Christ (Matthew 22:1-14). And it will be presented to Him as a bride "not having spot, or wrinkle" (Ephesians 5:22-33).

A third thing to recall is some of the mysteries in the Bible. The Church is a great mystery (Ephesians 5:32). Godliness is a mystery (I Timothy 3:16). And the Kingdom of God is a mystery (Mark 4:11).

In Revelations chapter 17, we meet "the great whore." She bears the name "MYSTERY, BABYLON THE GREAT, THE MOTHER OF HARLOTS AND ABOMINATIONS OF THE EARTH." And we encounter the mystery of the beast that "carrieth her." The beast has seven heads and ten horns. He is the Antichrist (Revelation 13:1-10); the culmination of "the mystery of iniquity" (II Thessalonians 2:7-12). Now let's put all this together. The true Church is a good woman, but Revelation chapter 17 is about a bad woman. The true Church is a mystery and Revelation chapter 17 is about a mystery. Godliness is a mystery. And iniquity is a mystery associated with Satan and the Antichrist.

Satan is a copycat. He tries to copy all that God does. God has the Bride of Christ. And Satan has the harlot of Antichrist. The conclusion: Mystery Babylon is the devil's church.

Many prophecy buffs believe the false church will be located in the seven-hilled city of Rome. This comes from verse 9 which tells us the woman sits on seven mountains. That may well be the most important center of religion following the rapture. But Satan's church will move to rebuilt Babylon sometime before the middle of the tribulation period (Zechariah 5:5-11). (See Babylon's Future in chapter 5 of this book.).

For nine days, between August 28 and September 5, 1993, leaders of the ten major religions of the world attended meetings of the World's Parliament of Religion in Chicago, Illinois. The meetings were sponsored by religious groups from all over the world including many Protestant and Catholic churches. And they hoped to lay the foundation for a "United Nations of Religions."

According to press reports, they produced a "Global Ethic," a new commandment (disarmament), and they condemned sexual discrimination. But all was not peace and harmony. Some Orthodox Christian leaders dropped out to protest the inclusion of "witches and other neo-pagan groups."

✦ *I will tell thee the mystery of the woman, and of the beast that carrieth her.*
(Revelation 17:7)

The Second Coming

Alleluia! Praise the Lord! Here comes heaven's best. Heaven was opened in Revelation 4:1 for the rapture of the Church. And now, in Revelation 19:11, heaven is opened again for the second coming of Jesus. In Revelation 4:1, His Church went into heaven. In Revelation 19:11, His Church comes out of heaven.

He is the KING OF KINGS, AND LORD OF LORDS. He is coming "to judge and make war;" to cast the Antichrist and his False Prophet into the lake of fire; to cast Satan into the bottomless pit; to put an end to evil; and to restore the kingdom to Israel. There will be no more Mark of the Beast; no more persecution of the righteous; no more famine, poverty, pestilence; and no more proud, boastful, unholy, unthankful characteristics of the Antichrist. What a wonderful day it will be. Jesus will reign. The earth will have peace. Alleluia! Praise the Lord! (Revelation 19:11–16).

✦ *And the armies which were in heaven followed him upon white horses.*
(Revelation 19:14)

When a Nation Rebels

A study of the Book of Judges reveals one verse of Scripture that is repeated over and over again. Seven times we read these frightening words, "The children of Israel did evil in the sight of the Lord." The people rebelled and each time they rebelled, they began a cycle that is repeated again and again. It has four steps-rebellion, retribution, repentance and restoration.

When God raises up a nation as He did with Israel (and America) and that nation rebels against His rule over it, that nation can expect to enter into a different relationship with Him. A nation in rebellion against God does not have the right to expect His blessings. It is not entitled to them and it will not continue to receive them as it did in the past.

When Joshua died, the children of Israel were being blessed by God. When they began to turn away from the Lord, He removed some of His help. When their rebellion grew worse, He sent retribution in the form of delivering them into the hands of their enemies.

What a disgusting sight it must have been; the people of God in servitude to pagans and foreigners; God's chosen people living in caves and dens in the mountains; the children of the covenant living in fear and poverty; the nation called to be a nation of priests, pure, strong, holy, and in communion with God, was dirty, destitute, weak and broken.

But this retribution from God did not come until the people rebelled against Him. The blessings were there until they began to break the relationship. Had they repented they would have been restored. And the blessings would have remained. But they did not.

America can expect no more than Israel. Our blessed nation is doing much evil in the sight of the Lord. God removed some of His help and we lost the Viet Nam War. We kept cruising down the river of ruin and we experienced hurricane Hugo, hurricane Andrew, the San Franscisco earthquake of 1989, the Los Angeles riots, the Oakland fires, the Midwest floods, and the Southeast drought to mention a few. It is quite possible we have passed the point of repentance. If so, our near future is dismal indeed. If we have not, then we need to humble ourselves and submit to God, without delay. We can repent and be restored or continue our moral decline and dare God to allow more retribution. "For if we would judge ourselves, we should not be judged" (I Corinthians 11:31). But what if we refuse to judge ourselves? (Read Amos 4:6–12.)

Chapter 8

Sequence And Timing

Anyone who even starts to discuss the sequence and timing of end-time events is quickly criticized and branded a "date- setter." Jesus said, *No one knows the day nor the hour of our Lord's return*. And some are so anxious to point it out, they will not even listen to what is being said. They do not understand the benefits of this information. And even though no date-setting occurs, they readily condemn any discussion of the subject. Many are genuine, God-fearing believers, but their minds are made up (and closed).

Nevertheless, the Scriptures tell us to watch, we will see the signs coming to pass, we can know when the kingdom of God is near, and we can see the day approaching. "Watching," "seeing," and "knowing" involves a knowledge of the signs, and their sequence and timing. Otherwise, we would err in our interpretation of end-time events.

Consider this example. Linda Robinson referred to the Cuban missile crisis in an article for U.S. News & World Report on January 20, 1992. Her story was entitled *Analysis* and she said, "the world came close to Armageddon nearly 30 years ago." The statement is descriptive, but completely inaccurate. The Cuban missile crisis could not have produced Armageddon because the rapture, the rise of Antichrist, the peace treaty, the rebuilding of the Jewish temple, and much more that precedes the great end-time battle, had not happened.

Before we look at the chronology it should go without saying, that this is a difficult subject and not everyone will agree with all the conclusions given in this chapter. Good Christians do disagree, and particularly on very complicated matters such as this. But even though some will hold different opinions on chronology, most are not likely to differ over the fact these events will occur.

The Rapture Precedes the Tribulation Period

Some refer to the rapture as "the next great event in prophecy." Others call it "the next great event in the life of the Church." If these statements are correct, it is obvious the rapture occurs before any other major event including the Russian invasion of Israel, the rise of the False Prophet, the rise of the Antichrist and so forth. The evidence is too weak to be dogmatic in every case, but these statements are probably true.

The New King James Version Prophecy Bible addresses the relation of the rapture to the tribulation period by saying,

> "We know that the Rapture will take place before the Tribulation because the Tribulation will be an unprecedented outpouring of the wrath of God (Revelation 6:17, as if any proof needed to be adduced that there has never been anything like the events of Revelation 6-18), and Jesus "delivers us (i.e., believers) from the wrath to come" (I Thessalonians 1:10; 5:9). The Thessalonians were extremely upset when they heard a rumor that the Tribulation (the Day of the Lord) had already come (II Thessalonians 2:1-12). The reason that they were upset was that they hadn't been taken. So Paul reminded them that certain things must happen before the Tribulation begins—things which hadn't happened yet."[1]

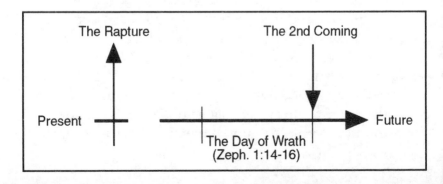

The rapture precedes the great outpouring of God's wrath. It is not that the Church is worthy to be protected. It is not. The pretribulation rapture is simply a matter of our blessed Redeemer's unlimited grace. He loves the Church, and has chosen not to lump it in with the Antichrist and his condemned followers. Those who sincerely repent of their sins and express a true personal faith in Jesus Christ are not about to be treated the same as those who trample underfoot the Son of God; who say His covenant to save people is worthless; who say the shed blood of Jesus is unholy; and who despise the voice of the Holy Spirit speaking to their heart. Live for the Lord and you will never experience even one fraction of a second of the great day of His wrath.

✦ *God hath not appointed us to wrath.*
(I Thessalonians 5:9)

The Rapture Precedes the Rise of the Antichrist

There are some who try to figure out who the Antichrist is. Since he will probably be alive and well when the Church is "caught up," they want to identify him. The problem is the Lawless One will not be revealed until after the Church is raptured.

The Apostle Paul taught this. He told the believers at Thessalonica the Antichrist will be revealed "in his time." But not until after the One who lets him rise is "taken out of the way" (II Thessalonians 2:6–8).

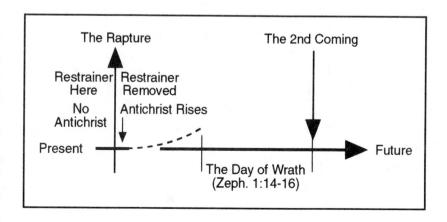

A strong Restrainer is preventing the rise of Antichrist. He indwells the Church and is taken "out of the way" when the Church is raptured. When His home leaves, He leaves. This powerful Restrainer is the Holy Spirit.

At the end of this age, the world will begin to oppose the true Church. God intends for His people and His Word to be respected. He will not tolerate the world's mockery and hostility for very long. He will rapture His Church. The Holy Spirit will go with it. And the door will be open for the rise of Antichrist.

✦ *He who now letteth will let, until he be taken out of the way.*
   (II Thessalonians 2:7)

The Rise of the Antichrist
Precedes the Tribulation Period

There will be an unspecified interval of time between the rapture and the tribulation period. This allows for the rise of the cruel Antichrist. There was some discussion of this in chapter six where it was shown The New King James Version Prophecy Bible, Hal Lindsey and Dr. David Hocking hold this view.

Bear in mind the tribulation period does not begin until this head of many nations signs a seven year covenant to protect the children of Israel (Daniel 9:27). His worthless signature on that highly touted covenant starts the terrible Day of the Lord. But remember too, he must rule over his kingdom in order to have the authority to make this ungodly agreement.

In Daniel chapter seven, we read about a vision the Prophet had. It was a vision of four beasts (four great powers). The fourth beast represents the rise of the revived Roman Empire (the EC). This fourth beast had ten horns (ten kings or rulers). And another little horn (the Antichrist) came up among them. He plucked up three of the original ten horns. And established himself over the remaining seven (Daniel 7:7, 8, 23-26).

This vision is telling us Europe will reunite in the last days. It will organize into ten divisions with a leader for each division. An eleventh leader—the Antichrist—will arise among them. He will be different from the other ten and will overthrow three of them. The remaining seven will subordinate themselves and allow him to become dictator over the entire group.

The New King James Version Prophecy Bible addresses this by saying,

> "The Antichrist will not simply be handed the control of this revived Roman Empire (also called the Western Confederacy or fourth kingdom by some scholars)—he will have to seize power. This Western Confederacy will initially comprise ten kings. These ten kings will be in place and reigning before the advent of the Antichrist. When the Antichrist comes forward, he will meet and overcome initial opposition from three of the kings. He will gain ascendency over the remaining seven kings.[2]"

There is more. After the bloody Antichrist comes to power, he must be recognized as a world leader. Otherwise he could not guarantee peace to Israel. He must gain the confidence of Israel. And have time to negotiate the covenant with the many parties who will agree to it. How much time this will require is unknown. Certainly some is needed.

✦ *He shall confirm the covenant with many for one week.*
   (Daniel 9:27)

The Russian Invasion of Israel

It seems important to recognize that there are a number of opinions, and no great consensus, on where to place the Russian invasion of Israel in the sequence of end-time events. David L. Cooper places it before the rapture.[3] Dr. Emil Gaverluk places it after the rapture and before the tribulation period.[4] Richard W. DeHaan places it after the rapture and before the middle of the tribulation period.[5] Hal Lindsey places it at the middle of the tribulation period.[6] Louis Bauman places it at the end of the tribulation period.[7] Arno C. Gaebelein places it at the beginning of the Millennium[8] and J. Dwight Pentecost says, "Still others teach the invasion takes place at the end of the millenium."[9] No matter where we place this invasion, several outstanding authorities would disagree.

The Russian Invasion is not the Battle of Armageddon

There are a number of reasons for declaring the Russian invasion is not the Battle of Armageddon. Some of them are as follows:

1. The Russian invasion is an attack on Israel (Ezekiel 38:11, 12), but the Battle of Armageddon is an attack on Jesus and His army (Revelation 19:19).

2. Russia's army is led by Gog (Ezekiel 38:2, 4, 7), but the Battle of Armageddon is led by the Antichrist (Revelation 19:19).

3. The Russian invasion excludes, and is questioned by, several nations (Ezekiel 38:13), but the Battle of Armageddon includes all nations (Revelation 16:14).

4. Russia's army is defeated by nature (Ezekiel 38:19-22) and infighting (Ezekiel 38:21), but the Antichrist is defeated by Jesus (Revelation 19:15).

5. Israel is dwelling safely at the time of the Russian invasion (Ezekiel 38:8, 14), but the Jews have fled the land when the Battle of Armageddon takes place (Matthew 24:16; Revelation 12:6).

6. Russia is pulled into the land of milk and honey by God (Ezekiel 38:4), but the armies are gathered to the Battle of Armageddon by three unclean spirits from the Satanic trinity (Revelation 16:13,14).

7. Jerusalem is captured in the Battle of Armageddon (Zechariah 14:2), but there is no indication of that in the Russian invasion.

8. The Russian invasion ends with the defeat of Russia and her allies (Ezekiel 38:19-39:7), but the Battle of Armageddon ends with the second coming of Jesus (Revelation 19:11–21).

The Russian invasion of Israel cannot be the Battle of Armageddon. Therefore, it must be treated as a separate war in the end-time sequence of events.

✦ *For they are the spirits of devils, working miracles, which go forth unto the kings of the earth and of the whole world, to*

gather them to the battle of that great day of God Almighty.
(Revelation 16:14)

The Russian Invasion is not the Attack by the King of the North

Some writers-Hal Lindsey, Dr. H. L. Willmington, Dr. J. Dwight Pentecost and others-identify the king of the North in Daniel 11:40 as Russia and merge his attack on the Antichrist with the Russian invasion of Israel in Ezekiel chapters 38 and 39. This places the Russian invasion of Israel near the middle of the tribulation period and has it igniting the Battle of Armageddon. While this writer is reluctant to disagree with these great men, it must be said their evidence is weak. Moreover, there is other evidence which suggests an entirely different scenario.

Here are some of the problems with merging Ezekiel chapters 38 and 39 with Daniel 11:40-45:

1. Those who fuse the two passages teach "dwelling safely" in Ezekiel 38:8,11& 14 means under the covenant with Antichrist, but there is no evidence of this and it seems to be more assumption than fact.

2. There are no ships in the Ezekiel chapters and it is unlikely the ships in the Daniel passage are airplanes.

3. The Ezekiel chapters make no mention of the Antichrist or the king of the South as does the Daniel passage.

4. The Ezekiel chapters mention Persia, Gomer and Togarmah, but these nations are not in the verses in Daniel.

5. Ezekiel has Russia defeated when it attacks Israel, but the army in Daniel enters the glorious land and moves on to defeat many nations including Egypt.

6. Some have the Russian forces entering Israel–after defeating Egypt-to fight armies from the East and West, but there is nothing like this in the Ezekiel passage.

7. Some have Russia moving into the Middle East to challenge the authority of the Antichrist (Daniel 11:40-45), but the Ezekiel passage has Russia attacking the luxuriant land, "to take a spoil, and to take a prey" (Ezekial 38:12).

These arguments make the merging of Ezekiel 38 and 39 with Daniel 11:40–45 highly suspect. We must conclude that these Scriptures refer to more than one attack.

> ✦ *He shall enter also into the glorious land, and many countries shall be overthrown.*
> (Daniel 11:41)

There Will be Two Russian Invasions

There are a number of people who suggest more than one Russian invasion. Rev. Noah W. Hutchings suggests Russia will be defeated in Israel (Ezekiel 38 & 39). Then a group of African nations (the king of the South) will form a military alliance for a brief interval of time (Daniel 7:6). Finally, the Antichrist will move in.[10] Concerning Daniel 11:44, Rev. Hutchings says,

> "Russia will suffer a great defeat when its forces march across the mountains of Israel as described in Ezekiel chapter thirty-eight. But it is evident that at the end of the tribulation, Russia will regather its armed forces and plan to march with communist China against the Antichrist. This is the only possible explanation at this time of verse forty-four . . . . And we are told here in Daniel 11:44 that another great and terrible battle will occur when this great army out of the north and the east will come against the Antichrist."[11]

Dr. John F. Walvoord and Dr. John E. Walvoord have this to say about two Russian invasions,

> "Daniel's prophecy also described a great army from Africa, including not only Egypt but other countries of that continent. This army, probably numbering in the millions, will attack the Middle East from the South. At the same time Russia and the other armies to the North will mobilize another powerful military force *to* descend on the Holy Land and challenge the world dictator. Although Russia will have had a severe setback three years earlier in the prophetic sequence of events, it apparently will have been able to recoup its losses enough to put another army in the field."[12]

Dr. Emil Gaverluk also sees two Russian invasions. He says,

> "Thus the first invasion can occur at any moment . . . It is in Daniel 11:40 that we see the second invasion from the north along with the 44th verse. This is the time of the Antichrist leading up to Armageddon."[13]

Two Russian invasions would solve many of the problems. First, there would be the invasion described in Ezekiel 38 with Russia's army and air force suffering a terrible defeat. Second, there would be the invasion described in Daniel 11:40-45 with Russia's navy taking it on the chin. This would explain why Persia, Gomer and Togarmah are in the Ezekiel chapters, but not the Daniel passage. And why the Antichrist is in the Daniel passage, but not the Ezekiel chapters. The first invasion could be to take a spoil and a prey and the second invasion could be to challenge the Antichrist.

The First Russian Invasion Precedes the Tribulation Period

We now refer to the assault in Ezekiel chapters 38 and 39 as the first Russian invasion of Israel. The attack by the king of the North in Daniel 11:40-45 will be the second Russian invasion. We will also accept the fact the second battle occurs near the middle of the tribulation period. The question at hand is where does the initial invasion fit into the prophetic sequence of events?

First, we know it cannot happen during the latter half of the tribulation period. Ezekiel tells us Israel will be *dwelling safely in the land* when the first attack occurs. But Israel will not be *dwelling safely in the land* during the last three and one-half years of the indignation. When the tribulation mid-point arrives, the Jews will be forced to flee into the mountains (Matthew 24:15, 16). This places the Ezekiel invasion in the first half of the tribulation period or before.

Second, the initial battle must occur before the Antichrist arrives on the scene; or at least, before he has had time to consolidate his power. Otherwise, it is difficult to imagine Ezekiel ignoring the willful king with global ambitions. This premise places it prior to the tribulation period.

Third, some teach the initial invasion occurs in the first half of the tribulation period. They believe "dwelling safely" in Ezekiel means under the covenant with Antichrist. But that is mostly supposition. As far as can be determined, there are no Scriptures to show Israel will not have other covenants (such as the 1979 "Camp

David" agreement with Egypt). And there are verses that seem to indicate the contrary. Dr. Emil Gaverluk believes the Jews will be tricked into signing one agreement giving them a false sense of security (Betakh in Ezekiel 38). And pushed into signing a second agreement (Gabar in Daniel 9:27) giving them a very strong covenant.[14] Apparently Israel negotiates the first treaty and signs it because the Jews are gullible. But they reluctantly agree to the second covenant under pressure from the Antichrist. This means the first Russian invasion can happen before the tribulation period.

Fourth, we are told it will take Israel seven months to bury the dead from the Ezekiel invasion (Ezekiel 39:12). Because the Jews must flee the land at the tribulation mid-point (42 months from the beginning), the invasion must begin no later than thirty-five months into the time of trouble. It will begin before then. But that is the latest date that will still allow seven months for burial before they flee.

Fifth, Ezekiel tells us Israel will burn the Russian weapons for seven years. The Jews cannot do this in the latter half of the tribulation period. They will be out of the land. Also, they cannot gather and burn weapons then. The Satanic Antichrist will be persecuting those in the land. And the Battle of Armageddon will be raging. By backing up seven years from the tribulation mid-point, we conclude the first Russian invasion must take place no later than three and one-half years before the covenant with the Antichrist.

Sixth, the Jews will be dwelling in their cities for a minimum of seven years following the first Russian invasion. We are told, *And they that dwell in the cities of Israel shall go forth, and shall set on fire and burn the weapons* (Ezekiel 39:9). Because the seven year burning time cannot overlap the last half of the tribulation period, the first Russian invasion must take place at least three and one-half years before the Day of the Lord begins (Zechariah 13:8; 14:2).

+ It will take seven years to burn the weapons.
  (Ezekiel 39:9)
+ It will take seven months to bury the dead.
  (Ezekiel 39:12)

✦ They that dwell in the cities of Israel shall burn the weapons. (Ezekiel 39:9)

The Rapture Probably Precedes the First Russian Invasion

We must emphasize the word "probably" because the evidence is scant. This does not mean it is wrong. It simply means the evidence does not support a concrete argument so we do not want to be dogmatic.

The evidence comes from a book by Dr. Emil Gaverluk.[15] He teaches The Jerusalem Bible translation of Micah chapter 7 gives us the chronology. This translation is highly acclaimed by some. But we find it troublesome that it is so different from the other more popular versions. We present the evidence because Dr. Gaverluk is highly respected and has extensive qualifications for this kind of study.

In The Jerusalem Bible, Micah 7:2 reads, *The devout have vanished from the land: there is not one honest man left.* The Living Bible reads, *The good men have disappeared from the earth; not one fair-minded man is left.* According to Dr. Gaverluk, this is Israel's cry when the Church is raptured and Israel is left alone in a hostile world.

In the same translation, Micah 7:4 reads, *Today will come their ordeal from the North, now is the time for their confusion.* The King James Version reads, *Now shall be their perplexity.* Dr. Gaverluk sees this as the first Russian invasion of Israel spoken of in Ezekiel chapters 38 and 39. Notice, it occurs after the godly people have disappeared from the earth. That will be the time of Russia's perplexity and confusion.

Still referring to the Jerusalem Bible, Micah 7:9 reads, *I must suffer the anger of Yahweh, for I have sinned against him, until he takes up my cause and rights my wrongs.* The King James Version reads, *I will bear the indignation of the Lord, because I have sinned against him.* "Indignation" is one of the names of the tribulation period (Isaiah 26:19, 20; 34:1-8; Jeremiah 10:10; Zephaniah 3:8) and this verse is saying, *Israel will go through the tribulation period because of her sin.* This verifies what the angel Gabriel said. It will complete the 490 years of judgment for sin he told Daniel about (Daniel 9:24).

The sequence here is the rapture first (vs. 2), the Russian invasion second (vs. 4) and the tribulation period third (vs. 9). This all depends upon the verses being accurately translated in The Jerusalem Bible and upon the chronology of these verses being the chronology of the actual events. Based on this, the rapture precedes the first Russian invasion of the good land.

The Sequence in the Book of Revelation

The Revelation of Jesus Christ is one of the most sequence oriented books in the entire Bible. Our Lord actually divides this prophetic book Himself using three main divisions and several subdivisions of sevens. His main divisions are:

1. The things which thou (John) hast seen;
2. The things which are;
3. The things which shall be hereafter (Revelation 1:19).

He subdivides "the things which are" into seven letters to churches. And He breaks "the things which shall be hereafter" into seven seals, seven trumpets, seven vials and so forth.

We should also note this book is written so the main divisions do not overlap. This is an important point because some want to take "things present" and apply them to the past or take "things hereafter" and apply them to the present. The first main division does not overlap the second, and the second does not overlap the third. Each division is a separate group of events for a specific period of time.

✦ *Write the things which thou hast seen, and the things which are, and the things which shall be hereafter.*
(Revelation 1:19)

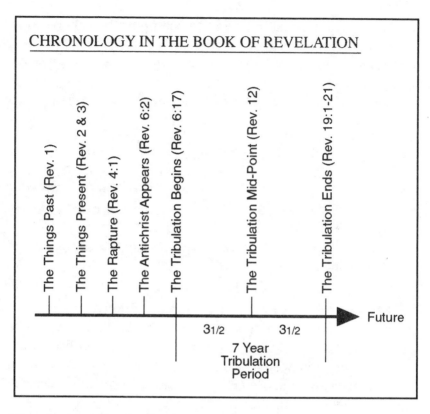

CHRONOLOGY IN THE BOOK OF REVELATION

The Things Which Thou Hast Seen (Past Events)

Chapter 1 is the first main division in the Book of Revelation. It describes what John saw when the resurrected Christ appeared unto him. Several of the verses are written in the past tense (Revelation 1:9, 10, 12, 17, 20).

✦ *And when I saw him, I fell at his feet as dead.*
(Revelation 1:17)

The Things Which Are (Present Events)

Chapters 2 and 3 contain the second part of God's outline. They describe seven churches which actually existed when John wrote the Book of Revelation. Those congregations were selected for this prophecy because their traits reveal the future of the Church. They actually represent the history of the Church written in advance and cover the period extending from Pentecost unto the rapture. Most of this period is behind us. We are rapidly approaching the end of this segment of God's outline. In other words, we are presently living in the last part of Revelation chapter 3.

✦ And the seven candlesticks which thou sawest are the seven churches.
(Revelation 1:20)

The Things Which Shall Be Hereafter (Future Events)

Chapter 4 begins the third part of God's outline. The same phrase used in Revelation 1:19 appears in Revelation 4:1. It lets us know "the things which must be hereafter" are about to be revealed.

✦ *Come up hither, and I will shew thee things which must be hereafter.*
(Revelation 4:1)

(1) The rapture

The first "thing hereafter" is the rapture. Revelation 4:1 begins with these words, "After this." We pause to ask, "After what?" The answer is, "After John saw the things which are (After he saw the events of the present age)." This is a break point in God's outline. There will be no more present events. From this point on, we will deal with future happenings.

What happened? John looked and he saw an open door to heaven. There was a sound like the voice of a trumpet saying, "Come up hither." The interesting thing is John described his summons to heaven with the same language the Apostle Paul used to describe the rapture of the Church (I Thessalonians 4:16-18). He left the earth just like the saints will go at the end of the age. This similarity is why a number of scholars believe Revelation 4:1 pinpoints the rapture of the Church.

There is more. The words "church" and "churches" appear nineteen times in the first three chapters of Revelation. But beginning with Revelation 4:1, the Church is not mentioned on earth again until the second coming of Jesus in Revelation 19. The absence of the Church from the prophetic visions on earth between Revelation

4:1 and Revelation 19 is another reason to conclude chapter 4 verse 1 is where the Church is raptured.

✦ *And the first voice which I heard was as it were of a trumpet talking.*
(Revelation 4:1)

(2) The Antichrist

We move from Revelation 4:1 to Revelation chapter 6. The four horsemen of the Apocalypse are unveiled. The first horseman is the rider on a white horse. Because the King of kings and Lord of lords comes forth on a white horse at His Second Advent (Revelation 19:11), some scholars take the position this rider with a bow and crown is Jesus. But the majority teach he is the Antichrist—an imitation of the King of kings and Lord of lords. Notice this first horseman comes forth in the Book of Revelation after the rapture of the Church. This is consistent with Paul's teaching in II Thessalonians chapter 2 (Revelation 4:1 = the rapture; Revelation 6:2 = the Antichrist).

✦ *And I saw, and behold a white horse: and he that sat on him had a bow: and a crown was given unto him: and he went forth conquering, and to conquer.*
(Revelation 6:2)

(3) The beginning of the tribulation period

Next, we jump over to Revelation 6:17 and "the great day of his wrath." This is the day the Old Testament prophets spoke of. Zephaniah said, *The great day of the Lord is near, it is near, and hasteth greatly, even the voice of the day of the Lord: the mighty man shall cry there bitterly. That day is a day of wrath, a day of trouble and distress, a day of wasteness and desolation, a day of darkness and gloominess, a day of clouds and thick darkness* (Zephaniah 1:14,15). This is the ghastly tribulation period. It follows the rapture (Revelation 4:1). And the rise of Antichrist (Revelation 6:2).

✦ *For the great day of his wrath is come.*
(Revelation 6:17)

(4) The middle of the tribulation period

Now we skip over to Revelation chapter 12. Many writers, but certainly not all, locate the middle of the tribulation period here. The temple must be in use before the middle of the tribulation period (Daniel 9:27). It is present for John to measure in Revelation chapter 11. The Jews were told to flee into the wilderness when the abomination of desolation stands in the holy place at the temple (Daniel 9:27; Matthew 24:15,16). They flee in Revelation 12:6 when the red dragon (Satan) attacks the sun clothed woman (Israel). God takes care of them for 1260 days (exactly three and one-half Jewish years).

> ✦ And the woman fled into the wilderness, where she had a place prepared of God, that they should feed her there a thousand two hundred and threescore days.
> (Revelation 12:6)

(5) The end of the tribulation period

The tribulation period ends with the second coming of Jesus. We find that in Revelation chapter 19. The chapter begins with the expression "After these things" which, in the Greek, is the same expression we saw in Revelation 1:19 and Revelation 4:1. "After these things" refers to what comes after the tribulation period; what comes after "the things which shall be hereafter."

> ✦ Salvation, and glory, and honour, and power, unto the Lord our God.
> (Revelation 19:1)

In Review

The sequence in the Book of Revelation is the same as the sequence presented for the other 65 books taken together. This is more than coincidence. It is verification the sequence is rightly understood.

The Rise of Israel vs. the Rise of the European Community

Several times we have noted the Antichrist confirms a seven year covenant pertaining to Israel. And he breaks it at the tribulation mid-point. For this to happen, a group of nations must arise out of the old Roman Empire and coexist with Israel. This covenant requires them to be contemporaries. Guess what? After several centuries of absence, both parties reappeared in the same year.

In 1948, the nation of Israel officially came back into existence. It fought its first war with the Arabs and won. Over in Europe, three nations (Belgium, the Netherlands and Luxembourg) formed an economic union called Benelux. Benelux is a word formed by the first letters in each nations name.

In 1949, Israel held its first election and signed its first armistice agreements (with Egypt, Syria, Jordan and Lebanon). The same year, The Council of Europe was established to achieve economic and social progress. It had no real power. But it worked toward the political organization of Europe. And the Benelux nations joined the group.

In 1955, Fedayeen Arabs, with Egyptian support, initiated terrorist raids against Israel from the Gaza Strip. The next year, Egypt seized the Suez Canal from its British and French owners. They nationalized it and barred Israeli ships from using it. Israel responded with an attack on Egypt. The second Arab-Israeli war was underway. Britain and France stepped in on the Israeli side and the war was soon over. Israel occupied the Gaza Strip and the Sinai Peninsula. Britain and France commanded the northern entrance to the Suez Canal. The next year, in 1957, the United Nations helped work out a settlement. The Suez Canal was reopened and a United Nations Emergency Force (UNEF) was organized to replace Israeli forces in the Gaza Strip and the Sinai Peninsula. Meanwhile, in Europe, the Treaty of Rome was signed which formed the Common Market and the European Atomic Energy Community (Euratom). This same year the European Economic Community (EEC) was organized. And the Benelux nations joined these groups.

In 1967, Syrian forces were initiating border clashes with Israel. And the Arabs asked the UN to remove its peacekeeping forces from the Gaza Strip and the Sinai Peninsula. Fearing an Arab attack, Israel struck first, capturing the Golan Heights, the West Bank, the Gaza

Strip and the Sinai Peninsula. The West Bank included the eastern half of Jerusalem and the all-important Temple Mount. These were officially annexed by Israel. Meanwhile, the European Coal and Steel Community (ECSC), the European Atomic Energy Community (Euratom) and the European Economic Community (EEC) all merged into one group. They came to be known as the European Community (EC).

In 1973, another Arab-Israeli war (the Yom Kippur War) broke out when Egypt and Syria attacked Israeli positions along the Suez Canal and in the Golan Heights. The Arabs had some initial success. But they were pushed back. And Israel gained additional Syrian territory. This was also a year of growth in the EC. It expanded from six to nine nations by taking in Denmark, Ireland and Great Britain. With the admission of these nations, the EC surpassed the United States in the production of steel and automobiles.

In 1979, Egypt and Israel signed the Camp David Accords. They agreed to a peace treaty with each other. While they were doing that, the EC was setting up the European Monetary System (EMS). Eight of its members agreed to participate.

In the early '90s, Israel grew by leaps and bounds. Large numbers of Jews emigrated to the homeland. And the EC made giant strides toward economic and political union. Its clout grew with the addition of several associate members.

> ✦ *And he shall confirm the covenant with many for one week: and the midst of the week he shall cause the sacrifice and the oblation to cease.*
> (Daniel 9:27)

What's Happening

The two main end-time world powers are walking in lockstep. Israel (God's battle ax during the tribulation period) and the EC (the land of God's adversary during the tribulation period) are simultaneously progressing on the scene. The stage is being set and the world is being propelled toward the great Day of the Lord.

The Time of Israel's Return

We have already learned the disciples asked Jesus, *What shall be the sign of thy coming, and of the end of the world* (Matthew 24:3)? In response, He told the parable of the fig tree. That means the re-establishment and regathering of Israel is a sign the Second Advent is near. We know the nation of Israel now exists. More than five million Jews live in the land. Thousands are returning each month. Several hundred thousand plan to return very soon. All of this was prophesied. Now look at something else. This is not setting a date, but the Bible actually provides a clue to the approximate time of Israel's return. The present return fits the information given.

Israel's Return is a Resurrection From the Dead

Ezekiel 37 gives us a very famous vision. It is called, "the vision of the valley of dry bones." God took Ezekiel to a valley full of dry bones. He asked, "Can these bones live?" And He answered His own question. He said, "I will cause breath to enter into you, and ye shall live." Some people will argue with a post, but there is general agreement this is a prophecy about the restoration of Israel. God even says, *These bones are the whole house of Israel* (Ezekiel 37:11).

His message teaches the nation of Israel will gradually be restored. He would begin with bones; place sinews upon them; add flesh to them; and cover them with skin. Finally, God would put breath into them. And they would live. Israel's restoration would not be one instantaneous act. It would be a step-by-step process.

The picture God uses for this process is important. It is the picture of a resurrection of the dead. He says, *Behold, O my people, I will open your graves, and cause you to come up out of your graves, and bring you into the land of Israel. And ye shall know that I am the Lord, when I have opened your graves, O my people, and brought you up out of your graves, And shall put my spirit in you, and ye shall live, and I shall place you in your own land* (Ezekiel 37:12-14).

This is what we have. God promised the children of Israel He would gradually restore them. He would bring them out of their graves which are the other nations of the world (Ezekiel 37:21). He would bring them into the land. And He compared the process of restoration and return to a resurrection from the dead. We are about to see this is very significant.

◆ Behold, O my people, I will open your graves, and cause you to come up out of your graves, and bring you into the land of Israel. (Ezekiel 37:12)

The Time of Israel's Resurrection From the Dead

The prophet Hosea lived during the time of the divided kingdom. He prophesied to the northern kingdom called Israel. He denounced the nation's sin and proclaimed God would scatter the people. This was done in 721 B.C.

But Hosea did not leave it there. He also foretold God would heal the people and bind them up (Hosea 6:1). The interesting thing is he compared this healing and binding process to a resurrection from the dead. And he foretold when God would do it. He said, *After two days will he revive us: in the third day he will raise us up, and we shall live in his sight* (Hosea 6:2). In other words, God would resurrect Israel and restore her to the land on the third day after her demise.

◆ *In the third day he will raise us up.*
(Hosea 6:2)

The Length of a Day

The Apostle Peter said, *One day is with the Lord as a thousand years, and a thousand years as one day* (II Peter 3:8). The idea is God does not view time like we do. We think in terms of time because it is an essential element of our lives. It is not that way with God. He is eternal and not subject to time. To Him one day is like a thousand years of our time.

When God said He would revive Israel after two days and raise her up in the third day, He was speaking in terms of His view of time. He was saying the resurrection of Israel will occur after 2,000 years, and during the next 1,000 years.

Upon examination, we see the northern kingdom of Israel fell around 721 B.C. (more than 2,700 years ago). The southern kingdom of Judah fell around 587 B.C. (more than 2,500 years ago). The two days have passed and we are now in the third day for both kingdoms.

✦ *A thousand years in thy sight are but as yesterday.*
(Psalm 90:4)

The 7,000 Year Theory

We know of no theory older than this one. It is not a new idea from unknown sources. It is the long-held understanding of several great men of God. Colin Deal provides a number of historical references for it.[16] He found information in the ancient books of I Enoch and Jubilees. Justin Martyr discussed it in three of his books. Irenaeus wrote about it in one of his books. And the Epistle of Barnabus (found in the Sinaiticus or Codex Aleph) implies it.

This theory begins with the fact God created all things in six days. And He rested on the seventh. It rationalizes God will deal with mankind for six days and rest on the seventh. It also assumes all the days of this week are of equal length.

The theory uses three Scripture selections to unveil the idea.

1. 2 Peter 3:8 which teaches one day with the Lord is 1,000 years.

2. Hebrews 4:4-11 which presents the Millenium as a day of rest.

3. Revelation 20:1-9 which gives us the idea of a 1,000 year Millenium.

The idea set forth is the six days God deals with mankind translate into 6,000 of our years. The seventh day is a 1,000 year day of rest called the Millenium. But there is something else. Four days passed between Adam and the birth of Jesus. Almost two days have passed since then. The second coming ushers in the Millenium. This makes the rapture imminent.

At this point, we want to issue a word of caution. As has been stated before, we do not know the date of our Lord's return. We are simply presenting a long-held Scripturally based theory. Barnabus was the Apostle Paul's companion. He lived before the New Testament was written. Justin Martyr and Irenaeus lived between 100–

200 A.D. They believed the Lord would return 6,000 years after the creation. We are almost there. This theory fits the others that have been presented.

> ✦ *Be not ignorant of this one thing, that one day is with the Lord as a thousand years, and a thousand years as one day.*
> (II Peter 3:8)

The Final Promise

It has been estimated the Bible contains approximately 7,500 promises personally made by God. The last promise in the Bible says, *Surely I come quickly.*

This does not mean Jesus promised to return immediately after the Book of Revelation was written. It means when the time of the second coming arrives, He will return very fast. It will be too late to prepare. The second coming will occur, and be over, in the twinkling of an eye. If you procrastinate, you could be eternally damned

> ✦ *Surely I come quickly.*
> (Revelation 22:20)

Chapter 9

Epilogue

Some remarks included here are provided at the request of my publisher. Others stem from my desire to keep this book up-to-date on late-breaking events.

The Four Beasts

In Daniel chapter 7, the prophet tells about four strange beasts that he saw in a series of God-given visions. For many years, the generally accepted interpretation held that he visualized four remarkable beasts which represent the same world kingdoms as those described in the enormous dazzling statue of Nebuchadnezzar's dream. (See Daniel 2, also Chapter 4 of this book.) Many scholars said the first beast, a winged lion, is the head of gleaming gold (Babylon); the second beast, a bear with ribs in its mouth, is the breast and arms of shining silver (Medo-Persian empire); the third beast, a four-winged, four-headed leopard, is the belly and thighs of brass (Greece); and the fourth beast, a dreadful and terrible animal, is the legs of iron, and the feet of iron and clay (Rome and the Revived Roman Empire). Dr. C. I. Scofield, Dr. J. Vernon McGee and Richard W. DeHaan are among those holding to this interpretation. There are other interpretations. Some modern expositors contend that the four beasts represent a line of prophetic events different from those interpreted in the vision of the statue. With this I am in agreement.

Here are some of the arguments to support the more recent thinking:

1. The symbols are different. Daniel saw beasts. Nebuchadnezzar dreamed about materials in a statue.

2. There are four beasts (lion, bear, leopard, dreadful beast). There there are five materials (gold, silver, brass, iron, a mixture of iron and clay).

3. The four beasts will appear in the future. They *are four kings which shall arise out of the earth* (Daniel 7:17). When Daniel received this vision, the head of gold, Nebuchadnezzar himself in Nebuchadnezzar's earlier vision (Daniel 2:38), was already dead for nearly ten years Babylon was no longer in the future. It was near demise.

4. The first three beasts will survive the fourth because it is the first to be destroyed. Daniel watched *till the (fourth) beast was slain* (Daniel 7:11). The lives of the other three beasts *were prolonged for a season and a time* (Daniel 7:12). The golden head did not survive the feet of iron and clay; the silver breast and arms did not outlive the feet of iron and clay; nor did the belly of brass.

5. The four beasts live at the same time. The first three witness the destruction of the fourth. The five materials of the statue did not live together as contemporaries. Each one was supplanted by a successor.

6. All the beasts will be alive when Jesus returns to destroy the fourth. The gold, silver and brass of the statue will not be alive at that time. They are past history.

7. When Nebuchadnezzar dreamed his dream, Daniel knew the head of gold was Babylon. When Daniel had his vision several years later, he did not know who the future winged lion would be.

The conclusion is that future events foretold in Daniel 2 and Daniel 7 are different. The four beasts must be looked at in terms of the last days. The winged lion was future history to Daniel, not past history or a contemporary event.

The Situation and Setting

Daniel *looked and the four winds of the heaven strove upon the great sea.* Winds are symbolic of demonic forces. Satan is *the prince of the power of the air, the spirit that now worketh in the children of disobedience* (Ephesians 2:2). The great sea is a Bible name for the Mediterranean Sea. *And the west border (of Israel) was to the great sea* (Joshua 15:12).

In the future, Satanic agitation will violently blow around the Mediterranean Sea. The children of disobedience will be stirred to defy God; moved to create disturbance and war. Satanic turmoil will push the nations toward the Battle of Armageddon.

✦ *The four winds of the heaven strove upon the great sea.*
(Daniel 7:2)

The Winged Lion

The first beast to arise is like a lion with eagle's wings. It begins as a combination of "the king of beasts" and "the king of birds." And it ends with human qualities. The symbol of England is the lion. And the symbol of the United States is the eagle.

The eagle's wings will be plucked off. And the lion will stand on its feet like a man.The symbol on the coat of arms of the throne of England is two standing lions. It is also significant to note that England's relationship with the United States is changing because of its membership in the EC. And let us not overlook the fact that the United States is on the decline; spiritually, morally, economically and militarily.

For decades, England and the United States worked together like Siamese twins to establish and strengthen the nation of Israel. They may even be *the merchants of Tarshish, with all the young lions* who jointly protest the first Russian invasion of Israel (Ezekiel 38:13). But the day will come, and it may not be far off, when the two will be separated. And the weakened England will be more like a man than a lion; more like the human prey and less like "the king of beasts."

✦ *The first was like a lion, and had eagle's wings: I beheld until the wings thereof were plucked, and it was lifted up from the earth,*

and made stand upon the feet as a man, and a man's heart was given to it.
(Daniel 7:4)

The Bear With Ribs in Its Mouth

The second beast to arise is like a hungry bear. While it still has three ribs (nations) in its mouth, it is called upon to devour more flesh. This seems to symbolize a hungry Russia whose national symbol is the bear.

Recall this from chapter three of this book. For many years, rumors have existed that the former Soviet leaders promised Islamic countries they would help liberate Palestine. Keep in mind that three such countries, Persia, Ethiopia and Libya, join in the first Russian invasion of Israel. Because Israel recently signed a peace treaty with the Palestine Liberation Organization (PLO), those countries now have only two choices: accept the peace, or call for an attack on Israel. They will try to use their influence with a hungry Russia to go after Israel's cattle and goods (Ezekiel. 38:5,13).

✦ *And behold another beast, a second, like to a bear, and it raised up itself on one side, and it had three ribs in the mouth of it between the teeth of it: and they said thus unto it, Arise, devour much flesh.*
(Daniel 7:5)

The Four-Winged, Four-Headed Leopard

The third beast to arise is like a four-winged (fowl's wings), four-headed leopard. In so far as we know, Scripture does not identify these nations. This seems to refer to a four nation Arab coalition—one that has not yet appeared—one that arises between the first Russian invasion of Israel and the appearance of Antichrist.

Just as the lion was supported with the wings of an eagle, this beast is strengthened with the wings of a fowl (not an eagle). It has an outside source of help; not the United States. *Dominion will be given to it* means it will not gain authority on its own. It will have authority delegated to it; the kind of authority the United Nations is trying to establish with the New World Order; the kind of authority it is exercising over the affairs of the nations of Iraq and Somalia. The EC will play the dominant role.

♦ *After this I beheld, and lo another, like a leopard, which had upon the back of it four wings of a fowl; the beast had also four heads; and dominion was given to it.*
(Daniel 7:6)

The Dreadful and Terrible Creature

The fourth beast to arise begins as a ferocious wild-looking beast with iron teeth, brass claws and ten horns. Quickly, it grows an eleventh horn that uproots three of the first ten. There is little doubt among conservative scholars that this is the humanistic kingdom of Antichrist; a fierce and oppressive Revived Roman Empire.

The iron teeth and brass claws signify the power and influence of Rome and Greece. The ten horns represent the ten kings who will rule over the initial ten sub-divisions of the Revived Roman Empire. The eleventh horn is the Antichrist. He will overthrow three of the other kings; become the dictatorial ruler of the Revived Roman Empire. He will speak great words of blasphemy against the most High; persecute Christians and Jews; try to change customs and laws; reign for seven years; and be brought to a swift end by the second coming of Christ.

♦ *The fourth beast shall be the fourth kingdom upon earth.*
(Daniel 7:23)

The Four Beasts and the Antichrist

In Revelation 13 the Apostle John reveals a vision that he had about these four beasts. They not only exist at the same time, but they also work together to aid the Antichrist during the tribulation period. John saw *a beast rise up out of the sea, having seven heads and ten horns, and upon his horns ten crowns, and upon his heads the name of blasphemy.* The ten horns are ten people (Daniel 7:24; Revelation 17:12). They are the ten rulers of the Revived Roman Empire. This beast is the little horn that rises up with them. He is a man; so terrible a man, the Bible calls him a beast (Revelation 13:18). Most interpret this being as the Antichrist.

John said he will be "like unto a leopard." The leopard beast represents an Arab coalition. This means the Antichrist and a group of Arab nations will act as one body. The EC and the Arabs will adopt the same goals and take a unified stand. The Arabs will go along with whatever the Antichrist wants.

John said his feet will be "as the feet of a bear." The bear beast represents Russia. This means the Antichrist will be supported by whatever is left of the Russian empire following the first Russian invasion of Israel.

John also said his mouth will be "as the mouth of a lion." The lion beast is England. And the young lions are those nations descending from, and established out of England. Since England is included in the EC, this means the Antichrist and those nations coming out of England will speak with the same voice. The English speaking nations will simply parrot what the Antichrist says.

The next revelation is terrible. John said, *the dragon gave him his power, and his seat, and great authority.* Remember the dragon? *He is that old serpent, called the Devil and Satan* (Revelation 12:9). The dragon (Satan) will give the Antichrist great power, dominion and authority—making the Antichrist the most powerful ruler in the world. He will give him the co-operation of these other groups of nations.

The Antichrist will be mortally wounded. But he will be healed. And all the world will marvel. Satan worship will surge across the face of the earth. Multitudes will bow down to the Antichrist and declare that no one can compare to him, that no one can stand up to him. He will blaspheme God; persecute and kill tribulation period believers.

Finally, John says, *If any man have an ear, let him hear.* Pay attention—whoever and wherever you are, : Think about the seriousness of terrible things. Satan and his Antichrist are going to rule this world. You and your family will not want to be here.

+ *And power was given him over all kindreds, and tongues, and nations.*
   (Revelation 13:7)

Gospel

Dr. Billy Graham is scheduled to preach the Gospel to the entire world via satellite in March of 1995. Interpreters will be used so people can hear it in their own language.

False Church

Pope John Paul II is now predicting the uniting of all religions into one religion within the next six years.

Temple

Among other things, the Israeli-PLO Declaration of Principles guarantees the Jews freedom of worship at religious sites. In a television interview following the signing ceremony, Yasser Arafat set forth the possibility of the PLO agreeing to the rebuilding of the Temple on the Temple Mount in exchange for the Arabs receiving certain unspecified rights in East Jerusalem. And King Hussein of Jordan has now suggested an interfaith dialogue to discuss sovereignty over the holy sites in Jerusalem. This suggests a willingness to give up sovereignty over some sites including the Temple Mount.

Ashes of the Red Heifer

Before the Jews can begin sacrificing animals on the Temple Mount, they ahve to be sprinkled with the water of purification containing the ashes of a red heifer (Numbers 19:1-22). Rev. Clyde Lott has been breeding a herd of these in Canton, Mississippi for several years. He is working closely with the Temple Institute in Jerusalem. And his first shipment of 500 red heifers is scheduled for delivery to Israel in November of 1994.

World Trade

A group called the World Trade Organization (WTO) is being established to control all buying and selling among the nations of the world. This group will try to plan and control the world's economy by setting, administering and enforcing all the rules of global trade. Several nations are competing to become the WTO headquarters. But the BIble teaches that this group will operate out of the rebuilt city of Babylon. Could it be that these people are laying the foundation for the Mark of the Beast?

The EC

In recent times, the EC has been less than the economic juggernaut predicted by the Bible. But the slumping U.S. dollar is now causing investors to shift their money to Europe. The coming juggernaut is now picking up steam.

The Antichrist

According to Margared Thatcher, "There is no real New World Order because the world lacks a leader." According to Ronald Reagan, "What the world needs now is leadership."

Russia

Moscow has now abandoned most of the economic reforms and removed the reformers who took over following the breakup of the Soviet Union. Hardliners have gained strength and their leader, Vladimir Zhirnovsky, stands a good chance of being elected president in 1996. He promises to restore the former Russian empire, is a self proclaimed dictator and is strongly anti-semitic. His book, *Last Dash to the South*, is making people nervous because he calls for Russia to suddenly and swiftly undertake a great historical mission to repartition the world. Whoever succeeds Boris Yeltsin will inherit a new constitution that grants the president the power to declare war by himself.

Iran

Radicals have gained strength in Iran. In exchange for oil, the nation is procuring missiles from North Korea. When launched from Western parts of Iran, these missiles have enough range to hit Israel.

Jerusalem

The Holy City is becoming more of a "cup of trembling" and a "burdensome stone" every day that goes by (Zechariah 12:2-3). Israel and the PLO are both claiming sovereignty over the city. On September 13, 1993, Yasser Arafat said the Palestinian flag "will fly over the walls of Jerusalem, the churches of Jerusalem and the mosques of Jerusalem." A secretly taped speech in Johannesburg, South Africa on May 10, 1994, caught him calling for "a jihad (holy war) to liberate Jerusalem." And he is now making it clear to the United Nations that he no longer considers valid the Declaration of Principles he signed with Israel. Jews now outnumber Arabs in the city and most of them are willing to go to war over this issue.

Peace

Now that the Israeli-PLO agreement has taken affect more treaties will follow. Jordan has approved the agreement and stands ready to ratify an accord of its own. Syria is negotiating and progress is being reported. It is only natural to believe the future looks brighter.

Remember that the PLO is only responsible for about half the terrorist attacks against Israel. No accords have been signed with, or approved by, such extremist groups as the Iranian-backed Hamas, the radical Popular Front for the Liberation of Palestine (PFLP), or the Democratic Front for the Liberation of Palestine (DFLP). President Rafsanjani of Iran has condemned the agreement and encouraged all Arabs to keep fighting. PLO Foreign Minister, Farouk Kaddoumi, refused to attend the White House signing ceremony. And Iraq and Iran are drawing closer to each other partly because of their opposition to this agreement.

It sounds nice to call this the beginning of peace. But it is more practical to recognize that some groups are committed to raising the level of violence now taking place. And while diplomats may say the PLO is the sole legitimate representative of the Palestinian people, that is more symbolism than substance. Many Palestinians are demonstrating against this accord. Others are killing their own people because of it.

Could this open the door for the first Russian invasion of Israel? Are we seeing the security agreement Ezekiel spoke about? Will Russia and Iran decide to attack Israel? Only time will tell, but the answer to these questions could be "yes." It would not be the first time the Jews cried, *Peace, peace; when there is no peace* (Jeremiah 6:14; 8:11).

The President Who Could Not Sleep

Chapter 4 of this book tells about the king who could not sleep. Nebuchadnezzar went to sleep, dreamed about a great statue, woke up and then could not go back to sleep. His dream pertained to the future and he wanted to know its meaning.

President Clinton went to bed about 10:00 PM on September 12, 1993. Aides said he woke up at 3:00 AM, but could not go back to sleep. He picked up the Bible and began to read the book of Joshua. Then he rewrote several parts of the speech he would deliver that day at the signing ceremony for the Israeli-PLO peace treaty. This is what he said, "The sound we heard today, once again as in ancient Jericho, was of trumpets toppling walls, the walls of anger and suspicion between Israeli and Palestinian, between Arab and Jew." There may be no connection, but Gog will soon say, *I will go up to the land of unwalled villages* (Ezekiel 38:11). He will form a coalition with Iran, Ethiopia, Libya and others. And they will try to invade Israel.

Peace and the EC

On April 18, 1994, Yasser Arafat received three ambassadors from the EC (Revived Roman Empire). He called for EC participation in the peace negotiations and EC involvement in some type of international protection for Israel and the PLO. The Vatican is even calling for "an international umbrella" guaranteeing the status of Jerusalem. This sounds very much like the Antichrist's seven year covenant to protect Israel is already being drawn up.

Invitation

In one of the most dramatic scenes in the Bible, The Apostle Paul stood before King Agrippa. The great missionary told the king his message was grounded in the Scriptures. He said he preached what the Prophets and Moses said would come to pass. He explained that he related current events about the death and resurrection of Jesus to prophecy and showed people *they should repent and turn to God, and do works meet for repentance* (Acts 26:20).

This book is an attempt to do the same thing. We are relating current events to prophecies and showing they are moving forward on all fronts. If there ever was a time when the stage was set for the terrible events of the last days, this is the time. If there ever was an hour when men and women should stop everything and consider their relationship with the Saviour of the world , that time is now.

There is good news. Our loving God has told us what He will do. He will give salvation to anyone who admits they are a sinner and sincerely trusts in Jesus as an offering for those sins. This is why we Christians think it is so important for people to believe on the Lord Jesus Christ. God has promised to give salvation to all who believe. And He will not and can not break His promise.

Reference Bibliography

Chapter 1

1. Graham, Billy, *Storm Warning,* pp. 29–30.
2. Anderson Robert, *The Coming Prince,* p. 128.

Chapter 3

1. McGee, Dr. J. Vernon, *Thru The Bible With J. Vernon McGee, Volume III, Proverbs-Malachi,* p. 512.
2. Kelly, William, *Notes On Ezekiel,* pp. 192–193.
3. Pentecost, Dr. J. Dwight, *Things To Come,* p. 328.
4. McGee, Dr. J. Vernon, Thru The Bible With J. Vernon McGee, Volume III, Proverbs-Malachi, p. 512.
5. Lindsted, Robert, *It May Be Sooner Than You Think,* p. 27.
6. Schofield, C.I., D.D., Footnote in The New Schofield Study Bible, Ezekiel. 38:2.
7. Pentecost, p. 328.
8. Taylor, Charles R., *Jesus Is Coming Soon,* p. 20.
9. Lindsey, Hall, *The Late Great Planet Earth,* p. 59.
10. Rimmer, Harry, *The Coming War and the Rise of Russia,* p. 62.
11. Bauman, Louis, *Russian Events in the Light of Bible Prophecy,* p. 38.
12. Pentecost, p. 330.
13. Gaverluk, Emil, M.Div., Ph.D., Ed.D., *The Rapture Before The Russian Invasion of Israel,* pp. 118–130.

Chapter 4

1. Lindsey, Hal, *There's A New World Coming,* p. 174.
2. Wilkerson, David, *Jesus Christ Solid Rock,* p. 29.
3. LaHaye, Dr. Tim F., *Revelation Illustrated and Made Plain,* p. 237.

Chapter 5

1. Bloomfield, Arhtur E., *Armageddon,* pp. 8–12.
2. Ibid., pp. 11–12.
3. *The World Book Encyclopedia,* 1990 ed., s.v. "Babylon."
4. Chambers, Rev. Joseph, *Babylon Rises Again,* pp. 3,23,28,29.

Chapter 6

1. *The Prophecy Bible,* Thomas Nelson Publishers, p. 1325.
2. Willmington, Dr. H. L., The King is Coming, p. 50.

3. Ludwigson, Dr. Raymond, *A Survey of Bible Prophecy,* pp. 136–146.

4. *The Prophecy Bible*, Thomas Nelson Paulbishers, p. 1319.

5. Lindsey, Hal, *The Rapture,* p. 151.

6. Hocking., Dr. David, *When Will Jesus Come Again,* The Biola Hour Ministries, Taped Message #3371.

7. Hocking, Dr. David, *Will We Go Through The Tribulation,* The Biola Hour Ministries, Taped Message #3374.

Chapter 7

1. Graham, Billy, *Storm Warning,* p. 226.

2. Lindsted, Dr. Robert, *Why I Believe . . . These Are the Last Days,* p. 166.

3. Ibid., p. 168.

4. Ibid., p. 169.

5. Church, J. R., *Guardians of The Grail,* p. 277.

Chapter 8

1. *The Prophecy Bible,* Thomas Nelson Publishers,, p. 1319.

2. Ibid., p. 1332.

3. Cooper, David L., *When Gog's Armies Meet the Almighty,* pp. 80–81.

4. Gaverluk, Dr. Emil, *The Rapture Before The Russian Invasion Of Israel,* pp. 122-129.

5. DeHaan, Richard W., *Israel And The Natons In Prophecy,* p. 91.

6. Lindsey, Hal, The Rapture, p. 110.

7. Bauman, Louis, Russian Events in the Light of Scripture, pp. 174–175.

8. Gaebelein, Arnol C., *The Prophet Ezekiel,* pp. 252–255.

9. Pentecost, J. Dwight, *Things To Come,* p. 349.

10. Hutchings, N. W., *Exploring The Book of Daniel,* pp. 160–161.

11. Ibid., p. 278.

12. Walvoord, John F. and John E. Walvoord, *Armageddon, Oil and the Middle East Crisis,* pp. 162–163.

13. Gaverluk, Dr. Emil, *The Rapture Before The Russian Invasion of Israel,* pp. 124–125.

14. Ibid., pp. 118–129.

15. Ibid., pp. 9–12; 37–41; 58–61.

16. Deal, Colin, *Armageddon & the 21st Century,* pp. 76–77.

Scripture Reference Index

All Scripture references are from the King James Version of the Bible unless otherwise stated. All Jerusalem Post quotations are from The International Edition.

Subject Index

Other Books by Starburst Publishers
(Partial listing—full list available on request)

On The Brink
Daymond R. Duck

Subtitled: *Easy-to-Understand End-Time Bible Prophecy.* Organized in Biblical sequence and written with simplicity so that any reader will easily understand end-time prophecy. Ideal for use as a handy-reference book.
(trade paper) ISBN 0-914984-586 **$9.95**

The Beast Of The East
—Alvin M. Shifflett

Asks the questions: Has the Church become involved in a "late date" comfort mode—expecting to be "raptured" before the Scuds fall? Should we prepare for a long and arduous Desert Storm to Armageddon battle? Are we ignoring John 16:33, *In this world you will have trouble?* (NIV)
(trade paper) ISBN 0914984411 **$6.95**

Political Correctness Exposed
—Marvin Sprouse

Subtitled—*A Piranha in Your Bathtub.* Explores the history of Political Correctness, how it originated, who keeps it alive today, and more importantly, how to combat Political Correctness. Contains 25 of the most frequently-told Politically Correct lies.
(trade paper) ISBN 0914984624 **$9.95**

Angels, Angels, Angels
—Phil Phillips

Subtitled—*Embraced by The Light...or...Embraced by The Darkness?* Discovering the truth about Angels, Near-Death Experiences and other Spiritual Awakenings. Also, why the sudden interest in angels in this day and age? Can we trust what we read in books like *Embraced By The Light?*
(trade paper) ISBN 0914984659 **$10.95**

Dinosaurs, The Bible, Barney & Beyond
—Phil Phillips

In-depth look at Evolution, Creation Science, and Dinosaurs in the media and toys. Reader learns why Barney, the oversized purple dinosaur, has become a pal to millions of children, and what kind of role model is Barney.
(trade paper) ISBN 0914984594 **$9.95**

Beyond The River
—Gilbert Morris & Bobby Funderburk

The first novel of *The Far Fields* series, **Beyond the River** makes for intriguing reading with high spiritual warfare impact. Set in the future and in the mode of *Brave New World* and *1984*, **Beyond The River** presents a world that is ruined by modern social and spiritual trends. This anti-utopian novel offers an excellent opportunity to speak to the issues of the New Age and "politically-correct" doctrines that are sweeping the country.
(trade paper) ISBN 0914984519 **$8.95**

Books by Starburst Publishers—cont'd.

TemperaMysticism—Exploding the Temperament Theory
—Shirley Ann Miller

Former Astrologer reveals how Christians (including some well-respected leaders) are being lured into the occult by practicing the Temperaments (Sanguine, Choleric, Phlegmatic, and Melancholy) and other New Age personality typologies.

(trade paper)   ISBN 0914984306   **$8.95**

Nightmare In Dallas
—Beverly Oliver

The hard-hitting account of the mysterious "Babushka Lady," Beverly Oliver, who at the age of seventeen was an eyewitness to the assassination of President John F. Kennedy. This is only the second book to be written by one who saw the event first-hand. Beverly was a personal friend of Jack Ruby and was married to a member of the Mafia. Beverly's film of the event (the only other known motion picture) was confiscated by two men who called themselves FBI agents. To this present day, neither she nor any other known person has been permitted to view the film. Why? This book tells the story.

(hard cover)   ISBN 0914984608   **$19.95**

The World's Oldest Health Plan
—Kathleen O'Bannon Baldinger

Subtitled: *Health, Nutrition and Healing from the Bible.* Offers a complete health plan for body, mind and spirit, just as Jesus did. It includes programs for diet, exercise and mental health. Contains foods and recipes to lower cholesterol and blood pressure, improve the immune system and other bodily functions, reduce stress, reduce or cure constipation, eliminate insomnia, reduce forgetfulness, confusion and anger, increase circulation and thinking ability, eliminate "yeast" problems, improve digestion, and much more.

(trade paper-opens flat)   ISBN 0914984578   **$14.95**

A Woman's Guide To Spiritual Power
—Nancy L. Dorner

Subtitled: *Through Scriptural Prayer.* Do your prayers seem to go "against a brick wall?" Does God sometimes seem far away or non-existent? If your answer is "Yes," *You* are not alone. Prayer must be the cornerstone of your relationship to God. "This book is a powerful tool for anyone who is serious about prayer and discipleship."—Florence Littauer

(trade paper)   ISBN 0914984470   **$9.95**

A Candle In Darkness —June Livesay

An exciting and romantic novel set in the mountains of Ecuador. The first in a series, based on fact, the story begins on market day in a small Indian village in Ecuador. Rolando, the eldest son of an alcoholic landowner and bedridden mother, is overprotective of his little sister Elena, who eventually runs away with her lover Carlos, a boy from "the other side of the tracks." Dragged home by her brother, Elena again runs away with Carlos only to find short-lived happiness—for lurking in the shadows of their life together is the kidnapping of their firstborn child, emotional breakdown, and death. Depression and alcoholism eventually drive Rolando to consider suicide. While on his way to commit the act he encounters a friend who offers him hope and help which leads him on the road toward happiness.

(trade paper) ISBN 0914984225 **$8.95**

Purchasing Information

Listed books are available from your favorite Bookstore, either from current stock or special order. To assist bookstore in locating your selection be sure to give title, author, and ISBN #. If unable to purchase from the bookstore you may order direct from STARBURST PUBLISHERS. When ordering enclose full payment plus $2.50* for shipping and handling ($3.00* if Canada or Overseas). Payment in US Funds only. Please allow two to three weeks minimum (longer overseas) for delivery. Make checks payable to and mail to STARBURST PUBLISHERS, P.O. Box 4123, LANCASTER, PA 17604. **Prices subject to change without notice**. Catalog available upon request.

*We reserve the right to ship your order the least expensive way. If you desire first class (domestic) or air shipment (Canada) please enclose shipping funds as follows: First Class within the USA enclose $4.50, Airmail Canada enclose $6.00.   10-94